THE WORLD'S CLASSICS

OVID
THE LOVE POEMS

A. D. MELVILLE was a scholar of King's College, Cambridge, where he gained a double First in Classics and won a Craven Studentship. His love of the Classics was kindled at Charterhouse and he discovered the seductive charms of Ovid at King's. After a long career as a solicitor in London, interrupted by distinguished service in the Second World War, he has returned to Ovid and translated first the *Metamorphoses* and now these poems.

E. J. KENNEY is a Fellow of Peterhouse and Emeritus Kennedy Professor of Latin in the University of Cambridge. His previous publications include a critical edition of Ovid's amatory poems (Oxford Classical Texts, 1961), an edition with commentary of Lucretius, *De Rerum Natura III* (1971), *The Classical Text. Aspects of editing in the age of the printed book* (1974), and *The Ploughman's Lunch. Moretum: a poem ascribed to Virgil* (1984). He is Editor of and a contributor to *The Cambridge History of Classical Literature*, Vol. II, *Latin Literature* (1982).

This is their second collaboration published by Oxford University Press. It follows their extremely successful edition of Ovid's *Metamorphoses*, which first appeared in 1986 and is also available in the World's Classics.

This volume contains 'Amores', 'Cosmetics for Ladies', and 'The Cures for Love' newly translated by A. D. Melville, and B. P. Moore's 1935 translation of 'The Art of Love' with small revisions by A. D. Melville.

OVID

The Love Poems

Translated by

A. D. MELVILLE

With an Introduction and Notes by

E. J. KENNEY

Oxford   New York

OXFORD UNIVERSITY PRESS

Oxford University Press, Walton Street, Oxford OX2 6DP

Oxford New York Toronto
Delhi Bombay Calcutta Madras Karachi
Kuala Lumpur Singapore Hong Kong Tokyo
Nairobi Dar es Salaam Cape Town
Melbourne Auckland Madrid

and associated companies in
Berlin Ibadan

Oxford is a trade mark of Oxford University Press

First published 1990 by Oxford University Press
First issued as a World's Classics paperback 1990

British Library Cataloguing in Publication Data

Data available

Library of Congress Cataloging in Publication Data
Ovid, 43 B.C.-17 or 18 A.D.
[Selections. English. 1989]
Ovid, the love poems / translated by A.D. Melville;
with an introduction by E.J. Kenney.
Translations from the Latin.
Bibliography: p.   Includes index.
1. Ovid, 43 B.C.-17 or 18 A.D.—Translations, English.   2. Love
poetry, Latin—Translations into English.   3. Love poetry, English—
Translations from Latin.   I. Melville, A. D.   II. Title.
PA6522.A2 1989   871'.01—dc20   89-9267

ISBN 0-19-814762-7
ISBN 0-19-282194-6 (Pbk)

3 5 7 9 10 8 6 4

Printed in Great Britain by
BPCC Paperbacks Ltd
Aylesbury, Bucks

UXORI NATISQUE CARISSIMIS

ET

IN PIAM MEMORIAM

L. P. W.

ACKNOWLEDGEMENTS

I am grateful for advice in matters botanical to Dr J. S. Heslop-Harrison and in matters legal to Professor J. A. Crook and Mr D. E. C. Yale. Mr Melville has read the Explanatory Notes in draft and his comments have led to the making of numerous improvements.

E.J.K.

CONTENTS

OVID (Publius Ovidius Naso) was born on 20 March 43 BC at Sulmo (now Sulmona) in the Abruzzi. The year of his birth was long remembered as that in which both consuls fell fighting Antony at Mutina, leaving Octavian (the future Augustus) in a position of strength which he exploited to become Triumvir and eventually sole ruler of the Roman world. In view of Ovid's fate at his hands it is not surprising that in the poem which is our chief source for his life (*Tristia* iv. 10) he lays some stress on these circumstances—more especially as there was a contemporary report that the deaths of both consuls had in fact been compassed by Octavian (Tacitus, *Annals* i. 10. 2, Suetonius, *Augustus* 11). By the time that Ovid came to manhood the combined forces of Antony and Cleopatra had been routed at Actium (31 BC) and the Roman Republic had been transformed into an (ostensibly) benevolent despotism.

Ovid's family was prosperous, and he was sent to Rome to study under the leading teachers of the day. For Roman boys education then and for centuries to come was verbal, literary and rhetorical, its principal aim the production of fluent and convincing extempore speakers. The reminiscences of the elder Seneca (*Controversies* ii. 2. 8–12, ix. 5. 17) illustrate vividly the effects of this kind of training on Ovid, in whom it encouraged and developed an obviously innate delight in words, their metrical arrangement and artistic manipulation. Possibly the encouragement went too far: Quintilian thought that he would have been a better poet 'if he had controlled his genius rather than letting it control him' (*Institutio Oratoria* x. 1. 98). His education was rounded off in the manner usual for the governing class, by the then equivalent of the Grand Tour through Greek lands. There followed on his return to Rome some minor judicial posts, but he soon decided (in spite of his father's discouragement) that his true vocation was poetry and abandoned his official career to dedicate himself to literature.

His earliest work, the *Amores* (Loves), was begun when he was a very young man, perhaps as early as c.25 BC. The original five books, circulated individually as each was completed, were reissued in the collected edition that we now have (see Ovid's Preface) not earlier than 16 BC, when the Sygambri first attracted public attention at Rome (*Amores* i. 14. 45 ff.; see McKeown, i. 79). In the interval Books i–ii of the *Ars Amatoria* (Art of Love) may have appeared (see Note on *Amores* ii. 18. 19); in their present form they are dated by the allusions at i. 177 ff. to about 1 BC. That there had been an earlier edition, to which this passage was later added, as argued by Syme, is debatable (see Note on *Ars* ii. 745–6). Book III of the *Ars* postdates the *Medicamina Faciei Femineae* (Cosmetics for Ladies) and the three-book edition of the *Amores* (*Ars* iii. 205–6, 343). The *Remedia Amoris* (Cures for Love) is dated by the allusion (155–8) to the eastern campaigns announced at *Ars* i. 177 ff. to not later than AD 2 (Henderson, xi–xii). Some if not all of the single *Heroides* (Letters of Heroines) had been circulated when *Amores* ii. 18. 21–6 was written (see Note); the double letters (16–21) may have appeared posthumously. The lost tragedy *Medea* is alluded to more than once in Ovid's running commentary on his poetic career; it may not have actually appeared until after the publication of the three-book edition of the *Amores* (see Note on *Amores* ii. 18. 18). There is much uncertainty as to the chronology and sequence of all these works (bibliography at McKeown, i. 74 n. 1), but even assuming a more even spread of activity than has been generally supposed (see Syme, 1–20), this body of work represents an ˋaltogether astonishing feat of literary productivity.

From about AD 1 onwards Ovid was simultaneously working on the *Metamorphoses* (Transformations) and the *Fasti* (Calendar). The first of these is an epic—Ovid's only surviving work in hexameters—in fifteen books, a vast collection of brilliantly told stories from classical and Near-Eastern legend describing or alluding to changes of shape. The second is a long elegiac poem in twelve books on Roman festivals and cults, an aetiological work inspired by Callimachus' *Aetia* (cf. Introduction, p. xiv). This was half completed and the *Metamorphoses* (so, in spite of Ovid's disclaimers, we must believe) substantially ready for publication, when disaster struck. In AD 8 Ovid, who was by then, since the deaths of Virgil and Horace, indisputably the premier poet of Rome, was suddenly sent into exile at Tomis (now Constanţa in Romania) on the Black Sea. The sentence was decided and pronounced personally by Augustus, the two causes of offence being *carmen*, a poem, the *Ars Amatoria*, and *error*, an unspecified indiscretion. The mystery surrounding this episode has never been cleared up; though Ovid in his exile poetry is sometimes surprisingly bold in pleading his case, and many of his contemporaries must have been in the secret, he nowhere allows a clear inference as to the nature of the *error*. The picture that emerges from such hints as he does give is that of involuntary complicity in some scandal, in which politics and morals were interlocked, affecting the Imperial house and Augustus in particular.

Of the poetry written by Ovid at Tomis the five books of *Tristia* (Sorrows) and the four of *Epistulae ex Ponto* (Letters from Pontus) were devoted to pleading his case, ostensibly before the Emperor, really before the bar of public opinion, to which he can be seen repeatedly appealing over Augustus' head. Tone and theme are constantly varied, but central to the whole campaign is Ovid's consciousness of his poetic vocation and his confidence in his identity as a poet. The second book of the *Tristia*, a single long elegy, is a witty and at times astonishingly outspoken defence of himself and his poetry. Standing apart from these works is the *Ibis*, a curse invoking many dire fates culled from Greek myth on an unidentified (and probably fictitious) enemy; its purpose was in all likelihood to uphold his reputation as a learned poet and so his claims to special consideration by the public and by posterity. Public and private pleading alike proved powerless to appease Augustus or Tiberius, who succeeded him in AD 14, and Ovid spent the rest of his life at Tomis, dying there in AD 17.

He was three times married, and had one daughter.

INTRODUCTION

Omnia uincit Amor: et nos cedamus Amori.
'Love conquers everything: we too must yield to Love.'

VIRGIL

Et mihi cedet Amor.
'Love too shall yield to me.'

OVID

I

IN his famous survey of Greek and Latin literature for the aspiring barrister Quintilian makes a relatively modest claim for Roman elegy. 'In elegy also [sc. as well as in epic] we challenge the Greeks', he writes.[1] He might have pitched it somewhat more strongly. In the hands of Ovid's predecessors, Gallus, Tibullus, and Propertius, the love-elegy took on almost the status of a new genre; and Ovid was to open up yet wider vistas of innovation.[2] Love, to be sure, had been a prominent theme of Greek elegy, especially of the elegiac epigram; but the elegiac love-poet as we meet him in Tibullus, Propertius, and Ovid is a Roman creation. This figure inhabits a world governed by a set of distinct, 'elegiac', values. His life is dedicated to love in the shape of service to a demanding, often cruel, not infrequently unfaithful mistress. This service he celebrates in a cycle of short elegiac poems in which both the relationship itself and the poetry inspired by it are written about in a manner perhaps best described as one of continuous critical assessment. Corresponding to this dual dedication is a rejection of 'un-elegiac' social and political values: marriage, public life, war, national and martial themes, the 'grand' genres of poetry, above all heroic epic.

In the long-running argument among scholars about the genesis of Roman elegy, the part played by Catullus is sometimes underestimated. Of the poems addressed certainly or probably

---

[1] *Elegia quoque Graecos prouocamus, Institutio oratoria* x. 1. 93.
[2] See the Explanatory Notes on *Remedia Amoris* 395–6. Subsequent references to the Notes are in the form '*Remedia* 395–6 n.', etc.

to 'Lesbia', a dozen or so are in elegiac couplets. These for the most part are short epigrams rather than elegies proper,[3] and Catullus' values are not identical with those of the later elegists; but there is clearly discernible in these poems the germ of the cycle of introspective poetry centring on the figure of the elegiac *domina*, the woman whom the poet can live neither with nor without. Too little survives of the four books of Gallus' *Amores* to allow his contribution to the development of the genre to be accurately assessed.[4] In the light both of the express testimony of Quintilian (loc. cit. n. 1) and Ovid (*Tristia* iv. 10. 53, *Amores* i. 15. 29-30, iii. 9. 63-4), and of the indirect evidence of Virgil's sixth and tenth Eclogues, there can be no doubt that it was substantial, possibly definitive. For actual examples of the genre in its brief heyday, however, we must turn to Tibullus, Propertius, and Ovid himself.

To Tibullus Ovid pays a striking formal tribute in a poem which, occupying as it does the central place of honour in Book III of the *Amores*,[5] must be given due weight for what may be implied as well as for what is actually said in it. One might guess that Tibullus' unostentatiously elegant[6] management of the elegiac couplet appealed more to Ovid, on the technical plane, than the often awkward and strained expression of Propertius. However that may be, it is in fact Propertius whose influence pervades the *Amores*, both as a source of themes, imagery, and phraseology for imitation and variation, and as the model of the collection as a whole. What may be called the 'plot' or scenario of the *Amores* may be viewed as a formalization—perhaps a *reductio ad absurdum* or burlesque (see section III below)—of that of the first three books of Propertius.[7] However, for Propertius any such term

---

[3] The long and difficult Poem 68 is in a class of its own; no successor chose to continue down the trail there blazed.

[4] Until 1978 all that was known was a single pentameter. In that year a papyrus was unearthed in Egypt containing fragments of ten verses generally attributed to him: text and commentary by Anderson, Parsons and Nisbet, *Journal of Roman Studies* 69 (1979), 125-55. As is often the way with such discoveries, the subsequent discussion has generated more questions than answers. See below, p. xv and n. 11.

[5] iii. 9; on the numbering and arrangment of the poems and the structure of the books see below, p. xvii f.

[6] The word is Quintilian's (loc. cit. above, n. 1).

[7] This point is not affected by the controversies about whether Propertius

as 'plot' would be misleading: there is no coherent narrative sequence linking his initial acceptance of Cynthia's domination over him, and the writing of the sort of poetry dictated by it, in the first elegy of Book I, with the final rejection of both at the end of Book III. But these initial and terminal positions are precisely defined; and the reader who turns from Book III to Book IV finds the implications of the shift from avowal to disavowal translated there into literary fact: a new kind of elegy, with a markedly aetiological cast and, when she reappears, a rather different Cynthia. This was the hint which Ovid took for his *Amores* and, being Ovid, proceeded to exploit *à outrance*.

II

Nowhere are Ovid's originality and independence of mind, as well as his sheer cleverness, more strikingly evident than in what is, for us, his literary début: the *Amores* as he finally approved them for the public eye. The first poem is itself a novelty: a brief epigram standing outside the sequence of elegies proper and containing a personal message from the book to the reader. In this is set out the publishing history of what awaits him: the five books of elegies (*libelli*) that had been put into circulation one by one as Ovid wrote them[8] have now been improved by being reduced to three and are reissued as a literary unit in that shape. How many poems were suppressed in this revision we have no means of knowing. If the lines are taken at their face value none were added. Given the neat arrangement and formal symmetry of the collection (see below), this is perhaps a little difficult to swallow (and cf. i. 9. 2 n.); and Ovid himself later hints (iii. 12. 41–2) that we are not bound to believe everything poets tell us. In any case, we can only read the collection as we now have it.

What follows is no less arresting and unexpected. Catullus, Horace, Tibullus, and Propertius had all opened their collections of poems with one addressed to a patron or dedicatee: Nepos,

'published' his books I–III as an entity or whether the present three books were originally four.

[8] This is what must have happened; there was never an 'edition' in five books.

Maecenas, Messalla, Tullus.[9] Ovid dispenses with any such introductory ceremony; he begins, epic-style, *in medias res*—for the very good reason that it is an epic that, as the curtain rises, we discover him writing. This is a far cry from the canonical self-introduction of the elegiac lover-poet. Nothing had been farther from his thoughts than love or elegy when he embarked on the composition of a successor to the *Aeneid* (i. 1. 1 n.), only to have Cupid appear and ruthlessly mutilate the metre, so turning him willy-nilly into an elegist. This is a brilliant per-version, both of generic posture and of well-known literary motifs. Of all possible subjects for an epic poem, a Gigantomachy, as this one is later revealed to be (ii. 1. 11–16), was the most offensive to Alexandrian critical taste,[10] therefore the least elegiac. That the poet should be deflected from such an undertaking into the approved, narrow, Callimachean, path by the intervention of a god was a motif familiar from contemporary poetics, most particularly in Virgil's adaptation (*Eclogues* 6. 3–5) of lines from the famous and influential proem to Callimachus' *Aetia* (frag-ment 1. 23–4 Pfeiffer). But such interventions were the pre-rogative of the Muses or of Apollo, their Chief, not of Cupid, whose uncalled-for appearance provokes a pained expostulation in Ovid's best manner on the subject of job-demarcation among the Olympian workforce (i. 1. 5–16).

In all this the poetic cart, so to say, is put before the amatory horse. Propertius and Tibullus had been moved to write poetry by love. Ovid is peremptorily drafted by Cupid into the ranks of the elegists; on protesting that he has nothing (i.e. nobody) to write about, he is told that Cupid can soon see to that:

> questus eram, pharetra cum protinus ille soluta
>   legit in exitium spicula facta meum
> lunauitque genu sinuosum fortiter arcum
>   'quod'que 'canas, uates, accipe' dixit 'opus.'
>   (i. 1. 21–4)

---

[9] Virgil's first *Eclogue*—which is in any case a dramatic dialogue—has no addressee, but 4 is addressed to the Muses, 6 to Varus, 8 to Pollio (?), and 10 to Arethusa.

[10] See Ovid, *Metamorphoses* tr. A. D. Melville (The World's Classics, Oxford 1987), p. xxvii f. and v. 319 n.

> I'd made my protest. He drew instantly
> An arrow from his quiver, chosen with care
> To lay me low, and braced against his knee
> His crescent bow. 'Here, poet, take
> This for the verses you next make.'

The poet's fate is sealed; with *'opus'* one can hear the plunk of the arrow hitting its target. The next two elegies go on to exploit the consequences of this witty inversion of literary cause and effect. In the second elegy the poet makes his formal submission to Cupid, figured as a Roman *triumphator*; and in the third he decides that he has found the girl who is to be the source and subject of the poetry that he is under contract to write. He opens his negotiations with her with a ritual protestation of undying love and faithful service, but the agreement between them is severely businesslike. She is to provide (literary) material in the shape of herself (see i. 3. 19 n.), and he will write the poetry about her that will make them both famous. The simple-sounding verse

> prouenient causa carmina digna sua (20)
> my verse will issue worthy of its source

has a double resonance. *Prouenient* connotes *prouentus*, the harvest or yield of an investment; and the phrase *carmina digna* is (as we now know) an echo of Gallus.[11] The fruit of this compact, that is to say, will be poetry that is worthy not only of its subject but of Gallus, implicitly acknowledged as the founder of the genre. Allusively and obliquely, as befits his pretensions, Ovid is pledging his poetic credit.

The sheer literariness of all this should operate as a check on speculation about the identity of the *puella* with whom the deal is struck in *Amores* i. 3. She is not named in that elegy or the next; 'Corinna' makes her first appearance in i. 5. In comparison with Catullus' 'Lesbia' or Propertius' 'Cynthia' or 'Tibullus' 'Delia',[12] Corinna is a colourless figure. She is of course ideally beautiful (i. 5)—perhaps in itself something that makes her too

---

[11] See S. Hinds, *The Metamorphosis of Persephone. Ovid and the self-conscious Muse* (Cambridge, 1987), pp. 122–4.

[12] All pseudonyms. The *locus classicus* for the conventions of naming the *domina* is Apuleius, *Apologia* ch. 10.

good to be true, more like the heroines of Greek romance than a credible contemporary mistress?, clever (ii. 19, 9), imperious (ii. 17. 5 ff.) and sensual (iii. 7. 25-6); but these traits of the elegiac *domina* are mostly conventional, as is the behaviour of all the girls in the *Amores*, whether specifically identified with Corinna or not.[13] Only in the abortion poems (ii. 13, 14) does the *persona* seemingly step out of line (see ii. 13. 2 n.). When Ovid notes that many have wanted to know who Corinna was (*Ars* iii. 538) and that there have been false claimants to the honour (ii. 17. 29-30) one may suspect that his tongue was in his cheek, and that Corinna's true place in Elysium is with Mrs Harris. The phrase by which he refers to her in his *apologia pro vita sua* (*Tristia* iv. 10. 60; cf. ii. 340) is ambiguous: *nomine non uero*, 'under a name that was not hers', does not necessarily imply that she actually existed. Discussion of that much-vexed question, the social status of the elegiac mistress, is therefore otiose in her case: enough that she provided the material for Ovid's exploration of the typical situations of the elegiac relationship. In connection with the *Ars Amatoria*, however, the question was to become painfully relevant.

III

The possibilities for poetical exploitation offered by the elegiac relationship were not unlimited, and might indeed have seemed to have been more or less exhausted by Ovid's predecessors. Such was evidently Propertius' feeling when he turned to the rather different type of elegy represented by his Book IV; and such is the lesson of the only substantial body of post-Ovidian love-elegy, the poems ascribed to 'Lygdamus', a tired *réchauffé* of conventional motifs and elegiac clichés.[14] In the initial pro-grammatic sequence of *Amores* i. 1-3 Ovid, as it were, takes the genre by the scruff of the neck and shows it who is to be master. By choosing to write love-elegy—the little charade with Cupid is Ovid's way of conveying that the choice of genre is his own— in the immediate wake of three distinguished predecessors[15] he

---

[13] She is named in twelve elegies out of the fifty.

[14] His poems are transmitted as Book III of the Tibullan corpus.

[15] Virgil and Horace, so far as Latin literature was concerned, broke new ground in the *Eclogues* and *Epodes*; and Lucilius was not recent enough to inhibit

was taking a calculated risk. If this gamble was to come off, some semblance at least of novelty had to be imparted to the genre as he had received it from Propertius and Tibullus.

Elegiac love-poetry is a symbiosis: love and poetry batten on and enrich each other. In Propertius' Books I–III the relationship finally goes into imbalance and dies. The *Amores* offers a cheerfully cynical commentary on this process in the shape of a caricature of it, in which every vicissitude of the lover-poet's attempt to make the genre 'work' is passed in review and the undertaking is followed through with relentlessly accurate observation to its fore-ordained collapse. The treatment of the themes and episodes is what is generally described as 'rhetorical': in each elegy Ovid propounds a thesis or posits a situation which is then systematically developed, using every resource of specious or even absurd argument until the possibilities are exhausted—or are apparently exhausted, for he will often return to attack the same idea from a different angle (see below). The effect may be compared with that intended by Professor Morris Zapp in David Lodge's brilliant novel *Changing places*, whose projected definitive edition of Jane Austen was not designed to enhance the understanding and enjoyment of her books but to put a stop once and for all to the production of any further garbage on the subject. After the *Amores* it was simply no longer possible to write love-elegy: Ovid had dealt the genre its death-blow.

His analysis does not proceed methodically through the affaire phase by phase; that would have been inartistic and—in this context the words are almost synonymous—implausible. It is evident that in Book III frustration and disillusion are the predominant emotions expressed, but they are by no means absent from Book I: the central elegy in that book (i. 8) is a revelation of the corruption and venality that are inherent in the elegiac relationship of its very nature, and it is shortly followed (i. 10) by a direct attack on the greed of his (unnamed) mistress. However, the movement, more clearly articulated than in Propertius, from the acceptance of elegiac love and elegiac love-poetry in i. 1 to the rejection of both in iii. 15 is unmistakable.

a would-be satirist. When Ovid wrote *Amores* i. 15 Propertius was evidently still alive: see i. 15. 9–30 n.

Formally the most noticeable difference between the two poets is that, whereas Propertius' overtly programmatic poems are distributed on no clear system,[16] Ovid punctuates the narrative or 'plot' of the Amores by a symmetrically ordered sequence of programmatic poems which serve as a sort of detached commentary on the whole undertaking, in which the poet defines and redefines his gradually evolving attitude to life, love and art: i. 1–3, 15; ii. 1, 18;[17] iii. 1, 15 (see nn.). Given this structural symmetry, it can hardly be accidental that, when certain easy and unforced adjustments are made to the conventional numeration of the poems, the total number of elegies in the collection turns out to be 50, made up of books of, respectively, 15, 20, and 15 poems.[18] Cultivation of round numbers, particularly multiples of five, was a feature of Augustan poetry-books,[19] as was that of symmetrical structures.[20] The exaggerated precision with which Ovid uses these devices to articulate the interaction between poet and poetry, lover and love, himself and his predecessors, in the Amores is peculiar to him and is in all probability part and parcel of their intended deflationary effect.

Within this framework the other elegies are arranged according to a well-understood principle of artful disorder (variatio, Greek poikilia); the reader is kept guessing and so expectant. Poems on the same or related themes are sometimes paired (e.g. i. 11, 12; ii. 7, 8; iii. 11, 11b), sometimes separated (e.g. i. 10, iii. 8; i. 4, ii. 5; ii. 3, iii. 4). Situation and mood may change abruptly, from exclusion and frustration (i. 4) to blissful consummation (i. 5) and back again to frustration (i. 6). Between what may be called poems of acceptance and hope and poems of rejection and despair there is, as has been noted previously, no obvious growth of

[16] ii. 1, 10, 34; iii. 1, 2, 3, 9. The term 'programmatic' is used by scholars of poems or passages in which the poet declares, usually in symbol or allegory, his poetic position.

[17] This poem is obviously and overtly programmatic, but its penultimate placing in the book seems anomalous. However, ii. 19, when attentively read, also offers programmatic features: see ii. 19. 25, 32 nn.

[18] The Somnium (Dream), iii. 5, is not Ovid's: see Kenney, Agon 3 (1969), 1–14. ii. 9 and iii. 11 are generally divided by editors into paired poems.

[19] Virgil, Eclogues (10); Horace, Satires I (10), Odes II (20), III (30), Epistles I (10); Tibullus I (10); Propertius I (20+2).

[20] e.g. (though scholars argue about the details) Virgil, Eclogues; Horace, Epistles I; Propertius I.

imbalance until Book III, where disillusion increasingly sets in after the second elegy and culminates in a sequence of poems in which in various ways the reader's attention is diverted to other subject-matter and other genres. Thus iii. 9, the lament for Tibullus, can be read as a valediction not only to the poet but to love-elegy itself; and in iii. 10 love is virtually edged out by mythical-aetiological themes, to be banished altogether in iii. 13 by the appearance of a figure from right outside the world of elegy—the poet's (real) wife (see iii. 13. 1 n.).[21] After this the formal leavetaking of iii. 15, with its glimpse of the wider literary vistas now calling the poet and already prepared for in his compact with Tragedy in iii. 1, comes as the predictable dénouement of the masquerade.

IV

Ovid had now finished with—had indeed finished off—love-elegy. He had not finished writing elegiac verse about love. In the *Amores* he had explored and mapped, tongue well in cheek and bucket of cold water at hand, the world of the elegiac lover-poet and, the exploration complete and the romantic mystery exploded, put the genre behind him, its literary usefulness exhausted. In the *Ars Amatoria* and the *Remedia Amoris* he turned to the real world of contemporary Rome. This is not to say that the kind of affaire poeticized by the elegists and by Horace in his erotic *Odes* took place in a purely literary Never-Never Land.[22] Roman society, like that of any rich cosmopolitan capital, was vivid and dissolute; the world of elegy was essentially urban, its backdrop the City of Rome. In the *Ars* and *Remedia* Ovid places his lovers firmly in that urban milieu, the streets, piazzas, colonnades, temples, shops, theatres, spectacles, dinner-parties of the Rome in which he and his readers lived. The sub-text, however, is identical with that of the *Amores*, though now overtly expressed:

---

[21] In the life of the elegiac lover-poet marriage plays no part. In the more realistic world of the *Ars* and *Remedia* husbands and wives figure as awful warnings, antitypes of the partners in a truly loving relationship. Cf. *Ars* ii. 155 n.

[22] See the important article by J. Griffin, 'Augustan poetry and the life of luxury', *Journal of Roman Studies* 66 (1976), 87–105 (= *Latin poets and Roman life* (1985), pp. 1–31), arguing cogently for the existence of a closer rapprochement between life and literature than many scholars have been prepared to allow.

the poet's complete mastery of his art and craft. Love and poetry are still symbiotic; the difference is that this symbiosis works.

Et mihi cedet Amor:[23] even the god whose universal power was acknowledged and feared by his fellow-gods (*Metamorphoses* v. 369–70) and who had (ostensibly) dictated the form of the poet's first literary venture, has now met his master. Even love (and Ovid's readers would have been cognisant of the genealogy that made Eros one of the primeval Powers of the universe) can be controlled by art. The premiss of the genre to which the *Amores* formally belongs is that in the bittersweet commerce of love (*Ars* iii. 331 n.) it is the bitter that inevitably predominates: suffering is the ordained lot of the elegiac lover.[24] That is the source of his poetry; laments and complaints, as Horace's *Ode* to Tibullus sardonically notes (*Odes* i. 33. 1–4), are his stock-in-trade. There is no poetic mileage in a happy affaire. Ovid will change all that. He will show, both that is possible to be happy, though in love, and also—and this, for him, is the essential point—that poetic capital can be made out of the paradox.

V

The poet of love was also necessarily a teacher of love. So Propertius:

> hoc, moneo, uitate malum: sua quemque moretur
>   cura, neque assueto mutet amore locum.
> quod si quis monitis tardas aduerterit auris,
>   heu referet quanto uerba dolore mea!

(i. 1. 35–8)

> Avoid, I warn you, this evil; let each of you cleave
> To the one he holds dear, nor change an accustomed love.
> But whoever is slow to heed my admonition
> Will recall, alas with what depth of sorrow
> These words of mine!

(tr. Ronald Musker)

---

[23] What an ancient reader saw in his text was *ET MIHI CEDET AMOR*; the crucial ambiguity between *amor* and *Amor* is obscured by modern conventions of capitalization.

[24] Cf. Propertius i. 1. 1 *Cynthia prima suis* miserum *me cepit ocellis*, 'It was Cynthia who first made me the unhappy captive of her eyes.'

It was, however, Tibullus who provided the actual prototype of
the *Ars Amatoria* in the shape of a lecture to the poet on love by
the ithyphallic garden-god Priapus (i. 4. 9–72).[25] The love in
question is that of boys, ignored in the *Amores* (see i. 1. 20 n.)
and expressly rejected in the *Ars* (ii. 684), and the treatment is
brief; but the hint was enough to set Ovid's ingenuity and
powers of invention to work. He had already experimented
with the didactic form in his poem on cosmetics, the *Medicamina
Faciei Femineae*, of which only the first hundred verses survive.[26]
On the face of it this belongs in the category of didactic trivia
cited (somewhat disingenuously) in his self-defence in *Tristia* (ii.
471–90); and so far as the recipes themselves are concerned, the
Medicamina represents a type of technical tour de force that
enjoyed a surprising popularity in classical antiquity and that has
been revived with more limited success in more recent times.[27]
The first fifty lines, on *cultus*, are another matter. The theme of
cultivation is closely related to the leitmotiv of the *Ars*[28] and
Remedia, the supremacy of art. Just as the complexion can be
improved by the application of modern scientific methods, so
(the message runs) can the quality of Roman love-life. The
poet's qualifications for his role as instructor are set forth in the
Amores; that is, as it were, his diploma. He now has his doctorate
and is equipped to found his own Open University:

> usus opus mouet hoc: uati parete perito;
>   uera canam. coeptis, mater Amoris, ades.
>
> (i. 29–30)

Experience prompts my labours. Heed the sage:
With truths, oh Venus! help me fill my page.

[25] In his defence of the *Ars* to Augustus Ovid draws attention to many other
passages in Tibullus which teach the arts of successful intrigue with women
(*Tristia* ii. 449 ff.).

[26] How much is lost is anybody's guess. Ovid's ingenuity was equal to any
amount of versified recipes and prescriptions, but a full-length *libellus* of some
seven or eight hundred verses on these lines would have taxed his readers'
patience, if not his resources.

[27] On Aratus and Nicander see below, p. xxiii; other subjects included
fishing, hunting, geography, precious stones, and volcanoes. In English one
may compare Armstrong's *The Art of Preserving Health* (1744), Dyer's *The
Fleece* (1757), and Grainger's *The Sugar-Cane* (1759).

[28] Cf. *Ars* iii. 101 ff. on *cultus*.

There is here a paradox that would not have escaped the attentive reader: an undertaking to master a god coupled with a rejection of divine revelation. Ovid clearly admired Lucretius: here he plays Epicurus on his own account. Venus is indeed invoked, as she had been invoked by Lucretius, but her part is that of the sensible mother who hands over her wayward son to a tutor in whom she has complete confidence.

In bringing the elegiac relationship out of its literary enclave into the light of common day Ovid was taking a risk, this time, however, not of a literary order—how great a risk was not to become immediately apparent. The social status of the girls of the *demi-monde* as we meet them in Horace and the elegists eludes precise definition. 'Between *libertinae* and prostitutes, between actresses and *meretrices*, even between some professionals and some *matronae*, the dividing line cannot have been so easy to draw as in theory, perhaps, it should have been.'[29] Corinna is a literary artefact, a type extrapolated from more sharply characterized individual figures such as Lesbia and Cynthia. In the *Amores* Ovid had described; in the *Ars* he prescribed, and the status of the women to be selected, pursued and possessed became of some consequence. He takes the precaution of entering a routine disclaimer at the outset: respectable freeborn girls and married women are out of bounds (*Ars* i. 31–2 n.). In a society in which married women notoriously intrigued with freedom and in a language in which *uir* meant indifferently 'lover' and 'husband', not many readers were likely to take this seriously, any more than Ovid himself, a wit and a sceptic, can have done. He recurs to and repeats this passage in his defence of the *Ars* in the *Tristia* (ii. 241 ff.), pointing out that Rome offered too many opportunities and incentives to lovely woman to stoop to folly for a mere book to make much practical difference. All perfectly true; but not calculated to appease an Emperor who was touchy on the subject of public morals, who had attempted to discourage adultery by legislation, and whose own private life was not above reproach. Ovid was not the first or the last political innocent to underrate the importance of humbug in keeping society on good terms with itself.

[29] Griffin, op. cit. (n. 22) 103=28.

VI

Had Augustus been disposed or equipped by nature to take a
historian's or critic's dispassionate view of the *Ars* he must have
recognized that it was no more a practical handbook of seduction
than Virgil's *Georgics* was a practical manual of agriculture. It is
not its utility, but its wit that recommends it. It belongs, like the
Medicamina, in the class of 'display' or ornamental didactic,
whose purpose is not to impart instruction but to show off the
poet's ability to transform technical subject-matter into poetry.
This was a Hellenistic development in the history of the genre:
famous examples are Aratus' poem on astronomy, the *Phaeno-*
mena, and Nicander's verse treatises on antidotes to poisons, the
Theriaca and the *Alexipharmaca*—the latter example being es-
pecially relevant to the *Remedia*, in which unhappy love is figured
as a disease and the poet as a doctor. As a subject for serious
philosophical enquiry love had preoccupied Plato and (some
might say) obsessed Lucretius. Ovid accordingly imparts a mock
significance to his theme by borrowing clichés of presentation
from the *De rerum natura* and the *Georgics*, and by the sustained
use of metaphors in which the progress of poet and reader
through the poems is depicted as a shared journey or voyage
towards the goal or haven of fulfilment or release.[30] Under this
pretence of serious and systematic enquiry the reader is regaled
with a kaleidoscopic sequence of vignettes, painted with affec-
tionate malice, of contemporary men and women in (or out of)
love—or rather playing the game of love according to the rules
of the elegiac affaire, now, we are told, reduced to a science.
This is a game at which anyone can play and in which nobody
need get hurt. And if after all something does go wrong, so that
a lover finds himself or herself really and unhappily in love, the
resources of science are not exhausted: what the poet taught he
can unteach. Some critics have thought that in the *Remedia*
Amoris the joke can be seen to be wearing thin, and indeed some
of its precepts amount to no more than a neat reversal of what
had been enjoined in the *Ars*. But this is by no means true of all
of them, and when all reservations are made, the exploitation of

[30] See *Ars* i. 3–8 n.

this single idea through four books of brilliantly accomplished verse with almost no longueurs is a tour de force hardly to be paralleled either in ancient or in modern literature.[31]

Lucretius and Virgil had illustrated and diversified their argument with a number of non-expository passages in which is contained some of the most powerful rhetoric and moving poetry to be found in the *De rerum natura* and the *Georgics*. These are the parts of the poems which make the strongest impression on their readers, a fact not lost on Ovid. The didactic precepts of the *Ars* and *Remedia* are interspersed and embellished with a series of narrative excursuses which offer some of the most entertaining writing in the poems. In tone and effect they vary greatly, ranging from the flippant revision of Roman history in the Rape of the Sabines (*Ars* i. 101–32) through an anthology of piquant episodes from the rich stores of Greek mythology— grotesque (Pasiphae, i. 289–326), marvellous (Ariadne, i. 527– 64), mildly lubricious (Achilles on Scyros, i. 681–704; Mars and Venus, ii. 561–92), enigmatic (Daedalus and Icarus, ii. 21–96), and tragic (Cephalus and Procris, iii. 685–746; Phyllis, *Remedia* 591–606). Ovid's gift for narrative was to attain its full expression in the *Metamorphoses*; the hexameter offered a more flexible and responsive vehicle than the elegiac couplet, with its built-in (and by Ovid actually enhanced) restrictions.[32] But whatever the limitations of the Ovidian couplet as a medium for narrative— limitations which he was to surmount with no less brilliance in the *Fasti*—it was ideally suited to the terse, nervous, and epigrammatic style of the *Amores*, *Ars* and *Remedia*.

VII

To grasp something of the technical problems faced by the translator of these poems some understanding of their Latin form is desirable.[33] The elegiac couplet is formed by a verse consisting of six metrical units ('feet'), the hexameter, followed by another with five, the pentameter. Thus the removal of a foot from a hexameter converts it to a pentameter (*Amores* i. 1.

---

[31] 'Ovid's best' was Macaulay's verdict on the *Ars*.
[32] See below, p. xxviii f.
[33] For more detail see the Note on Ovid's metre, below pp. xxvii ff.

4)—though it is worth noting that (as will be seen from the metrical analysis below), this cannot be done merely by lopping off a foot at the end of the line. In usurping Apollo's function Cupid has to know his metrical onions. Like all the metres of classical Latin poetry this one was borrowed from the Greeks, but in borrowing it the Roman poets changed its character in certain important respects. In Greek elegiacs sense and grammatical construction often flow on freely from one couplet to the next, whereas in Latin each couplet, even when it forms part of a sentence extending over several couplets, is as a rule syntactically self-contained. True enjambment between couplets is rare, in Ovid virtually unheard of, though within the couplet it is freely and effectively used, as in the opening lines of *Amores* i. 1:

> arma graui numero uiolentaque bella parabam
>   edere, materia conueniente modis.

> Fighting and violent warfare in a serious metre I was preparing
> To tell of, the matter fitting the metre.

Here sense and construction flow without a break from hexameter to pentameter; the comma in line 2 is strictly unnecessary, a concession to modern conventions.[34] But the quasi-autonomous nature of the couplet makes the form highly suitable for a balanced and antithetical treatment both of hexameter and pentameter and of the halves of the verses. A particularly striking example is:

> conscius esse uelis?   domina est obnoxia seruo.
>   conscius esse times?   dissimulare licet.
> scripta leget secum: matrem misisse putato;
>   uenerit ignotus;   postmodo notus erit.
>
> (Amores ii. 2. 17–20)

> Would you like to be an accomplice?
>   Then the mistress is in the servant's power.
> Do you fear to be an accomplice?
>   You can always pretend to be unaware.

---

[34] There was no consistent and generally observed system of punctuation in use in Latin books; generally readers punctuated for themselves, if they cared to take the trouble.

> You'll see her reading a letter in secret:
> assume it's from her mother.
> An unknown man will appear:
> before long you'll know him.

The number of changes that can be rung on these and other patterns is limitless, and Ovid's ingenuity in exploiting them inexhaustible; in the foregoing example one may note the avoidance of monotony (over even so short a sequence as four verses) achieved by the switch from questions in the first couplet to statements in the second. For the crisp sententious wit of these poems the form is ideally suited. For an English reader with no Latin the heroic couplets of Pope afford some sort of approximation to the effect of Ovid's elegiacs, but the analogy cannot be pressed too far. Nothing could be more Ovidian in spirit than *The Rape of the Lock*; but Pope's couplets, compared with Ovid's, lack both rhythmical and structural variety, and the effects of rhyme have no counterpart in Latin.

Thus, though at first sight the heroic couplet would seem to be the obvious form for an English translation of Ovid's elegiacs (cf. B. P. Moore, quoted below, p. xxx), the differences between the two metres impose caution; and the technical difficulties of such an attempt are formidable. Compact as English, with its wealth of monosyllables, can be, an inflected language sometimes has the advantage in respect of conciseness. It would not be easy to pack more point into six words than Ovid manages in

> spectatum ueniunt, ueniunt spectentur ut ipsae.
> *(Ars* i. 89)
> They come to look and to be looked at too.

Moore's version renders the basic sense perfectly, but the elegant verbal architecture of the original is only dimly visible: 'come' . . . 'too' answers very imperfectly to the emphatically pointed repetition and juxtaposition of 'ueniunt, ueniunt'. Moreover, as against the unvarying twenty syllables per couplet of the English heroic measure, Ovid had at his disposal a more flexible scheme offering from twenty-five to thirty-one syllables,[35] to say nothing of more varied rhythmical possibilities. Hence the translator who chooses heroic couplets is apt to find that there is often

---

[35] As in the holodactylic *Amores* i. 1. 1–2 quoted above.

simply too much in the Latin, especially if some stroke of linguistic wit is to receive its due, to fit comfortably into the English form. Even Moore's version, which is indeed a tour de force, shows the strain. Similar restrictions, *mutatis mutandis*, operate in the case of the metre devised by Mr Melville, mitigated however by a less exacting rhyme-scheme and by the ingenious use of four- or six-line groupings as explained in the Translator's Note. The result seems to me to come as close to conveying to a twentieth-century reader a sense of what Ovid is like as is humanly possible, and I like to think that Ovid himself would not have disapproved it.

NOTE ON OVID'S METRE

For readers wanting a more detailed account of the mechanics of Ovid's metre the following brief description may, it is hoped, be serviceable. The metre of English verse is accentual: the words bear their natural stress, and it is on the regular recurrence of this stress in some fixed scheme (with more or less subtle variations and inversions according to the art of the individual poet) that the metre depends. Greek and Latin verse is quantitative: the ordinary spoken accent (pitch or stress or both) is ignored (but see below), and the metre consists of patterns of syllables classified as either 'long' or 'short' according to the time taken to pronounce them.[36] The pattern of the elegiac couplet is:

1	2	3	4	5	6

quī mŏdŏ| Nāsō| nīs fŭĕ|rāmūs |quīnquĕ lĭ | bēllī

1	2	5/1	3	4	5/2

trēs sŭmŭs| hōc īl| lī | prāetŭlĭt | aūctŏr ŏ | pŭs.[37]

---

[36] This sharply dichotomous distinction must have been somewhat arbitrary, though less so than it would be in English, where there is a considerable range of gradations between the times needed to pronounce (e.g.) 'it' and 'strength', both of which can be either stressed or unstressed in English verse. Modern writers on ancient metre tend to prefer the terminology 'heavy' and 'light' to distinguish the metrical quantity of the syllable from the length of the vowel contained in it: see W. S. Allen, *Vox Latina*, 2nd edn. (Cambridge 1978), pp. 89–92.

[37] There is classical authority for this analysis, as for the alternative:

1	2	3	4	5

tres sumus | hoc il | li prae | tulit auc | tor opus.

The point is worth mentioning as it illustrates a pervasive interest in linguistic

In the first four feet of the hexameter and the first two of the pentameter dactyls (–∪∪) and spondees (––) are interchangeable. The variety thus achieved is counterbalanced by the uniformity required at the ends of the verses, where the patterns –∪∪|–⌣ and –∪∪|–∪∪⌣ are (respectively) almost and absolutely invariable. The last syllable of either verse may be 'long' or 'short'. The other fundamental rule concerns what is called the *caesura* (cutting). This is designed to ensure that in the middle of the verse the boundaries of words and feet do not coincide. Thus in the hexameter the third foot is usually divided after the first (long) syllable, giving the so-called 'strong' caesura:

$$\overset{3}{}$$
qui modo Naso|nis||fue|ramus quinque libelli.

This is the commonest pattern, with or without subsidiary caesuras in the second and/or fourth feet. With a so-called 'weak' caesura after the second (short) syllable of a dactylic third foot, 'strong' caesuras in both second and fourth feet are usual:

$$\overset{2}{} \qquad \overset{3}{} \qquad \overset{4}{}$$
at Phoe|bus||comi|tesque¦no|uem||ui|tisque repertor.

In the pentameter there must always be word-division after the first half of the divided fifth foot, cutting the verse in two in an unvaryingly regular pattern:

tres sumus hoc illi || praetulit auctor opus
at leuior demptis || poena duobus erit
edere materia || conueniente modis.

Thus the relatively flexible hexameter is always followed by a relatively inflexible pentameter.

The tendency to autonomy of the individual couplet inherent in this basic pattern was accentuated by two developments. Whereas in Greek the pentameter could end with a word of any number of syllables up to seven, Propertius appears to have initiated (or possibly revived) and Ovid with a tiny number of exceptions rigidly adopted a rule that it should always end with

---

minutiae; the grounding received by Ovid's readers was such as to equip them to appreciate the technical implications of Cupid's intervention in *Amores* i. 1 (cf. above, p. xxv).

a disyllable. The reasons for this limitation are disputed, but appear (like the comparable but rather less stringent limitations imposed on the end of the hexameter and the rule of the caesura) to be connected with the incidence of the stress-accent at these places in the verse. Ovid furthermore increasingly tended to use colourless words such as personal pronouns or parts of the verb 'to be' in this final position. The result was to throw the verbal interest of the pentameter, its centre of gravity, so to say, back into the body of the verse and so intensify the punctuating effect of the metrically invariable cadence of the distich.

E.J.K.

TRANSLATOR'S NOTE

OVID wrote all the poems in this volume in Elegiac couplets, an hexameter followed by a pentameter, the metre appropriate to the subject matter, as he explains in the first poem. He was following a long-established tradition. For more than five hundred years verse in this form had had a prominent place in the literature of the Greeks. Now in the sophisticated literary circles of Augustan Rome it had become de rigueur for love poetry, the rules of its versification increasingly refined in poems of polished elegance. Of this verse form Ovid was the supreme master; it was perfectly suited to his talents and temperament, the ideal vehicle for a young man's virtuosity.

The translator's task is to match in English, if that were possible, the sophistication of the Latin. For this purpose rhyme is in my opinion essential; without rhyme the brilliance of Ovid's couplets cannot be reproduced. By English translators from Marlowe onwards for some 350 years this view was accepted; the tradition of using rhyming couplets (the so-called heroic couplet) was firmly established. But in recent years, despite the examples of Moore, Wilkinson, and Watts, aberrations of taste have led to the belief that rhyme is outdated; and the translations that have resulted prove my point.

In this volume the *Art of Love* is translated in heroic couplets. I recalled the brilliant version of Moore, first published in 1935, and believed it could not be bettered. I suggested that it should be used and am delighted by its inclusion. (Moore wrote that heroic couplets are the only metre 'which adequately reproduces the snap and tang of the Ovidian elegiac'.) The translations of the *Amores*, the *Cosmetics for Ladies* and the *Cures for Love* are my own. I decided to experiment with a variety of metres, though in the Latin the metre is always the same, partly to please myself and partly to reduce the risk of monotony which some readers may find in the original where the theme is constant and the metre unvaried. For some of the poems of the *Amores* I have used heroic couplets, for others different metres that took my fancy (always of course rhyming). For most of them and for the

Cosmetics and *Cures* I have evolved a verse form which I believe more closely than any other gives the feeling of Ovid's couplets. A five-foot iambic line with a feminine ending alternates with a standard five-foot line and the shorter lines (corresponding to Ovid's pentameters) rhyme. The result is a sequence of four-line groups. Ovid did not formally join his couplets in pairs, but I have been agreeably surprised to find how often the sense of the Latin falls into groups of four or six lines. The use of an occasional six-line group, with a triple rhyme, provides the flexibility needed to fit the form to Ovid's couplets. With this verse form formality and elegance can be achieved and at the same time lightness and speed. In some of the poems of the *Amores* the groups are shown as stanzas, while in others they are not; thus further variety is obtained.

Elegance and sophistication would be enhanced if the longer lines rhymed as well as the shorter:

> And often they point out the passing poet,
> 'That's him, the fellow scorched by Cupid's flame.'
> And you're the whole town's talk, though you don't know it,
> While you boast what you've done and show no shame.
> *(Amores* iii. 1. 19–22)

This would require a Byronic virtuosity, but I hope that one day such a version may be achieved.*

I have of course profited from the versions of my predecessors. Marlowe translated the *Amores*, and his slim volume was published possibly in 1596. His is a line-for-line version in heroic couplets, a difficult task for which his technique proved inadequate, despite his many felicities; his vocabulary is by now often obsolete and his understanding of the Latin not always sound. I have adapted three of his versions (i. 5, iii. 7, iii. 14) with little change, and in homage to a great poet wished to adapt more, but found that to make them acceptable to a modern reader would involve changes so extensive as to

---

* It is interesting that on occasion Ovid rhymed his pentameters:

> Tempus erat quo uos speculum uidisse pigebit,
> et ueniet rugis altera causa dolor.
> Sufficit et longum probitas perdurat in aeuum
> perque suos annos hinc bene pendet amor.
> *(Cosmetics* 47–50)

frustrate my purpose. Dryden and a number of collaborators translated the *Amores* in heroic couplets with varying degrees of success; these versions, typical of their age, were paraphrases rather than translations. When interest revived in the twentieth century Guy Lee, some twenty years ago, rejected heroic couplets and defended his use of 'free verse'. His loose translation catches the spirit of the original pretty well. I have found pleasure and profit in reading it, but his style gives no hint of the elegance and virtuosity of Ovid's elegiacs.

Dryden translated Book I of the *Art of Love*, a vigorous and pleasing paraphrase; the rest was translated by others less successfully. The volume appeared in 1709 and included a version of the *Cures for Love* by Nahum Tate (better known as the author of the hymn 'While shepherds watched their flocks by night'). His is a very readable version with much to be admired, but he added a good deal of his own embroidery and when faced with difficulties preferred to invent.

All these poems were translated by Riley in the middle of the last century. His stilted Victorian prose is a helpful guide to the meaning of the Latin. The Loeb translation, dating from 1929 and revised in 1978, is helpful in the same way, but would not claim literary distinction. In 1982 there appeared translations of all these poems by P. Green; of his versions let it suffice to say that his views of a translator's duty to Ovid differ profoundly from mine.

Moore's translation of the *Art of Love* is now more than fifty years old. Some small amendments to modernize his style seem desirable. For instance I have changed 'thou', thine', etc., to 'you', 'yours'; ''tis' and ''twere' have gone; and a very few lines have been revised to correct the sense or remove a word that has become obsolete. These minor alterations will, I hope, enhance the reader's enjoyment and admiration of Moore's achievement. His version is line-for-line, particularly difficult in heroic couplets when the meaning is so accurately conveyed. My versions of the *Cosmetics* and *Cures* are also line-for-line, but my style needs fewer rhymes and my task has been that much easier.

Ovid's attitude to women, so clearly displayed in these poems, may well be judged offensive by many readers. I share that opinion; and it is no excuse, because it is not true, to say that

Ovid is less concerned with real life than with the fantasy world of the erotic genre. This is not the mellow poet of the *Metamorphoses*; these poems are the products of a younger man, brilliant and heartless. His contemporaries no doubt found them vastly amusing. From an early age, like Byron, he was famous. The entertainment is not always innocent and many readers will find it none the worse for that. But I prefer innocence; and when I had finished my translation of the Metamorphoses it was not my intention to tackle these poems. My defence (if defence were needed) is that I was provoked by Green's recent translation, which is widely available and in my view wholly unsatisfactory, and my publishers urged me to provide an alternative. Much—perhaps all—should be forgiven to a poet who writes with such sparkling wit and unfailing elegance. That wit and elegance I have endeavoured to reproduce; let that endeavour be my justification.

In making my translation I have had the great advantage of the expert guidance of Professor Kenney; he has suggested many improvements and I am most grateful. I have received, too, much advice and encouragement from my family and friends; to all of them I express my thanks. In these poems Ovid has given me much to admire and enjoy; I hope my readers will share my pleasure.

A.D.M.

SELECT BIBLIOGRAPHY

GENERAL

R. O. A. M. Lyne, *The Latin love poets from Catullus to Horace* (Oxford, 1980).

P. Veyne, *Roman erotic elegy. Love, Poetry, and the West*, tr. D. Pellauer (Chicago and London, 1988).

E. K. Rand, *Ovid and his influence* (London, 1926).

L. P. Wilkinson, *Ovid recalled* (Cambridge, 1955).

J. W. Binns (ed.), *Ovid* (London, 1973).

J. Barsby, *Ovid* Greece & Rome New Surveys in the Classics, 12 (Oxford, 1978).

E. J. Kenney, 'Ovid', in *The Cambridge History of Classical Literature*, II, *Latin Literature*, ed. E. J. Kenney and W. V. Clausen (Cambridge, 1982), 420–57=*The Age of Augustus* (Cambridge, 1983), 136–63.

LIFE AND CHRONOLOGY

R. Syme, *History in Ovid* (Oxford, 1978).

THE LOVE POEMS

Text

E. J. Kenney (Oxford Classical Texts: Oxford, 1961).

Translation and commentary

P. M. Green (Harmondsworth, 1982).

AMORES

Text and commentary

J. C. McKeown (4 Vols., Liverpool, 1987–).

F. Bertini (Milan, 1983) (in Italian, with translation).

Commentary

P. Brandt (Leipzig, 1911) (in German).

Book I: J. Barsby (Oxford, 1973) (with translation).

Interpretation

I. M. Le M. DuQuesnay, in Binns (op. cit.), 1–48.

MEDICAMINA FACIEI FEMINEAE

Text and commentary

F. W. Lenz (Berlin, 1960) (in German, with translation).
G. Rosati (Venice, 1985) (in Italian, with translation).

ARS AMATORIA

Commentary

P. Brandt (Leipzig, 1902) (in German).
Book I: A. S. Hollis (Oxford, 1977).

Interpretation

A. S. Hollis, in Binns (op. cit.), 84–115.
Molly Myerowitz, *Ovid's games of love* (Detroit, 1985).

REMEDIA AMORIS

Text and commentary

A. A. R. Henderson (Edinburgh, 1979).

Interpretation

A. S. Hollis, in Binns (op. cit.), 84–115.

AMORES

PREFACE

[to the second edition]

We who before were Ovid's five slim volumes
    Are three: he thought it better to compress.
Though reading us may still give you no pleasure,
    With two removed at least the pain is less.

BOOK ONE

I

I'd meant in solemn metre to rehearse
A tale of arms and war and violence,
Matching the weighty matter with my verse,
All lines alike in length—no difference;
    But Cupid laughed (they say)
    And filched one foot away.

Cruel boy, who made you judge of poetry?
We're not your rabble, we're the Muses' choir.
Shall Venus snatch blonde Pallas' weaponry,
Blonde Pallas fan the flames of passion's fire?
    And who'd approve if Ceres stood
    Queen of every upland wood?

Or shall the warrior Virgin rule the byre,
Long-haired Apollo learn to use the lance,
While Mars on Helicon strikes up the lyre?
Great is your reign, too strong your dominance.
    Why, greedy child, should you
    Go for this work that's new?

Is all the world then yours? The Muses' shrine
Yours too? Even Phoebus' lyre not now secure?
On the new page arose my proud first line,
Then came the next, unstringing me for sure;
    And there's no theme of mine
    Can suit that slighter line,

No boy, no girl with long and lovely hair—
I'd made my protest. He drew instantly
An arrow from his quiver, chosen with care
To lay me low, and braced against his knee
    His crescent bow. 'Here, poet, take
    This for the verses you next make.'

Poor me! That boy's sure arrows never stray.
I'm burning. In my vacant breast love reigns.
So in six beats my verse must rise today,
And settle back in five. Farewell, you strains
   Of steely war! Farewell to you,
   And to your epic metre too!

Muse, wreathe your golden tresses
   With myrtle of the sea,
And in eleven stresses
   Compose our poetry.

2

What can it be that I should find my bed
So hard, the blankets slipping, sleep quite fled,
And through the night, so long, I lie awake,
Tossing about until my tired bones ache?
I think I'd know if love were teasing me,
Or does his damage steal on secretly?
That's what it is. He's shot his subtle dart;
Love's in possession, tossing my poor heart.
So shall I yield, or feed the flame and fight?
I'll yield: a load borne readily lies light.
From torches waved I've seen the flame leap high;
When no one brandishes, I've seen it die.
Oxen that fight first yokes are beaten more
Than those who've learnt the plough's a pleasant chore.
A proud horse finds a hard bit brings distress;
One that's submissive feels the bridle less.
Love strikes the stubborn far more savagely
Than those who will confess their slavery.
Look, Cupid, I confess—your latest prize—
I hold out abject hands, my heart complies.
No need of war. Favour and peace are all;
No praise for you—unarmed to arms I'll fall.

Harness your mother's doves and wreathe your hair
With myrtle. Your stepfather, I declare,
Will give a fitting chariot, where you'll stand
As crowds triumphant shout on either hand.
Deftly you'll drive your birds and, following,
A train of captive youths and girls shall bring
A triumph that shall make the welkin ring.
Myself, new prize, my wound just made shall wear,
And in my captive heart fresh fetters bear.
In the triumphal train Good Sense you'll see,
Hands bound behind her back, and Modesty—
Whatever stands against Love's armoury.
All things fear you. In welcome loud and long
The cheering crowd will chant the triumph song.
Endearments, Madness, Wanderings of the brain,
Shall be your escort in the happy train,
Constant supporters, following your cause.
With these fine troops you vanquish in your wars
Both men and gods: their service lost, you'd be
All undefended in your nudity.
Your mother from Olympus' peak in joy,
Delighting in the triumph of her boy,
Her plaudits and her praises shall bestow,
And scatter roses to adorn your brow.
With jewelled wings and jewelled locks, behold,
You'll ride in golden state on wheels of gold.
And, if I know you, you'll ignite then too
Your furnace in the hearts of not a few.
Then many a wound you'll deal as you pass by:
Even should you wish, at rest your bow can't lie;
Your fierce flame scorches when its heat is nigh.
So Bacchus marked his Indian victory—
Though you are drawn by doves, by tigers he.
Therefore, since in your triumph I form part,
Don't waste your victor's wealth on my poor heart.
See how your kinsman Caesar's victories go:
The conqueror protects the conquered foe.

3

I ask for justice; she who's caught me now
Must either love me or ensure that I
Love her for ever. No, I aim too high.
Just to be loved—let her but that allow
And Venus will have met my dearest vow.

Take one who through long years would slave for you;
Take one who'd love with purest loyalty.
I've no proud names of ancient ancestry,
My line stems only from a knight, it's true.

No ploughs unnumbered work rich land of mine,
Both parents keep good watch on what they spend—
Little enough your lover to commend.
But on my side are Phoebus and his nine
Companions and the inventor of the vine,

And love who gives you me, and loyalty
That yields to none, and frank sincerity,
A blameless life and blushing modesty.
A thousand charmers give no joy to me;

I'm not love's acrobat to leap from bed
To bed. Believe me, you'll be mine always:
With you may heaven let me pass my days
Through the span granted by the Sisters' thread,

And die with you there weeping. Offer me
Yourself, a happy subject for my verse:
My verse will issue worthy of its source.
So many owe their fame to poetry—

Poor Io whom her cow's horns terrified,
Leda duped by the swan's adultery,
Europa whom the false bull bore to sea,
Horns held in virgin hands on either side.

We too shall live in verse the whole world through,
And my name shall be ever linked with you.

4

Your husband will be there at the same dinner—
  I wish your husband his last meal tonight.
I'm just a guest then, gazing at my darling
  While at your touch another takes delight?
And you to warm another's breast will snuggle,
  While round your neck his arm at will he throws?
No wonder that for fair Hippodamia,
  When wine went round, the Centaurs came to blows.
I'm no half-horse, my home's not in the forest,
  Yet I can hardly keep my hands from you.
Now, don't just give the winds my words of wisdom;
  Listen, and understand what you must do.

Arrive before your husband. Not that I can
  See quite what good arriving first will do;
But still arrive before him. When he's taken
  His place upon the couch and you go too
To sit beside him, on your best behaviour,
  Stealthily touch my foot, and look at me,
Watching my nods, my eyes, my face's language;
  Catch and return my signals secretly.
I'll send a wordless message with my eyebrows;
  You'll read my fingers' words, words traced in wine.
When you recall our games of love together,
  Your finger on rosy cheeks must trace a line.
If in your silent thoughts you wish to chide me,
  Let your hand hold the lobe of your soft ear;
When, darling, what I do or say gives pleasure,
  Keep turning to and fro the ring you wear.
When you wish well-earned curses on your husband,
  Lay your hand on the table, as in prayer.
If he pours you wine, watch out, tell *him* to drink it;
  Ask for what *you* want from the waiter there.

I shall take next the glass you hand the waiter,
    And I'll drink from the place you took your sips;
If he should offer anything he's tasted,
    Refuse whatever food has touched his lips.
Don't let him plant his arms around your shoulder,
    Don't rest your gentle head on his hard chest,
Don't let your dress, your breasts, admit his fingers,
    And—most of all—no kisses to be pressed!
You kiss—and I'll reveal myself your lover;
    I'll say 'they're mine'; my legal claim I'll stake.
All this, of course, I'll see, but what's well hidden
    Under your dress—blind terror makes me quake.

No squeezing thigh to thigh, no playing footsie!
    Don't link your tender foot with his hard one.
I fear so much because I've been so naughty—
    I'm tortured by the dread of what I've done.
Often my girl and I in sudden passion
    Beneath her cloak have had our happy fling;
You won't do that, but, still, to kill suspicion
    Just take it off—remove the knowing thing.
And urge your man to drink—but, mind, no kisses!
    When he's not looking try to lace the brew.
If wine and sleep have got him nicely settled,
    The time and place will tell us what to do.
And when you rise to leave and all rise with you,
    Make sure you're in the middle of the crush;
You'll find me in the crush, or I'll find you there;
    If you can touch me, give me a soft push.

Alas, a few short hours for words of wisdom!
    I'm forced to leave my girl at night's command.
At night he'll lock her in; in tears I'll follow
    To his cruel door—where I shall have to stand.
Now he'll take kisses, now not only kisses.
    You'll give him as his right, because you must,
What you give me in secret. Make it grudging
    (You can do that) like any girl who must.

Let love be sullen—no sweet words—just silence.
　If prayers of mine have power, I pray he too
May get no sort of pleasure; if he likes it,
　I pray at least no pleasure comes to you.

　　But yet, whatever lot the night may send,
　　Next day maintain you didn't—to the end!

5

[Marlowe's version, slightly modernized]

In summer's heat and mid-time of the day
To rest my limbs upon a bed I lay.
One shutter closed, the other open stood,
Which gave such light as lies within a wood,
Like twilight shade at setting of the sun,
Or when night's gone and yet day not begun.
Such light for bashful girls one should provide,
In which their shyness may have hope to hide.
In came Corinna in a long loose gown,
Her white neck hid with tresses hanging down;
So to her many lovers came Lais,
Or in her bedroom fair Semiramis.
I snatched her gown; being thin the harm was small,
Yet strove she to be covered therewithal,
And striving thus as one who wished to fail,
Was simply beaten by her self-betrayal.
Stark naked as she stood before mine eye,
No blemish on her body could I spy.
What arms and shoulders did I touch and see,
How apt her bosom to be pressed by me!
Belly so smooth below the breasts so high,
And waist so long, and what a fine young thigh.
Why detail more? All perfect in my sight;
And naked as she was, I hugged her tight.
And next—all know! We rested, with a kiss;
Jove send me more such afternoons as this!

6

Porter!—too bad you're chained by your hard shackle—
  Open this tiresome door, undo the bar.
I don't ask much—a little gap to take me
  Squeezing through sideways when it's just ajar.
Long love has shrunk me for this sort of business,
  Slimmed me and shaped my body the right way.
Love shows one how to slip past watching sentries
  And guides one's footsteps not to trip or stray.
Yet once I feared the night and empty phantoms,
  Amazed when people in the dark would go:
Cupid laughed in my ear with his sweet mother,
  And whispered 'Ovid, you'll be brave, you too.'
And in a trice love came. Now I'm not frightened
  By flitting ghosts or hands unsheathed to kill;
It's you I fear, so stubborn, you I flatter;
  You wield the bolt to ruin me at will.
Look (and draw back the ruthless bars to see it),
  Look how the door my flowing tears bedew.
You know that once when you stood stripped for flogging,
  I begged your mistress, I spoke up for you.
So does that favour then that did you service—
  So much for gratitude!—serve me no more?
Give me my due: you've got the chance to give it.
  The night is slipping by; unbolt the door.

Unbolt! May you not always drink slaves' water,
  But shed the chain you've worn so long at last.
Useless! You hear me but you're stony-hearted;
  The door is solid oak and still stuck fast.
Locked gates are good to guard beleaguered cities:
  Why are you scared of force? We're not at war!
What hope for foes, if you lock out a lover?
  The night is slipping by: unbolt the door.

I'm not escorted by a force of soldiers:
    Were cruel Love not here, I'd be alone,
Nor, if I wanted, could I make him leave me,
    I'd need leave first this body of my own.
So here is Love with me, a little fuddled,
    Hair oiled and garland slipping more and more.
Who'd fear that force? Who would not go to meet it?
    The night is slipping by; unbolt the door.

Still stubborn? Or asleep, your ears—confound you!—
    Rejecting words of love for winds to take?
Yet I recall when I first wished to elude you,
    Until the midnight stars you stayed awake.
Perhaps you've got a girl-friend sleeping with you:
    Alas! more luck for you than me in store.
If I'd that luck, I'd love to wear those shackles!
    The night is slipping by; unbolt the door.

Am I deceived or are the hinges creaking,
    Was the door pushed to give that tell-tale groan?
No, I'm deceived: the lively wind beat on it.
    Ay me! how far the breeze my hope has blown.
Boreas, if you recall raped Orithyia,
    Strike these deaf portals with your whirlwind's roar.
The whole town's silent now, and damp and dewy
    The night is slipping by; unbolt the door

Or I'm all set to raid your haughty mansion
    Myself with my strong sword and torch's flame.
The night and love and wine urge no forbearance,
    Wine and love free from fear and night from shame.
I've tried—tried everything—but I can't move you
    With prayers or threats; the door's less hard than you.
You are not fit to guard a lovely lady,
    To be a prison warder is your due.

And now the Morning Star on frosty axles
    Rises; the cock calls men to toil anew.
Here from my mournful locks I'll take my garland;
    Let it lie all night long on the hard sill;
My girl will see it thrown there in the morning,
    Witness of all the time I've spent so ill.
Goodbye, for what you're worth. I pay you tribute:
    Stubborn—lover locked out—a nasty knave.
Goodbye too, granite step and cruel door-posts
    And hard oak door, yourself, like him, a slave.

7

Put handcuffs on me, friend, if any friend's here,
    (My hands deserve it) till my frenzy clears.
My frenzy roused rash hands against my mistress,
    My mad hands hurt her and my girl's in tears;
So mad, I could have outraged my dear parents,
    Or at the holy gods hurled savage spears.

Well, Ajax, master of the sevenfold buckler,
    Seized herds and over wide fields laid them low;
Orestes, evil champion of his father,
    For battle with the Furies sought a bow.
So could I really tear those elegant tresses?
    Yet ruffled hair became my mistress' brow:

Quite beautiful—she looked like Atalanta
    Out hunting on the hills of Arcady,
Or Ariadne weeping when gales wafted
    False Theseus with his promises to sea,
Or (save her sacred priestess-band) Cassandra
    In chaste Minerva's shrine on bended knee.

Everyone calls me brute, they call me madman.
    She said no word: her tongue was stopped in fear.
But silent looks conveyed her sad reproaches;
    Speechless, she held me guilty with a tear.
I wish my arms had fallen from my shoulders;
    That part of me I usefully could spare.

To my own loss I've used my might in madness,
   My valour only punishment has won.
Hands, you're not mine, you means of crime and slaughter;
   You're sacrilegious: have those handcuffs on.
I'd suffer if I struck Rome's humblest citizen:
   Shall I have greater rights over my loved one?

Diomede's crime bequeathed the worst example:
   He first to strike a goddess, second me.
His guilt was less; I hurt the girl I worshipped;
   Diomede raged against his enemy.

Come, conqueror, get your fine triumph moving;
   Set laurels on your locks, fulfil your vow,
With crowds beside your chariot all shouting
   'Brave hero, hail—a girl's his conquest now.'

Put her in front, sad captive, tresses tumbled,
   All white but for the bruises on her face.
It should have been my lips that did the bruising;
   It should have been my love bites left that trace.

Why, if I stormed on like a swollen torrent,
   And rage, so blind, had got me for its prey,
Surely a scaring shout had been sufficient
   With thundered threats not over-strong that day.
I could have ripped her dress from top to middle
   To shame her—with her belt to bar the way.

Instead, brute that I was, I mauled her forehead,
   I used my nails to scratch her delicate face.
She stood distraught, her features pale and bloodless,
   Like marble quarried from the hills of Greece.

I saw her numb and faint, her body quivering,
   Like aspens trembling when soft breezes blow,
Or slim reeds rustling in a gentle zephyr,
   Or wrinkling waves when warm winds slide and go.
Her tears, long-hanging, down her cheeks came flowing,
   As water trickles from a bank of snow.

Then the first guilty feelings welled within me;
  It was my blood that flowed in every tear.
Three times I tried to kneel and beg for pardon;
  Three times she thrust my hands away in fear.

My darling, sweet revenge will soften anguish:
  Don't wait, just use your nails and scratch my face;
My eyes, my hair, don't spare them, show no mercy;
  Rage helps the weakest hands in such a case;
Or—so my crime's sad signs may last no longer—
  Set your hair straight and put it back in place.

8

There's an old hag, an old hag, name of Dipsas,
  A bawd, so listen if you'd like to know.
Her name speaks for itself—she's never sober
  Enough to see Aurora's rosy glow.
She knows the magic arts, the spells of Circe,
  Her skill turns back broad rivers to their source;
The flux of mating mares, the herbal mixtures,
  The whirling wheel, she knows their baleful force.
At her behest clouds mass across the heavens,
  At her behest day shines clear in the sky.
I've seen the stars drip blood, if you'd believe me,
  And on the moon's fair face a bloody dye.
At night she changes shape; with her old body
  Thick-feathered through the dark I think she flies;
I think, and so it's said; and double pupils
  Flash lightning and gleams dart from dual eyes.
From ancient tombs she calls past generations
  And splits the solid earth with sorceries.

This hag proposed to desecrate a marriage;
   Of baleful eloquence she had rich store.
Chance let me overhear her long instructions
   (I was concealed behind the double door).
'Yesterday, my dear, a rich young fellow found you
   Pleasing; he stopped and gave you a long stare.
And why not please? You're lovely—no girl lovelier;
   It's sad you're let down by the things you wear.
I'd like your luck to match your peerless beauty;
   When you are wealthy, I shall not be poor.
Your hopes were hurt with Mars in opposition;
   Now Mars is gone and Venus' place secure.
See how her coming helps. A wealthy lover
   Wants you; he's keen to fund whatever's short.
His good looks too with yours will bear comparison,
   And should he not buy you, he should be bought.
She's blushing! Shyness suits a pale complexion,
   A boon, if faked, a barrier if true.
You'll keep your eyes fixed on your lap demurely,
   Suit your regard to what each brings to you.
Maybe in Tatius' reign the frumpish Sabines
   Rejected more than one man with disdain;
Today in foreign wars Mars shows his mettle;
   In her son's city now it's Venus' reign.
Pretty girls play. She's chaste? Well, no one asked her.
   She asks herself, unless she's too illbred.
A matron too whose brows are wrinkled—shake them:
   From wrinkles many a mischief may be shed.
Penelope used a bow to test her suitors,
   To prove their prowess that great horny bow.
Winged time slips by in secret and deceives us,
   And galloping away the seasons go.
Coins shine with use, a fine dress asks for wearing,
   Abandoned buildings moulder in neglect.
Beauty needs use and fades without a lover,
   And one or two don't have enough effect.
With plenty plunder's surer—less ill-feeling;
   Full flocks give wolves a fine prey to select.

Look, what except new verses does that poet
    Give you? You'll get a lover's thousand things.
The poet's god himself in golden mantle
    On gilded lyre plucks his melodious strings.
Value a giver higher than great Homer;
    Believe me, giving too's a subtle art.
And don't despise a slave who's bought his freedom;
    A whitened foot won't mean a blackened heart.
And don't let busts in stately homes deceive you;
    He's poor; off with him and his blue blood too.
He'll ask a night for nothing, he's so handsome;
    His man-friend should pay him, then he'll pay you.
Keep your price down till the trap's set, in case they
    Escape; once captured roast them as you please.
No harm if love's a lie; let him think you love him
    And take good care your love's not lacking fees.
Often refuse a night: pretend a headache,
    Or your excuse will be it's Isis' day.
Then take him back before he's used to patience
    And love, repulsed too often, ebbs away.
See your door's deaf to pleas but oiled to presents;
    The voice outside your man inside should hear.
He's hurt? Be angry, seem hurt first: his charges
    Before your counter-charge will disappear.
But never give a lot of time to anger;
    Anger that lingers makes for enmity.
What's more, you ought to learn to weep to order,
    And wet your cheeks with tears of jealousy.
You'd cheat? Swear falsely, never fear. For love-games
    Venus adopts a deaf divinity.

Procure a well-trained lady's maid and servant
    To teach him what's the best to buy for you,
And ask small tips themselves; small tips from many
    Are straws to make a huge pile soon come true.
Get sister, mother, nurse to fleece your lover;
    The plunder's swift with many hands to take.
When you've run out of reasons for a present,
    Say it's your birthday and produce the cake.

Don't let his love feel safe, without a rival;
    Take care; if love's to last it must compete;
So let him see your neck all bruised with love-marks
    And traces of a man across the sheet.
Above all show him someone else's presents,
    And if you've got none, ask the Sacred Way.
When you've got lots, but there's still some remaining,
    Ask for a loan—which you will not repay.
Make your tongue mask your meaning; charm him, harm him:
    Sweet honey hides the poison down below.
If you'll do what I've learnt by long experience
    And my words aren't all lost to winds that blow,
Time and again while I'm alive you'll bless me,
    And pray my bones lie easy when I'm dead . . .'
Her words flowed on, when my shadow betrayed me;
    I could hardly keep my hands from her white head,
That wispy straggling hair, those cheeks all wrinkled,
    Those red wine-bleary eyes. May you be cursed
With want in your old age and long hard winters,
    No roof above your head and endless thirst!

9

Lovers are soldiers, Atticus. Believe me,
    Lovers are soldiers, Cupid has his corps.
The age that's fit for fighting's fine for Venus;
    Old men are shamed in loving, shamed in war.

The spirit captains look for in a soldier
    A pretty girl will look for in her man.
Both keep night watches, on the hard ground resting,
    Each for his girl, or captain, guardian.

Long marches are a soldier's job: a lover
    After his girl to the world's end will go.
High mountain barriers, rain-doubled rivers
    He'll cross and trudge his way through drifts of snow.
At sailing time he'll not plead dirty weather,
    Or wait for stars to tell him when to row.

Soldier or lover, who but they'd put up with
    The rain, the sleet, the snow, the cold of night?
One's sent to spy upon a dangerous enemy,
    One keeps his rival, like a foe, in sight.
Besieging cities, or a hard girl's threshold,
    On barbicans—or doors—they spend their might.

It often pays to catch the enemy sleeping,
    And rank and file unarmed with arms to slay.
Thus fell the fierce brigade of Thracian Rhesus;
    The captured horses left their lord that day.

And likewise lovers use a husband's slumber
    And launch their weapons on a sleeping foe.
Soldier and wretched lover, it's their business
    To foil the watch and past the sentries go.
Venus is chancy, Mars unsure; the vanquished
    Rise, those you thought could never fall, lie low.

So chuck it, anyone who thinks love's lazy!
    Love's for a dashing soul who dares the most.
Achilles was aflame for lost Briseis—
    Take your chance, Trojans, smash the great Greek host!

When Hector left Andromache's embraces
    To fight, his wife gave him his casque to tie;
When Agamemnon saw wild-haired Cassandra
    They say that great commander's heart leapt high.
Mars too was caught and felt the blacksmith's meshes;
    No tale in heaven had more publicity.

I was born idle, for unbuttoned leisure,
    Just lying languid with the shade above.
A pretty girl spurred me from my slack habits
    And bade me in her camp my service prove.
So now you see me brisk, a brave night-fighter:
    Yes, if you'd not be lazy, you should love.

10

You were like Helen on the Trojan galleon,
    Stolen from Troy to make two husbands fight,
And you were Leda whom the crafty lover
    Inveigled as a swan with wings of white;
You were Amymone lost in parched meadows,
    With on her head her pitcher poised above,
And for your sake I feared the bull, the eagle,
    And everything that love has made of Jove.
Now I've no fear; I'm cured of those delusions,
    Those looks of yours attract my eyes no more.
Why am I changed? Because you ask for presents—
    That's why you cannot please me as before.
While you played straight, I loved you, soul and body,
    But now your beauty's marred by your offence.
Love is a naked boy; his years unblemished
    And lack of clothes attest his innocence.
Why bid him price himself, the child of Venus?
    He's got no purse to stow the pelf away.
Fierce war he's just not fit for, nor his mother;
    Such gentle gods should not draw soldiers' pay.
A whore stands at her price for all to purchase,
    And, body under orders, seeks her fee.
Yet on the grasping pimp she piles her curses:
    She's forced to do what you do willingly.

Take the unreasoning animals' example:
    Shame if brute beasts have softer hearts than you!
Cows don't claim gifts from bulls, nor mares from stallions,
    A ram won't bring a gift to charm his ewe.
Only a woman's proud her man to plunder,
    Auctions her body, offers nights for hire,
And sells what pleases both, what both were seeking,
    And sets a price that's gauged by her desire.
The love that gives the pair an equal pleasure,
    Why should the woman sell it, the man buy?
Why should that joy be my loss, be your profit,
    That man and woman share in unity?

It's not right to be bought and bear false witness,
    Nor for a judge to give his palm to grease;
It's shame when paid tongues plead for poor defendants;
    When courts make fortunes, that's a foul disgrace.
It's shame to swell a heritage by a bed's income,
    With beauty prostituted for a fee.
Thanks are deserved for things one doesn't pay for;
    No thanks when beds are hired so shabbily.
The hirer pays for everything; that settled,
    In debt for service done he'll not remain.
So cease, you beauties, pricing a night's favours;
    No good can ever come from sordid gain.
Tarpeia priced too high the Sabine armlets,
    When she was crushed beneath the pile of arms.
Alcmaeon's sword transfixed the womb that bore him,
    In vengeance for the fatal necklace' charms.
Yet it's no shame to ask rewards from rich men;
    You ask—they have the wherewithal to pay.
When vines are brimming pick the hanging bunches;
    Alcinous can give his fruit away.
A poor man's coin is zeal and trust and service—
    To give his all to her who holds his heart.
It's my dower too to hymn girls who deserve it;
    The chosen one's made famous by my art.
Dresses get torn and gold and jewels broken;
    The fame that verses bring will always live.
Being asked a price—not giving—'s vile and hateful;
    No—if you ask. Stop wanting—and I'll give.

II

Nape, you're not just any lady's maid;
You're skilled at dressing hair that's disarrayed,
You're known for stealthy services at night,
And shrewd at giving signs kept out of sight;
And often when Corinna was in doubt
Whether to come to me and venture out,
You urged her to be bold, and often too,
When things went wrong, I found you tried and true.
I wrote these lines this morning. Take them now
And give them to your mistress. Don't allow
Yourself to be delayed and take good pains.
You have no steely heart or flinty veins;
As maids go, you're no bumpkin; you've got brains.
I can believe that Cupid's wounded you;
Defend, by helping me, *your* standards too.

If she should ask you how I am, just say
In hope of nights with her I live all day.
The rest incised by my fond hand she'll see.
Time flies. Give her the tablets when she's free,
But yet make sure she reads them urgently;
And as she reads, observe her brow and eyes:
Mute looks can tell you how the future lies.
And when she's finished reading, instantly
Tell her to write me back a long reply.
Fine wax that's mostly blank's a hateful sight,
So let her squeeze the lines of writing tight;
Right to the margin let the letters go
To hold my eyes and make my reading slow—
But why tire fingers writing a long screed,
When just the one word 'come' is all I need?
Triumph! With bay those tablets I'll entwine
And set them in the midst of Venus' shrine,
And underneath I'll write: 'These servants true,
Kind Venus, Ovid dedicates to you'—
Though just now they were worthless squares of yew.

12

Weep for my failure. Tablets back to say—
All gloom and doom—'Not possible today.'
Omens *are* something. When she meant to go,
Against the doorstep Nape stubbed her toe.
Next time you're sent, cross it more carefully;
Be wary, see your foot's raised properly.
Out of my sight, you tiresome coffin-wood,
And wax packed tight with words that say 'No good'!
From the tall hemlock's flower I'm sure you come,
With Corsica's notorious honeycomb,
Deep-dyed with cinnabar to make you ruddy,
A colour that in truth was simply bloody.
You useless wood, at crossroads you should lie,
Shattered by wheels of wagons passing by.
Yes, and the man who shaped you from a tree
Had hands, I'm certain, steeped in devilry.
That tree made gallows for some wretch to die,
It made a ghastly cross to crucify.
It gave screech-owls its shameful shade for rest,
To hawks and vultures lent its boughs to nest.
Did I—so mad—entrust my love to this,
To bring my darling words that meant a kiss?
That wax was fitter for a bailbond's screed,
For some hard-faced practitioner to read.
With ledgers and accounts it ought to lie,
Where misers mourn lost wealth in misery.
So, like your name, I've found your dealings double;
Duplicity's a recipe for trouble.
What curses shall I call to match my rage?
Mould, rot, and worm to crumble your old age!
And may that wax of yours all waste away,
And whiten filthily in foul decay!

13

Across the ocean from her ancient husband
   Golden, on frosty wheels she brings the day.
'Dawn, why the hurry? Wait—so may your Memnon's
   Birds act their blood-rite in the ancient way.

Now in my darling's arms I love to linger
   And now, if ever, feel her close to me.
Now sleep is rich, the air is cool, and birdsong
   Pours from slim throats a liquid melody.

Why such a hurry when you're so unwelcome?
   Hold in with rosy hands your dewy rein.
Before your rising sailors watch stars better
   And do not wander lost across the main.

When you come, wayfarers, however weary,
   Must rise and soldiers gird fierce arms again.
It's you who are the first to see the farmhands
   Burdened with heavy hoes to till the plain.

And you're the first to summon the slow oxen
   Beneath their curving yoke to plough the rows.
You cheat schoolboys of sleep and hand them over
   To masters for their palms to take hard blows.

You send men into court to give their pledges,
   Huge losses suffered from a single word;
You bring no joy to counsel or attorney,
   Both forced to rise to have fresh cases heard;
And you when women's labours might have respite
   Call back the spinners' hands to tasks deferred.

All this I could endure; but who could ever
   Endure that pretty girls should rise at dawn,
Except some fellow who had never had one,
   And spent his long nights lonely and forlorn?

Often I've wished night would not yield before you,
    The stars not take to flight when you arrive;
Often I've wished the wind would break your chariot
    Or massed clouds trip your steeds and make them dive.

Why hurry, jealous creature? Your son Memnon
    Was black; his mother's heart is dyed the same.
I'd like to hear Tithonus tell your story:
    There'd be no tale in heaven of greater shame.

You fly from him because he's ages older,
    Your hateful wheels rise from him at first light.
But if your arms were round your darling Cephalus,
    You'd cry: "Run slow, run slow, you steeds of night."

Shall my love suffer because your husband's senile?
    Your old man's match, was that a plan of mine?
See what long sleep the Moon gave her Endymion,
    And yet her beauty's not a whit less fine.

Jove—for his joy—to see you not so often,
    Made one night into two without a day'—
My last rebuke; she blushed; no doubt she'd heard me.
    But day dawned promptly in the usual way.

14

'Stop dyeing your hair.' How many times I told you.
    And now you've none to dye and you're disgraced.
But if you'd let it be, none more abundant,
    It reached so far, right down below your waist.

It was like silk, so fine you feared to dress it,
    Fine as the gauzes yellow Chinese wear,
Or gossamer spun by a subtle spider,
    His web hung from a beam high in the air.

Its colour wasn't black, it wasn't golden;
   Though it was neither, gold was shot with dark,
Like, in the watered dales of hilly Ida,
   A lofty cedar when one peels the bark.

Obedient it was and fit for countless
   Fashions and never gave you cause to chafe.
It wasn't frayed or torn by combs or hairpins;
   The maid who managed it was always safe.

I've often watched her dress it, but my darling
   Never once snatched a pin to do her harm.
You often lay, hair loose still, in the morning
   On purple pillows, propped upon your arm;

Lovely then too, all ruffled, like a Bacchante
   Lying relaxed and weary on the sward.
But though your locks were downy-soft and delicate,
   What trials they bore, their sufferings how hard!

The iron and fire, how patiently they faced them
   To coil the ringlets spiralling so far!
'A crime', I cried, 'a crime to burn those tresses!
   Spare them, iron girl, they're lovely as they are.
No force, no violence! They're not for burning;
   Those tongs can learn a lesson from your hair.'

Those lovely locks are ruined, locks Apollo
   And Bacchus would have wished to call their own;
To those of naked Venus I'd compare them
   Held dripping, in the famous picture shown.

Why complain hair so badly treated's ruined?
   Why, silly, put the mirror down so sad?
It's no good gazing with the eyes you used to;
   You must forget yourself if you'd be glad.

You've not been hurt by magic of a rival,
    No treacherous witch has washed you in her brew;
No illness—heaven forbid!—has hit and harmed you;
    No jealous tongue made those thick tresses few.
You made the loss you feel, *your* hand was guilty;
    The poison on your head was put by you.

Now Germany will send you captured tresses;
    A conquered nation's gift will save your day.
You'll blush—how often!—when a man admires them;
    'It's what I've purchased makes me please', you'll say;

'Instead of me he's praising some Sygambrian,
    Yet once I know that glory was my own.'
Dear me. Her hand is raised to hide her blushes—
    Those dainty cheeks—tears almost tumbling down.

Her lost hair's in her lap, she's gazing at it,
    A gift, alas, unworthy to be there.
Make up your face, your mind; all can be mended.
    You'll soon be turning heads with home-grown hair.

15

Devouring Envy, why find fault with me
For years of sloth and call my poetry
Work of an idle wit, and grudge that I,
Unlike my forebears, while youth holds me high,
Will not pursue a soldier's dusty life,
Or study wordy statutes and the strife
Of courts of law or make my thankless choice
In politics to prostitute my voice?
Your aims are mortal, mine's eternal fame,
That the whole world may ever hymn my name.

Homer will live while Tenedos still stands
And Ida, and across the Trojan sands
The torrent of swift Simois is borne;
And Hesiod will live as long as corn
Falls to a scythe and grapes swell on a vine.
Callimachus throughout the world will shine,
In art supreme, in genius less fine;
Sophocles' plays from harm will be secure,
Aratus long as sun and moon endure;
Menander lives while fathers rage, slaves cheat,
Pimps have no shame and whores charm in the street.
Ennius' rough art and Accius' ardent strain
For evermore a name unfailing gain;
Of Varro too what age shall not be told,
And Jason's Argo and the fleece of gold?
Sublime Lucretius' verses shall not die
Till one day ends the world in tragedy;
Aeneid, Eclogues, Georgics shall be read
As long as Rome's the conquered globe's great head;
While Cupid's weapons still are torch and bow,
Your polished lines, Tibullus, men will know;
The lands of east and west know Gallus' fame,
And linked with Gallus his Lycoris' name.

And so, though rocks and ploughshares wear away,
Yet over poetry death has no sway.
To poetry let pomp of kings yield place
And all the gold that Tagus' banks embrace.
Let boors like dross; to me may Phoebus bring
His goblets filled from the Castalian spring.
I'll wear frost-fearing myrtle round my head
And much by anxious lovers I'll be read.
Envy feeds on the living. When men die,
It rests—each has his honour due; so I,
When the last flame devouring me has gone,
Shall still survive and all that's best live on.

BOOK TWO

I

This too I, stream-fed Sulmo's son, have written—
    Ovid, the poet of my naughtiness.
This too Love ordered. Prudes, keep off! My tender
    Strains are not fit for your ears, I confess.

Let girls read me who're warm towards their true-loves,
    And boys untutored, touched by Love's first dart.
I hope some lad, like me by Cupid wounded,
    Will recognize the flame that makes him smart,
And ask, amazed, what spy has taught this poet
    To versify the fortunes of *his* heart.

I'd dared relate Heaven's wars and hundred-handed
    Giants, I well recall—of words no lack—
Earth's fell revenge, and, piled upon Olympus,
    High Ossa with steep Pelion on its back.

I'd got storm-clouds, I'd got Jove with his lightning,
    A bolt Jove well might hurl to save his sky.
My darling slammed the door. Jove with his lightning
    I dropped; great Jove just slipped my memory.

Forgive me, Jove. Your weapons didn't help me.
    That slammed door has a stronger bolt than yours.
So back to coaxing couplets, my own weapons;
    Soft soothing words have softened stubborn doors.

Verses pull down the moon, blood-red, from heaven,
    Call back the sun's white steeds upon their course;
Verses split serpents' fangs and draw their venom,
    And send back rivers running to their source.

To verses doors give way; the bolts that bar them,
    Even the strongest oak, to verses yield.
What use to me is either son of Atreus?
    What good Achilles with his famous shield,

Or he who spent such years in wars and wandering,
    Or Hector whom Greek horses dragged along?
But praise a pretty girl—she'll come in person,
    Herself the payment for the poet's song.

A fine reward! Farewell, you famous heroes!
    I get no thanks from you that's fit for me.
Girls, turn your pretty faces to my verses—
    Love, blushing Love, dictates my poetry.

2

One moment, please, Bagoas, our fair lady's
    Attendant, just a few words in your ear.
In the arcade that's got the rows of Danaids
    I saw her yesterday as she strolled near.
I liked her looks, wrote promptly for a meeting.
    'It's not allowed', she wrote back nervously,
And when I asked why not, she gave the reason
    That you attend the girl too tiresomely.

If you're a *wise* guard, you'll stop making enemies;
    Fear someone, and one wants him dead and gone.
Her husband's a fool too. Why bother guarding
    When nothing would be lost with no guard on?
Well, let him keep his crazy style of loving,
    And think what charms so many's chaste and true.
Give her the gift yourself of furtive freedom,
    So what you give her, she'll give back to you.
Be her accomplice—slave's then mistress' master.
    You'd be afraid of that? Well, just pretend.
She reads a note, pretend her mother sent it;
    A stranger comes, at once he'll be a friend.

She'll go to see a 'sick' girl-friend—who isn't;
    In your view she's unwell; why bother more?
She comes back late, don't wear yourself out waiting;
    You can just settle chin on chest and snore.
Don't ask what might go on in Isis' temple,
    Or in the theatre fear something wrong.
Good pickings never fail a good accomplice—
    And what's less tiring than to hold your tongue?—
He's popular, upsets the home unpunished;
    He's powerful—the rest a scurvy crew.
To keep her husband from the facts use fictions,
    So what suits her alone will suit him too;
And when he's frowned and scowled and made a rumpus,
    Then what his wheedling girl has willed he'll do.

But with you too at times you'll let her bicker,
    Call you a brute and feign a tear or two.
Charge her in turn with something safely answered;
    Charge falsely, and the truth will not ring true.
This way you'll gain respect, pile up your savings;
    Take my advice, you'll very soon be free.
I'm sure you've seen chains round the necks of tell-tales;
    A filthy jail rewards disloyalty.
Tantalus grasps at fruit in vain, seeks water
    In water; that's what gossiping has given.
When Argus kept his watch too close on Io,
    He died before his time, but she's in heaven.
I've seen a man with legs in chains for forcing
    A husband, cuckolded, to know his shame.
That evil tongue hurt two—got off too lightly—
    The man was grieved, the girl lost her good name.

No husband ever welcomes accusations,
    Believe me; no one's pleased to hear the bad.
If he's lukewarm, your scandal won't disturb him,
    Or, should he love, your service makes him sad.

A lapse is hard to prove, though clear as daylight;
    The girl's safe in her biased judge's eye.
He'll not trust what he's *seen*, if she denies it;
    He'll blame his sight and give himself the lie.
And if he sees his darling's tears, he'll blubber
    Himself, and say 'He'll pay, that gabbling chap.'
Why fight with odds against you? You'll be beaten,
    Flogged, while she's sitting in her judge's lap.
We're on no course of crime, nor met for mixing
    Poisons, our hands no gleaming sword-blade bear.
We beg of you the means to love in safety:
    What could be more innocuous than our prayer?

3

Poor guardian, you're neither man nor woman;
    The joys of mutual love you cannot know.
He who was first to mutilate boys' manhood
    Ought to have borne himself his own blade's blow.
You'd be obliging, first to do a favour,
    If love had warmed your heart to any girl.
You're not a trooper, you weren't born for battle,
    A soldier's spear your hand's not fit to hurl.
Leave that to men; lay down your hope of manhood;
    Your mistress' standard is the place for you.
Give *her* true service; profit by *her* favour;
    Without your mistress what good can you do?
She's charming too, her youth just right for love-games;
    Shame if her beauty perished by neglect!
She could have tricked you, though you're thought so tiresome;
    What two have willed won't fail to find effect.

    But asking first's the decent thing to do.
    We ask; you've got the chance; it's up to you.

4

I would not dare excuse my dreadful morals,
    Or with a war of lies my faults defend.
I own my sins—if good can come from owning—
    Madman, I own them—and I still offend.

I hate myself, but can't not do the thing I
    Hate, though I try. How hard a burden seems
One longs to shed! My self-control has failed me,
    I'm swept away like boats on rushing streams.

The looks that lure my love have no set pattern;
    Reasons are legion why I'm kept in love.
Maybe a girl will drop her eyes demurely;
    I'm fired, those bashful looks my pitfall prove.

Or if she's pert I'm caught; she's not a peasant—
    She's nimble, I can hope, between the sheets;
Or if she's stern and apes the rigid Sabines,
    She'll yield, no doubt, though deep in her deceits.

She's educated, those rare skills are pleasing;
    Or crude, then pleasing her simplicity.
She'll say, compared with mine Callimachus's
    Poems are rough—I like her liking me.

She'll criticize my poems and the poet,
    I'd cuddle that hard critic blissfully;
Her walk is lithe, I love it; or she's stony,
    A man can touch the stone and lithe she'll be.

She's a fine singer, quite a virtuoso;
    I'm longing, as she sings, to snatch a kiss.
She sweeps the plaintive strings with clever fingers;
    Who could not fall in love with hands like this?

Another girl I like's a ballet dancer
  Who spins and pirouettes with art divine;
Don't talk of me, I'm always hooked, but even
  Hippolytus would be a libertine.

A girl who's tall as in the times of heroes
  From top to bottom of the bed can lie.
A short one too is fine; they both undo me;
  Both long and short, they suit my lover's eye.

She's dowdy—I dream what would suit her better.
  She's dressed to kill—her dower's on display.
I fall for blondes, I fall for girls who're auburn,
  A dusky beauty charms in the same way.

If dark hair dangles down a snowy shoulder,
  Her sable locks were Leda's crowning glory;
Or if they're gold, Aurora charmed with saffron;
  My love adapts to every ancient story.

Youth tempts me. So do riper years. Youth's prettier,
  Yet older women's ways have me in thrall;
Yes, every worthwhile girl in Rome's great city,
  My love's a candidate to win them all.

5

No love is worth so much—away, cruel Cupid!—
  That makes it now my dearest prayer, to die.
I pray to die, recalling how you've wronged me,
  Girl born to make my life a misery.

No surreptitious note lays bare your actions,
  No furtive present proves you've done me wrong.
I wish I'd arguments too weak for winning;
  Alas, alas! Why is my case so strong?

Happy the man who dares defend his loved one,
   To whom his girl can say 'I'm innocent.'
The man who'd prove her guilt in bloody triumph
   Is hard as steel, on his own pain intent.

I saw your crimes my wretched self at dinner;
   I wasn't drunk although you thought I dozed.
I saw you both speak volumes with your eyebrows,
   And by your nods much meaning you disclosed.

Your eyes, my girl, weren't dumb, and on the table
   No lack of letters written in the wine.
I noted phrases full of hidden meaning,
   And words that served to send a coded sign.

And now the crowd of guests had left the table,
   Just one or two young lads dead drunk still there.
I saw you then and your outrageous kisses,
   Tongue kisses, clear enough, is what they were;

Not what a sister gives a strait-laced brother,
   But what a warm girl gives her willing man;
Not what you'd think Apollo gives Diana,
   But what Mars gets from Venus when he can.

'What are you at?' I cried, 'those joys are mine you're
   Spreading around. My legal claim I'll stake.
They're yours and mine, and mine and yours, together,
   Our property—third parties shan't partake!'

That's what I said, and more as rage dictated,
   And she—upon her cheeks a blush of shame,
Like rosy skies Tithonus' wife had painted,
   Or a young bride who to her bridegroom came;

Like roses shining set among white lilies,
   Or the moon bewitched and labouring in the sky,
Or ivory a Lydian woman tinted
   Lest it grow yellow as long years glide by.
Like this she blushed or that, or one or other,
   And never looked more lovely to my eye.

Her looks were sad, her sad looks well became her;
   Her eyes downcast, downcast eyes gave her grace;
Hair smart, that sleek smart hair I felt like tearing,
   I'd half a mind to scratch her tender face.

Then as I gazed, my brave arms dropped. My darling
   Was safe and sound with her own armoury.
I, savage brute, was humble, even begged her
   To give some kisses, no less good, to me.

She laughed and gave her best, whole-hearted kisses,
   They'd shake the three-pronged bolt from Jove's fierce hand.
Torture to think that fellow got such good ones!
   I wish they hadn't been of the same brand.

What's more, these were much better than I'd taught her,
   She seemed to have some knowledge that was new.
They pleased too well—bad sign. Her tongue was in them,
   Tongue kisses, and my tongue was kissing too.

Nor is this all that hurt. I grudge hot kisses,
   But it's not only kisses that are hot;
Nowhere except in bed could she have learnt them;
   A splendid fee some teacher must have got!

6

Her parrot, flying mimic from the Indies,
   Is dead. Come, every bird, come flocking round,
Beat wings on breasts, tear tender cheeks with talons,
   All at her obsequies, in duty bound;
Like mourners' tresses rend your ruffled plumage,
   And with your wings supply the trumpet's sound.

Why wail for Tereus' crime, sad Philomela?
   It's had its day, that ancient song of woe.
To this rare bird now turn your mournful dirges—
   Though great your grief, Itys died long ago.

Mourn, every bird that in the bright air poises,
   But chiefly you his friend, the turtle-dove.
Your whole lives passed in harmony together,
   And steadfast to the end your loyal love;
Like Pylades' devotion to Orestes,
   So loyal to his parrot was the dove.

But what avail were loyalty, rare colours,
   Your voice's brilliant gift of mimicry,
The joy that from the first you gave my darling?
   Glory of birds, poor parrot, dead you lie.

Your wings could dim the blaze of brittle emeralds,
   Your crimson beak was tinged with saffron hue.
No bird in all the world a better mimic—
   Your lisp could echo every word so true.

Fate's envy took you. You fought no fierce battles;
   For peace and calm and talk your love was strong.
But look at quails that spend their lives in fighting;
   Perhaps that's why they often live so long.

The least thing filled you full. Your love of talking
   Left you no time to have a hearty feed.
Your fare a nut, and poppy seeds for slumber,
   And for a drink plain water met your need.

The kite that circles round, the greedy vulture,
   Live on, and daws that make the rain arrive;
The crow lives on, Minerva's pet aversion,
   After nine generations still alive.

He's died, that mimic of our human voices,
   The parrot, gift that came from the world's end.
The best are grasped first by Fate's greed so often,
   The worst their full long tale of years may spend.
Thersites sees Protesilaus' funeral,
   And Hector's brothers over his ashes bend.

What use the vows of my poor frightened darling?
   Those vows the stormy gales swept out to sea.
The seventh dawn could find no dawn to follow,
   Exhausted now the thread of destiny.
But still that fainting tongue was unbewildered;
   'Farewell, Corinna' was its dying cry.

Below an Elysian hill a grove of ilex
   Stands dark; the earth is moist, grass always green.
There—trust the tale—the good birds have their heaven,
   While nasty birds are banned and never seen.

There roams the bird unique, the long-lived Phoenix,
   And harmless swans, wide-feeding, range abroad;
There Juno's peacock spreads her splendid feathers,
   The dove with kisses charms her cooing lord.

Among them in the grove the parrot's welcomed,
   And all the good birds turn to hear his words.
His tomb's a mound, a mound to match his stature;
   A small stone space for two lines just affords:

   'My mistress' joy in me this tomb can teach;
   Beyond a bird I had the art of speech.'

7

So I'm to face fresh charges every day!
   I win, but all those battles are a bore.
If my eyes wander when we're at a play,
   You'll choose one in the gods to make you sore.

A pretty girl gives me a silent look,
   You claim that silent look some sign revealed;
I praise her—my poor hair your sharp nails hook;
   I fault her—you suppose some guilt's concealed.

If I look well, you say I'm cold to you;
  If pale, for love of someone else I'm dying.
I wish I'd really got some guilt to rue;
  When punishment's deserved it's not so trying.

By your wild charges and credulity
  You just deny your anger any weight.
The long-eared ass, poor creature, don't you see,
  The more he's thumped, the slower is his gait.

And now a new offence. Your clever maid,
  Cypassis, does her mistress wrong—with me!
Heaven grant me better, if my fancy strayed,
  Than such a low-class slut for company.

What man who's free would want a slave to share
  Love's joys, put arms around a lash-scarred waist?
Besides, her duty is to dress your hair,
  A service you enjoy—such skill and taste.

What! I ask favours from your faithful maid?—
  And find myself rejected and betrayed!
I swear by Venus and her winged offspring
  I am not guilty of the charge you bring.

8

Cypassis, so supreme in styling hair
  (None but a goddess' should by you be dressed),
In our sweet stolen joys so debonair
  (You suit your mistress well, but suit me best),

What gossip whispered we were intimate?
  How did Corinna hear of our amour?
Did I let slip some word to indicate
  Our secret? Did I blush? Not I, for sure.

What if I did say, if a man could fall
   For a slave, he'd want his head examining?
Briseis held Achilles' heart in thrall,
   The slave Cassandra fired the great Greek king.

Achilles? Agamemnon? I'm no higher;
   What's right for kings, shall I think wrong for me?
Well, when she stared at you with eyes on fire,
   Your face was one big blush, as I could see.

But I, more on the spot, (d'you call to mind?)
   By mighty Venus swore my loyalty.
Dear lovely goddess, bid the warm south wind
   Waft that white lie across the Aegean sea!

For that good turn, my dear dark girl, today
   Give me your loving self, my sweet fee due.
Be grateful, don't say no, pack fears away;
   Just serve one master well—you can't serve two.

   But if you're stupid and refuse, I'll tell
   Your mistress all, betray myself as well;
   Yes, where and when I had you, I'll make clear,
   And in how many ways and what they were.

9a

Cupid, no words can match my indignation—
   Boy lounging in my heart as days go by.
Why hurt *me*, when I've never left your colours?
   In my own camp I'm wounded—tell me why.
Why does your torch burn friends, your bow transfix them?
   You'd get more glory by defeating foes.
Achilles, when his spear had wounded Telephus,
   Doctored him later—so the story goes.
Hunters give chase, and when they've caught their quarry,
   Leave it, and ever onward quests the hunt.
But you're so slack, so slow to fight resistance.
   It's we, your faithful flock, who bear your brunt.

Love's left me skin and bone, so what's the good of
    Blunting barbed arrows on a skeleton?
So many men, so many girls are loveless;
    It's there your glorious triumph should be won.
Had Rome not pushed her power the wide world over,
    She'd be a huddle of thatched huts today.
Old soldiers are retired to their small holdings,
    Worn race-horses to grass are sent away.
Ships are laid up in dry dock; gladiators
    Put swords aside and claim safe wooden foils;
I too in Love's campaigns have done long service;
    It's time to live in peace and end my toils.

9b

If some god said to me 'Live without loving',
    I'd pray for mercy—girls are such sweet bane.
Yes, I've been bored, the fire a feeble flicker,
    Then some strange whirl of torment strikes again.
Like a horse bolting with his rider tugging
    The foaming bit, to hold him, helplessly,
Or when a sudden wind almost at landfall
    Sweeps a ship, making harbour, out to sea.
So I'm the sport of Cupid's chancy breezes;
    Love aims again his well-known shafts at me.
Shoot, boy! You find me naked and defenceless;
    Here's valour for you, here's your gallantry.
On me your arrows home—they're automatic;
    They know their quiver hardly better than me.
Pity a man who spends the whole night sleeping,
    And fancies slumber sweet felicity.
Fool! What is sleep but cold death's imitation?
    The Fates will give long time for R.I.P.
Just let a girl's beguiling voice deceive me;
    My hopes at any rate will bring delight.
She'll charm me and she'll chide me: I'll enjoy her
    Often, be driven often from her sight.

The chanciness of Mars is your fault, Cupid,
   Stepfather modelling his wars on you.
You're light, you've flighty wings, but you're more flighty;
   Joys given or grudged, your word does not ring true.
But if you hear my prayer, you and your mother,
   Come, in my heart as king unchallenged dwell.
Let girls, that tribe too nomad, join your kingdom,
   And you'll be worshipped by their sex as well.

10

No man can love two girls at once, you told me,
   Graecinus—I remember it was you.
It's all your fault I'm tricked and caught defenceless;
   You see me shamed—in love at once with two.

They're both good lookers, elegant and *soignée*;
   Which more accomplished, difficult to say.
This one's more beautiful, and so's the other,
   Each more attractive in her own sweet way.

I waver like a yacht when winds are warring;
   This love, that love, they keep me torn in two.
Why, Venus, make my endless troubles double?
   Could one girl not give me enough to do?
Why give the forest leaves, the ocean water,
   Why give the crowded sky more stars to strew?

Yet this is not so bad as lying loveless.
   God grant my enemies high moral tone;
God grant my enemies a bed that's empty,
   To sprawl there in the middle all alone.

I want wild love, to shatter sluggard slumber,
   Mine not the only weight the blankets bear.
Then clear the decks and let my girl undo me,
   If one can do it; if not, I'll take a pair.

I'm up to it; I'm slender, but I'm wiry;
   I may lack weight but not virility;
And fun's the food that fortifies performance—
   No girl has ever been let down by me.

I've often spent a night in dissipation,
   And still been fit and strong when morning came.
Happy's the man who dies amid love's duels;
   Heaven grant the cause of my death be the same!

Let soldiers get their chests stuck full of arrows,
   And buy eternal glory with their gore;
Let traders in their greed criss-cross the ocean,
   And swill it, with their swindles, far from shore.

May my death find me fainting in love's ferment,
   And in mid-act may I expire in bed;
And may some mourner weeping at my funeral
   Comment 'Your death well matched the life you led'.

11

That pine first taught the evils of seafaring,
   Felled on high Pelion in the hills of Greece,
Braving the clashing cliffs—how the waves wondered!—
   And fetching back the famous Golden Fleece.
I wish the Argo'd sunk, and drunk disaster,
   And men had left the long sea-lanes in peace!

Corinna's set to leave sweet home, sweet bedroom,
   And on those treacherous highways venture forth.
What fears the winds of east and west will bring me,
   What dread the balmy south, the icy north!

There you'll admire no cities, there no forests—
   Only the unjust ocean's same blue reach.
The deep sea has no shells or coloured pebbles;
   For those one lingers on the thirsty beach.

The shore's where lovely girls should leave their footprints;
   That far it's safe, but blind the way ahead.
Let others tell you tales of winds in conflict,
   Seas Scylla and Charybdis fill with dread,

The stormy reefs below the Thunder Mountains,
   The bay where Syrtes' quicksands lie in wait.
Let them tell tales; and what each tells, believe it;
   Belief's not hurt by storms, however great.

Too late to look back landwards, when the anchor's
   Weighed and the ship runs to the boundless main,
And winds are wild and anxious sailors shudder,
   And near as the next breaker see death plain.

And what if Triton stirs the storm-waves higher—
   How pale you'll turn, your cheeks white as a sheet!
You'll pray to those twin stars, the sons of Leda,
   And envy all whose land's beneath their feet;
Safer to snuggle down and read a novel,
   Or on your lyre make music soft and sweet.

But if my words are swept away by storm-winds,
   May sea-nymphs cherish your ship's company.
The Nereids and their father will be guilty,
   Should such a lovely girl be lost at sea.

Think of me as you go, and on your passage
   Back home may favouring breezes fill your sails,
And mighty Nereus slope the ocean homewards
   With the sea-swell abaft and no strong gales.

And you must pray soft winds will swell your canvas,
   And trim the bulging sails with your own hand.
I'll be the first to see your well-known vessel
   And say 'She brings my goddess back to land.'

I'll carry you ashore, with countless kisses;
   The victim vowed for your return shall die;
And on the beach some mound can be our table,
   We'll shape a couch of sand where we can lie.

Over the wine you'll tell me many a story,
   How the wide sea almost engulfed your bark,
How, hastening to me, you dreaded neither
   The wild south wind or night's unfriendly dark.

I'll take it all as fact, although it's fiction.
   Why shouldn't I indulge my fantasy?
May Lucifer, the brightest star in heaven,
   Urge his steeds on to bring that hour to me.

12

Come, laurels, crown me with your wreath of triumph!
   I've won! Look, in my arms Corinna lies,
Despite the watch and ward of husband, escort,
   And stubborn door, so many enemies.

Here's victory that's worth a special triumph,
   Winning a prize of war no blood has stained,
No town with puny walls and tiny ramparts—
   A girl is what my generalship has gained.

When Troy was overwhelmed in ten years' warfare,
   What praise, among so many, had Atreus' son?
But my fame is my own, no soldier shares it;
   None can claim credit for the war I won.

I was the general, the standard-bearer,
   The troops, the horse, the foot; I gained my goal.
The triumph's mine, won by my own exertions;
   In my success luck never played a role.

And my war's nothing novel. But for Helen
  Europe and Asia never would have fought.
A woman set the Lapiths and the Centaurs
  To shameful fighting when the wine was brought.

A woman in the realm of just Latinus
  Drove Trojan troops to draw the sword once more.
The women, when Rome's city was just founded,
  Sent fathers against husbands into war.

I've seen bulls battling over a white heifer;
  She watched and fired their hearts as she stood by.
Me too like many (but for me no bloodshed)
  Cupid's called up to join his soldiery.

13

Aiming to end her pregnancy—so rashly—
  Corinna lies exhausted, life in doubt.
To run such fearful risks without my knowledge
  Should make me rage, but fear's put rage to rout.
But still I got her pregnant—or I think so;
  I often take as fact what could have been.
O Isis, patroness of Paraetonium,
  Of Memphis, Pharos, and Canopus queen,
And where the swift Nile glides in its broad channel,
  And through seven mouths goes forth into the sea,
Now by revered Anubis, by your sistrums
  I pray—and may Osiris endlessly
Cherish your ceremonies, and the languid
  Serpent go gliding round your treasury,
And in the pomp and pride of your procession
  Great bull-horned Apis keep you company—
Turn your eyes here; on her—and me—have mercy;
  You will give life to her and she to me.
She's often sat to serve you on your feast days,
  Where the priests wet your laurel's greenery.

You too, kind Ilithyia, who take pity
   When girls are locked in labour, and relieve
Their hidden load, be present, hear my prayer;
   Give her the help she's worthy to receive.
I, robed in white, will cense your smoking altars;
   The gifts I've vowed before your feet shall lie,
Labelled 'From Ovid for Corinna's safety',
   If gifts and label you'll but justify.

If in such fears a man may give advice,
   You've fought this battle once; let that suffice.

14

What good for girls to be exempt from warfare,
   No shields, no line of march to meet the foe,
If they get wounds, in peace, from their own weapons
   And blindly arm themselves to their own woe?

She who first from the womb wrenched life's beginnings
   Deserved to die by her own warring hand.
Can you, just so that lines shan't mar your belly,
   Face mortal combat on the tragic sand?

If in times past that practice had found favour,
   The crime would have destroyed the race of men,
The empty world would need someone for throwing
   The stones of our creation once again.

Who'd have crushed Priam's power, had the sea-goddess,
   Thetis, refused to bear her womb's due weight?
The queen of cities would have lost her founder,
   Had Ilia aborted her twin freight.

Had Venus in her womb assailed Aeneas,
   The world would be without its Caesars too;
And *you*'d have died—unborn to be so lovely—
   If your own mother'd tried the same as you.

I, better meant to die of love, would never
   Have seen the light, against my mother's will.
Why pick—so cruel—fruit that's green and bitter,
   And steal the growing grapes the vine would fill?

Let ripe fruit fall by nature; let beginnings
   Grow on; life's no slight prize for small delay.
Why poison unborn children, why take weapons
   To probe the womb and delve the life away?

We blame Medea by her sons' blood spattered,
   For mother-murdered Itys we lament;
Both mothers cruel, but both had cause for tragic
   Vengeance on husbands in that shared blood spent.

Tell me what Tereus or what Jason drives you
   To violate yourself in such distress.
No tigress in Armenian dens would do it,
   Her cubs aren't murdered by a lioness.

But gentle girls do that, though not unpunished;
   Killing their wombs' young life, they often die.
Die, and they're on the pyre with hair dishevelled,
   And 'Serve them right' say all those standing by.

But may these words of mine bear no bad omen,
   But vanish in the wind, and I'm content.
Ye gracious gods, let her sin once in safety;
   Enough—next time impose your punishment.

15

Go, little ring, whose worth will prove
Nothing except the giver's love.
Circle my fair one's finger, be
A pleasing gift to her from me.
I hope she'll welcome you and over
Her knuckle slip you, from her lover,
And straightaway you'll neatly hug
Her finger, fitting just as snug
As she fits me. O happy ring,
That to the girl I love can cling!
I envy now my gift's new home.
Would I might suddenly become
That gift myself (the magic change
Circe or Proteus could arrange).
Then when I would her bosom press
A d slip my hand inside her dress,
I'd squeeze myself from her dear finger
(However tight, I wouldn't linger)
And working loose by magic art
Drop to the fold beside her heart;
Or if she wrote a secret letter,
To help me seal the tablets better,
(My stone not dry, the wax quite free)
My darling's tongue would moisten me—
Provided I was never set
To seal a note that I'd regret.
And if she ever had in mind
To lock me in her box, she'd find
I wouldn't go; I'd shrink and fight her,
And circle round her finger tighter.
I'd not embarrass you, my dear—
No weight your finger wouldn't wear.
Wear me when your bath is warm,
Don't fear the stone may come to harm,
Though, seeing you naked, I'd expect
That virile ring to rise erect.

Vain fantasies! Go on your way,
You little gift of mine, and may
My darling realize with you
I give her love that's staunch and true.

16

I'm at Sulmo, here in Pelignian country;
    It's small, but healthy with its channelled streams.
Even when the Dog-star shimmers in high summer,
    And the sun cracks the soil with burning beams,

Clear waters wander through the fields of Sulmo;
    The ground is soft, the grass is lush and green.
The land is good for corn, for vines far better,
    And olives here and there are often seen,
And where brooks glide along through water-meadows
    On soft wet soil the fresh sward spreads a screen.

But my heart's flame's not here—no, one small error—
    The kindler's far away, the flame is here.
Though I were placed between Castor and Pollux,
    I'd hate to be in heaven if you weren't near.

May those who scored the world with roads lie restless
    Beneath a weight of unforgiving clay,
Or if roads have to score the world, they should have
    Made girls go with their lovers all the way.

Then, though I tramped the windy Alps, half frozen,
    With my girl there the journey would be kind;
With my girl there I'd cross the Syrtes' quicksands
    And spread my sails before the wild south wind;

And I'd not fear the curves of Cape Malea
    Or savage Scylla's howling hounds of Hell,
Or whirlpools of wreck-surfeited Charybdis
    That sucks and spews and sucks the ocean's swell.

But should the windy power of Neptune triumph,
 The gods that guard us lost in the wild sea,
Throw your two snowy arms around my shoulders,
 I'll bear the lovely burden easily.
Leander often swam the strait to Hero
 Until the last blind night brought tragedy.

But here without you, though the vineyard's busy,
 And lazy rivers float along the leas,
And peasants lead the water down their channels
 And cooling airs caress the leafy trees,

I can't think this is home, this healthy Sulmo,
 My birthplace, my ancestral countryside,
But wastes of Scythia or woad-blue Britain
 Or the wild rocks Prometheus' red blood dyed.

Elms love their vines, their vines do not desert them;
 My girl and I, must we so often part?
Why, you had sworn to stay with me for ever—
 By me and by your eyes, stars of my heart.

Lighter than falling leaves are words of women,
 The playthings of the whims of wind and wave.
But if you feel at all for me left lonely,
 Begin to keep the promises you gave.

Make haste, get out your trap and lightfoot ponies,
 And crack the whip above their flying manes;
And may you find the hills sink down before you,
 And in the winding valleys easy lanes.

17

Anyone who thinks it shame to be a girl's slave,
    Will surely judge me guilty of that shame.
Give me disgrace, if I'm just burnt less badly
    By her whom Paphos and Cythera claim.
Since I was bound to be a beauty's victim,
    I wish a kinder girl had taken aim.

Beauty breeds pride. Her beauty makes Corinna
    Stormy. Alas, how well she knows her face.
She gets her pride from what her mirror shows her—
    But doesn't look till everything's in place.

Although your beauty reigns so wide—too widely—
    That beauty born to hold these eyes of mine!—
Because I can't compare with you don't scorn me;
    For lesser things with great may well combine.

It's said the nymph Calypso loved a mortal
    And kept him though he tried to get away;
And Nereid Thetis shared her bed with Peleus,
    Egeria with Numa, so they say.

Venus has Vulcan too, though when he's left his
    Anvil he limps and shuffles clumsily.
My metre here's shortfooted, but the heroic
    Line couples with the short one perfectly.

Take me on any terms you like, my darling;
    In open court, dear, lay your edicts down.
I'll not disgrace you, and you'll not regret me;
    This love of ours we'll never need disown.

Instead of wealth I have my happy couplets,
    And many a girl has hopes of fame from me.
There's one I know who broadcasts she's Corinna;
    What would she not have given to really be!

But cold Eurotas can't share the same channel
    As far-off poplar-fringed Eridanus,
And none but you'll be sung in my slim volumes,
    And none but you inspire my genius.

18

While in your poem ending with the wrath of
    Achilles, heroes swear their oaths for war,
I'm idling, Macer, in the shade of Venus;
    Love wrecks the fine themes I'd have faced before.
Time and again I've told my girl to leave me—
    And in a trice back in my lap she'll be.
I told her I'm ashamed; in tears she answered
    'Oh dear, are you ashamed of loving me?'
And wound her arms around my neck and gave me
    Kisses a thousandfold that laid me low.
I've lost, and I've demobilized my talents;
    Back to the front at home my verses go.

Still I did grasp the sceptre; I was suited
    To writing tragedy; my efforts pleased.
Love mocked my tragic robes and coloured buskins
    And sceptre my unroyal hand had seized.
And this too my girl's stopped—divine injustice—
    And Love has triumphed over the buskined bard.
So—what's allowed—I teach the art of loving—
    Poor teacher hoisted with my own petard;
Write love-letters, Penelope to Ulysses,
    Compose abandoned Phyllis' tearful screed,
Appeals for Paris, Macareus, and Jason,
    And Theseus and Hippolytus to read,
The last words of the loving Lesbian lyrist,
    And wretched Dido, naked sword in hand.
How soon from the world's ends my friend Sabinus
    Returned with letters from each foreign land!

Penelope recognized Ulysses' signet,
    And Phaedra read the words her stepson wrote;
Aeneas, duty-bound, has answered Dido,
    And Phyllis, if she's living, gets a note.
Hypsipyle receives sad news from Jason,
    Sappho (loved now) to Phoebus gives her lyre.
You, Macer, too, within your epic limits
    In midst of warfare sing love's sweet desire—
Paris and Helen, famous guilty lovers,
    Laodamia, loyal to the last.
You'd rather write of love than war, I'm certain,
    And from your camp to mine you'll soon have passed.

19

You fool! If for yourself you will not guard her,
    Guard her for me, to make me want her more.
Love by another's leave's so cold and callous,
    What's banned blows up the blaze, what's free's a bore.
Lovers need hope and fear, need both together;
    The odd rebuff leaves room to dream again.
A girl's no good who'll never double-cross me,
    And I don't love what never causes pain.
Corinna, clever girl, had seen my weakness,
    And knew how best to catch me, cunning thing!
How many times she feigned a fearful headache
    And sent me off when I was lingering!
And often said she'd wronged me, though quite guiltless,
    And guilty all the same she seemed to be.
Then, when she'd roused me, fanned the fading embers,
    She was my girl again, just made for me.
Such winning whisperings, so many kisses,
    Ye Gods, what kisses, what sweet witchery!

You too, my dear, the latest to attract me,
    Should often seem afraid, often say no,
And let me stretch my length upon your doorstep,
    Enduring the long night of frost and snow.

Thus my love lasts and through long years grows stronger.
  That does me good; that gives my heart strong meat.
Love cloys that's free and easy, fed too richly,
  Like indigestion when the food's too sweet.
Had Danae not been locked in the bronze tower,
  Jove never would have sired the son she bore;
While Juno watched the heifer that was Io,
  Poor Io pleased Jove better than before.
What's lawful, easy—if that's what you're after,
  Drink from a river, pick leaves from a tree.
For a long reign a girl must fool her lover—
  May my advice not cause me misery!
What follows me, I flee; what flees, I follow,
  And, come what may, permission ruins me.

So you, who guard your pretty girl so poorly,
  Start locking your street door at day's last light.
Start asking who comes tapping at the window,
  Why dogs are barking in the silent night,
What messages the clever maid delivers,
  And why your wife so often sleeps apart.
Give me a chance to practise my deceptions,
  And let such worries sometimes gnaw your heart.
Anyone who can love a tomfool's lady,
  Can steal sand from the shore's wide empty line.
I give you warning: if you don't start guarding
  That girl of yours, she'll start to stop being mine.
I've suffered long enough. I've hoped so often,
  As you'd stand guard so I'd slip past your door.
No husband should endure what you're enduring;
  For me, if love's allowed, it's love no more.

What, shall I never be refused admission,
  My nights from threats of vengeance always free?
Never be scared? no sighs, no broken slumbers?
  No reason why your death I'd long to see?
What good to me's a milksop pimp for husband—
  Depravity corrupting our delight?
Find someone whom your pimping patience pleases!
  If you want *me* to be your rival, fight!

BOOK THREE

I

There stands an ancient grove unhewn for ages
    Wherein some deity might well reside.
It has a holy spring, a rock-roofed grotto,
    And birds pour their sweet plaints on every side.
There in the woodland shadows I was strolling
    And wondering what my Muse' next work would be,
When Elegy appeared, her coiled hair perfumed,
    And limping, one foot short, it seemed to me,
Her gauzy dress and loving looks quite charming,
    And graced too by her foot's infirmity.
Then Tragedy strode up, a stormy presence,
    Scowling, her mantle trailing on the ground,
Her left hand brandishing a royal sceptre,
    And on her feet high Lydian buskins bound.

She spoke first: 'Won't you ever end your loving,
    You poet clinging to your chosen line?
Your naughty morals are the crossroads' gossip,
    The after-dinner tattle over wine;
And often they point out the passing poet,
    "That's him, the fellow scorched by Cupid's flame";
And you're the whole town's talk, though you don't know it,
    While you boast what you've done and show no shame.
It's time you felt a weightier inspiration;
    You've loafed enough, begin some greater task.
Your subject cramps your talent; sing of heroes;
    "This field", you'll say, "is all that I could ask."
Your Muse was trifling—tender girls' love-lyrics;
    Your youth's been spent on young men's poetry.
I'm Roman Tragedy, now make me famous;
    You know my rules and you will rise to me.'
With that, poised on her painted boots, she shook her
    Head with its long thick locks from side to side.

Then Elegy smiled slyly, I remember,
 Holding—was that a myrtle wand I spied?
'Proud Tragedy, why load your weighty words on
 Me?' she said, 'Can't you use a lighter tone?
You've deigned indeed to strut in foot-short couplets;
 You've fought me in the metre that's my own.
I'd not compare my strains with your high drama,
 Your palace dwarfs my tiny door, poor thing.
I'm light, and light with me's my darling Cupid,
 And I'm no tougher than the theme I sing.
But Venus without me would be a bumpkin;
 I organize her loves, I'm at her side.
The door you can't unbolt with your tough buskin
 Before my winning words flies open wide.
Corinna learnt from me to elude her escort,
 And shake the loyalty that locks the door,
Slipping away from bed in her loose nightdress
 And never stumbling as she crossed the floor.
Indeed I've earned more power than you by standing
 Much that your haughtiness would never bear.
How often I've been pinned on some hard doorpost,
 For passers-by to read, and I'd no fear!
Why, I remember hiding in a maid's dress,
 Poor me, until her escort went away.
Yes, when you sent me for that crude girl's birthday,
 She tore me, washed me down the drain that day.
I gave your happy genius germination;
 If *she* is after you, it's thanks to me.'

She'd finished. I began myself: 'I beg you,
 Both of you, listen to my timid plea.
One honours me with sceptre and tall buskin,
 My narrow throat swells with a surge of song.
The other gives my love eternal glory;
 So, Elegy, combine short lines with long.
Please, Tragedy, allow your bard a breather.
 You are eternal toil, her wants are short.'
She gave me leave. Quick, Loves, while I've the leisure!
 A greater work is waiting to be wrought.

2

I don't sit here because I'm keen on bloodstock,
    Though may the horse you've backed the winner be.
I came to talk with you, to sit beside you,
    So that you'll learn the love you've lit in me.
You watch the course, and I watch you; together
    Let's both watch what we want and feast our eyes.
Happy the charioteer who's found your favour!
    That fellow's got the luck; it's him you prize.
I wish that luck was mine. I'd get the horses
    Galloping from the start, I'd be so brave;
I'd give them rein, I'd use my whip, as need be,
    And with my nearside wheel the post I'd shave;
But seeing you as I swept by I'd falter,
    My hands would drop the reins and loose they'd lie.
How nearly Pelops fell to Oenomaus
    When fair Hippodamia caught his eye!
And yet he won, you know, through his girl's favour;
    So may your favour give us victory!

Why edge away? It's no use; the line keeps us
    Close—one good thing about the seating here.
You on the right there, careful, please. You're hurting
    The lady with your elbow; you're too near.
And you on the seat behind us, draw your legs back,
    And mind your manners. Keep your hard knees clear.
Your dress, my dear, is on the ground, it's trailing.
    Lift it—or look, I'm lifting it for you.
Mean, jealous dress to cover legs so lovely!
    The more one looks—mean, jealous dress, how true.
Such were the legs of lightfoot Atalanta,
    Legs that Milanion longed to have and hold;
So painters show the legs of swift Diana,
    The huntress than her own bold prey more bold.
I was on fire before. What, now I've seen them?
    You're adding flames to flames and seas to seas.
They make me sure that all the rest that's hidden
    Beneath your gauzy gown is bound to please.

But would you like a soft breeze while we're waiting?
　　My programme here can fan the heavy air.
Or is the heat my heart's, and not the weather,
　　And in my breast the flames of passion flare?
Look, your white frock—some dust there, while I'm talking.
　　Away, vile dust, don't soil her snowy lap.
But hush! Attend! The great procession's coming,
　　The gold procession, everybody clap!
In front, look, Victory wide-winged is leading.
　　Come, goddess, grant my passion victory.
Cheer Neptune, all who over-trust the ocean;
　　The sea's not my concern: dry land for me.
Cheer your Mars, soldiers. I hate war and weapons;
　　It's peace I like, and love that peace can bring.
Let Phoebus foster augurs, Phoebe huntsmen,
　　Let arts and crafts the praise of Pallas sing.
Let farmers honour Ceres and kind Bacchus,
　　Boxers to Pollux, knights to Castor bow.
But I cheer Venus and the boy, her bowman.
　　Smile, charming goddess, on my venture now,
And warm my new girl's heart to let me love her.
　　She's nodded! That's a favouring sign for me.
She's promised; give your promise too; and pace
　　Venus, you'll be a greater deity.
The crowd, the gods' procession be my witness
　　You'll always be my girl, my love won't fail.
But look, your legs are dangling. If you want to,
　　Why don't you rest your toes here on the rail?

They've cleared the course—the great event—the praetor's
　　Started the four-horse chariots. Off they go!
That's yours. The one you back will be the winner;
　　Your wishes even the horses seem to know.
Oh, Hell! What is he at? The fellow's taken
　　The post too wide. They're neck and neck again.
What are you at, you idiot? You're wrecking
　　The girl's best hopes. Left rein! Hard now, left rein!

We've backed a snail. Recall them, give the signal,
  Good Romans! Wave your togas everywhere!
Look, they're recalled. My cloak can give you shelter,
  So waving togas won't disturb your hair.
And now again the starting-gates are open,
  All those bright colours galloping away.
Come on now, take the lead down those wide furlongs,
  And make her hopes and mine come true today.
My girl's hopes have come true; *my* hopes are waiting.
  He's won his palm; my palm is still to wear.
She smiled; those bright eyes surely promised something.
  Enough for here. Give me the rest elsewhere.

3

Believe in gods, oh, yes! She swore and broke her
  Oath, and her lovely looks are lovely still.
Her hair was long before her heart was perjured,
  Her hair's as long now, though she's hurt heaven's will.

Her cheeks were snowy white with rosy blushes,
  Roses are blushing still amid the snow.
Graceful and tall she was, still tall and graceful,
  Foot tiny then, foot very dainty now.

Bright eyes she had, and still like stars they're shining,
  Eyes that so often spoke such lies to me.
Even the eternal gods let girls swear falsely—
  Of course—and beauty too's a deity.

She swore the other day, I well remember,
  By her own eyes and mine—and *my* eyes hurt.
Tell me, you Gods, if she tricked you unpunished,
  Why did *I* suffer so for her desert?

But then, you doomed Andromeda to die for
  Her mother's sin and reckoned that no shame.
It's bad enough that heaven's a worthless witness:
  Scot free with gods—and me—she plays her game.

Am I to be the cheater's cheated victim,
    I punished to redeem her perjury?
Either a god means nothing, just a bogy
    Fooling mankind in crass credulity,
Or, if he's there, he loves the little darlings
    And gets them given total liberty.

Against us men Mars buckles on his broadsword,
    At us Pallas' unfailing lance takes aim,
At us is bent the bow of great Apollo,
    On us Jove's high right hand hurls heaven's flame.

The slighted gods won't dare offend these lovelies;
    Girls don't funk them; it's they who're in a funk.
Who bothers to burn incense on their altars?
    We men, for sure, should show a deal more spunk.

Jove with his fire blasts sacred groves and towers,
    But he makes sure the bolts he hurls are barred
From perjured girls. So many have deserved them,
    But only Semele, poor soul, was charred.

That poor girl's punishment was her own doing
    Because she gave herself, but had her heart
Shrunk when her lover came, for infant Bacchus
    The father'd not have played the mother's part.

But why complain? Why abuse the whole of heaven?
    Gods too have eyes, gods too have hearts that beat.
Were I a god, I'd let girls dupe my godhead
    Unscathed—unpunished they could lie and cheat.

I'd swear it was the truth the girls were swearing,
    Not I a god for taking a hard line.
But use their gift, my dear, with more discretion—
    Or anyway please spare these eyes of mine.

4

Guarding a pretty girl, you brute, gets nowhere;
  A girl's good morals are the guard you need.
A girl who doesn't since she mustn't, does it;
  A girl who's chaste unforced is chaste indeed.

The body you may guard—the mind is guilty;
  No means of guarding a girl's thoughts from sin.
Nor can you guard the body, all doors bolted;
  Bolt as you will, a lover lurks within.

When sin's allowed, a girl sins less; the licence
  Debilitates the seeds of naughtiness.
A veto provokes vice, believe me. Chuck it,
  You'll gain your object by objecting less.

I saw a horse one day that went like lightning,
  Fighting against the curb of bit and rein;
As soon as he was given his head he halted,
  The leathers lying on his flowing mane.

We fight for what's illicit, want what's vetoed,
  So for forbidden drink a sick man drools.
Argus had eyes both back and front, a hundred;
  Love, single-handed, made the whole lot fools.

A bower of stone and steel imprisoned Danae;
  A virgin she went in, but got a mate:
Yet with no guard among so many suitors
  Penelope remained inviolate.

What's locked away one wants the more; precautions
  Invite a thief; few love by someone's leave.
It's not her looks delight them, but your loving;
  There's something there that gets you, they believe.

Locks never make girls good, just put the price up;
   Fear more than figure puts the value on.
Fuss as you will, there's charm in joys forbidden;
   Unless she says 'I'm frightened', she's no fun.

And locking up a freeborn girl's illegal,
   Let foreign women go in fear of that.
Shall she be chaste—to give her guard the credit,
   Your slave to have a feather in his hat?

A man's a country-bumpkin if he's hurt by
   Adultery. He doesn't know the form
At Rome where Mars' twins, Romulus and Remus,
   Were bastards—Ilia set the naughty norm.

If you must have her chaste, why go for beauty?
   In no way can they couple—not those two.
Be sensible! Don't look so stern and starchy;
   Give in to her—don't claim a husband's due.

Just cultivate the lots of friends she'll bring you;
   No effort, but a fine reward will come:
You'll always have a chance to join stag-parties,
   And see the gifts *you* didn't give at home.

5

'One night when sleep on tired eyes weighed
I had a dream and was afraid.
Below a sunny hill there stood
With serried trunks an ilex wood,
Whose branches many birds concealed,
And by the wood a lush green field,
A damp and grassy tapestry
With water softly purling by.
There, seeking shelter from the heat,
In the leaves' shade I'd made my seat
(The heat struck through them all the same),
When cropping grass and flowers came
A fine white cow before my eyes,
Whiter than first fresh snow that lies
Not melted yet by warmer skies,
Whiter than milk that hisses to
The foaming pail and drains the ewe.

A bull I dreamed was with her now,
And lay beside his darling cow
On the soft grass, her happy swain;
And while he lay and chewed again
Slowly the food he'd cropped before,
Sleep bowed his brawny neck, I saw,
And head and horns were lying there
When, lightly gliding through the air,
There came a carrion crow that cawed
And settled on the grassy sward.
And then against the white cow's breast
Three times its probing beak it pressed
And tore away white tufts of hair.
The cow a long while lingered there,
Then left—but on her breast she bore
A big black bruise and when she saw
Bulls in lush fields not far away
(Some bulls were grazing there that day)

She ran to join their company,
In hope some lusher grass to see.
Say now, whoever you may be,
Interpreter of dreams for me,
What do these things I saw foretell,
If truth at all in them may dwell?'

Then, weighing every word I'd said,
The interpreter this answer made:
'The heat from which you sought to gain
Shelter, and shelter sought in vain
Beneath the rustling leaves is love's.
The white cow, as the colour proves,
That cow's your girl, and apt its hue.
The bull, her mate (her man), is you;
The crow that pecked her breast stands for
An ancient bawd enticing her;
That the cow lingered and then left,
Means you'll lie cold in bed bereft;
Her breast's black bruise declares to me
A heart dyed with adultery.'

The blood fled from my cheeks, and night
Stood deep and dark before my sight.

6

Pause now, you muddy-margined, reed-lined river,
    I'm hurrying to my love; I pray you pause.
You have no bridge nor any cable-ferry
    To carry me without the stroke of oars.
Once you were small, I didn't fear to ford you,
    My ankles, I remember, almost dry.
But now the snow has melted from the mountain,
    A huge high murky spate goes swirling by.
What good were hours of rest cut short, a journey
    Uniting night and day so urgently,
Just to stand here, and have no means of setting
    Foot on the further bank that faces me?

I want the wings of Perseus, when he carried
　　Medusa's head with ghastly snakes all round;
I want the flying chariot that transported
　　The seeds of Ceres first to virgin ground—
All lies, the fairy tales of ancient poets;
　　Such things were not and never will be found.
Rather, you flooding river (may you always
　　Flow on!) glide in your proper bed today.
Believe me, you'll be loathed beyond endurance,
　　Should word get round you barred a lover's way.

Rivers should do their best to help young lovers;
　　Rivers have felt love too and learnt its charm.
Inachus, so they say, for love of Melie
　　Ran pale and all his icy waves grew warm.
The ten year siege of Troy was not yet finished
　　When Xanthus to Neaera lost his heart.
And was it not true love of Arethusa
　　That made Alpheus flow to lands apart?
Peneus spirited away to Phthia
　　Creusa, who was Xuthus' bride to be;
Asopus, you recall, adored Mars' daughter,
　　Thebe, and mother of five girls was she.
If I ask Achelous where his horns are,
　　The rage of Hercules wrenched them away—
Not Calydon nor Aetolia was worth it,
　　Just Deianira worth the world that day.
The famous, wealthy Nile, whose mouths are seven
　　And hides so well his mighty waters' home,
The flame Asopus' child, Evanthe, kindled
　　His swirling floods could never overcome.
Enipeus bade his waters stop to let him
　　Embrace Tyro; they stopped and dry was he.
And there's the stream that rolls through rocky channels
　　And laves the orchard lands of Tivoli,
The stream that Ilia charmed, though so dishevelled,
　　Cheeks torn and tresses torn in her distress.
Mourning her uncle's crime and Mars' wrong-doing,
　　She wandered barefoot through the wilderness,

And from his roaring rapids Anio saw her,
   And in his waters rose and eagerly
'Why do you pace my banks', he cried, 'so troubled,
   Ilia, child of Troy's long ancestry?
Why do you walk alone? Why so bedraggled,
   With no white band of braid to bind your hair?
Why those hot tears, why spoil your eyes with weeping,
   And why your breast in frenzy bruised and bare?
He who's not touched by tears on cheeks so tender,
   Iron and flint must form his hard heart's core.
Ilia, fear no more! My halls await you,
   My waves will hail you. Ilia, fear no more!
A hundred nymphs or more dwell in my waters,
   Queen of a hundred nymphs or more you'll reign.
Princess of Troy, I pray you, don't despise me,
   Gifts richer than my promises you'll gain.'

She stood abashed, her eyes downcast and weeping,
   Her tender bosom wet with many a tear.
Three times she tried to flee, three times stood rooted
   By those deep waters, frozen, numbed with fear.
At last, tearing her hair with angry fingers,
   In trembling tones these bitter words she said:
'Would I had died while I was still a virgin,
   And in my father's tomb my bones been laid.
Why am I offered marriage, I, a Vestal
   Disgraced, rejected by the Trojan flame?
Why linger on, a whore for folk to point at?
   Perish the face that bears the brand of shame!'
So saying, before her swollen eyes she held her
   Dress, and so threw herself into the flow.
The river, to her breasts his sly hand sliding,
   Made her his consort in the stream below.

You too, I well believe, found some girl warmed you,
   But trees and woods conceal your wicked course.
Even as I speak, your swelling waves flood wider,
   Your deep bed can't contain your waters' force.

Why pick on me, wild river, so ill-mannered,
  Breaking my journey, thwarting joys I share?
Perhaps, were you a proper stream, or famous,
  Renowned throughout the world beyond compare—
But you've no name—a flood of falling freshets—
  You've neither source nor home to call your own.
For source you have the rain and melting snow-drifts,
  The riches lifeless winter brings you down.
Either when days are short you're brown and muddy,
  Or summer sees a dry and dusty bed.
And then what thirsty wayfarer would drink you,
  What grateful voice call blessings on your head?
Losses you cause to herds, and more to ploughlands;
  They'll worry others, my loss worries me.
How mad of me to list the loves of rivers!
  A shame to name such names unworthily,
Telling of Inachus and Achelous,
  Naming the Nile before this nobody!
I wish you your deserts, you murky torrent,
  Suns fierce and scorching, winter always dry.

7

[Marlowe's version slightly modernized]

Yes, she was beautiful and well turned out,
The girl that I'd so often dreamed about,
Yet I lay with her limp as if I loved not,
A shameful burden on the bed that moved not.
Though both of us were sure of our intent,
Yet could I not cast anchor where I meant.
She round my neck her ivory arms did throw,
Her arms far whiter than the Scythian snow,
And eagerly she kissed me with her tongue,
And under mine her wanton thigh she flung.
Yes, and she soothed me up, and called me sire,
And used all speech that might provoke and stir.
Yet like as if cold hemlock I had drunk,
It humbled me, hung down the head, and sunk.

Like a tree trunk, a useless weight, I lay,
And were I ghost or body, who can say?
What will my old age do, if I have one,
When in my prime my force is spent and done?
I blush that being youthful, hot, and lusty
I prove not youth or man, but old and rusty.
Pure rose she, like a nun to sacrifice,
Or one that with her tender brother lies.
Yet boarded I the golden Chlide twice,
And Libas and the white-cheeked Pitho thrice.
Corinna craved it in a summer's night
And nine sweet bouts we had before daylight.

What, am I poisoned by some witch's charms?
Do spells and drugs do me, poor soul, such harms?
Did she my image in red wax procure,
And with her needles' points my liver skewer?
Charms transform wheat to weeds, and make it die,
Charms make the running streams and fountains dry.
Through charms oaks acorns shed, from vines grapes fall,
And fruit from trees when there's no wind at all.
Why might not then my sinews be enchanted,
And I grow faint as with some spirit haunted?
To this add shame: shame to perform it quailed me,
And was the second cause why vigour failed me.
But what a girl I only touched and saw,
Just clinging to her like the robe she wore!
Yet might her touch old Nestor's youth renew,
And make senile Tithonus lusty too.
Yes, I had her, and she had me—in vain.
What might I crave more, if I ask again?
I think the great gods grieved they'd offered me
The gift that I abused so shamefully.
I wished to be received in, in I get me,
To kiss, I kiss; to lie with her she let me.
What good such luck? Why, given the crown, refuse it?
I had a miser's gold and could not use it,

Like Tantalus in the pool who told too much,
Looking upon the fruits he cannot touch.
Does any man rise thus from a young maid
As she might straight have gone to church and prayed?

　　Perhaps she did not kiss me as she should,
Nor used the sleight and cunning which she could.
No! *She* could oaks and adamant have stirred,
And her sweet words deaf boulders would have heard.
Worthy she was to stir all living men,
But neither was I man nor living then.
Can deaf ears take delight when Phemius sings?
Blind Thamyras enjoy bright painted things?
Yet what sweet ways of love did I not frame,
How many fantasies in silence came!
But notwithstanding, like one dead it lay,
Drooping more than a rose picked yesterday.
Now, when he should not be, he's bolt upright,
And craves his task and seeks to have his fight.
Lie down in shame and see you stir no more!
You've caught me with your promises before.
You've tricked me, got me captured weaponless,
And I've endured great shame and sore distress.
Nay more, the wench did not disdain a whit
To take it in her hand and play with it.
But when she saw it would by no means stand,
But still drooped down, regarding not her hand,
'Why mock me so', she cried, 'or, if you're ill,
Who bade you lie down here against your will?
Either you've been bewitched and you're half dead,
Or you came jaded from some other's bed.'
With that, in her loose gown, she leapt from me
(Her bare feet were a pretty sight to see),
And lest her maids should know of this disgrace,
To cover it, spilt water on the place.

8

The liberal arts—does anyone respect them,
    Or think there's value in love-poetry?
Time was when gold was thought worth less than genius;
    Now having nothing's sheer vulgarity.
Though my girl gives my work a warm reception,
    I cannot go myself where my books go.
She's praised them, but her door's shut on her praises;
    My genius in disgrace drifts to and fro.
A *nouveau riche* whose wounds have made his money,
    A blood-devouring knight usurps my place.
That man, my dear, can your sweet arms embrace him?
    Can you, my dear, lie in that man's embrace?
That head, you may not know, once wore a helmet,
    The flank that serves you bore a sword of steel.
That left hand, where his new ring's so unsuited,
    Carried his shield; his right hand there—just feel—
Did bloody murder—can you bear to touch it?
    Alas, where is your soft heart's tenderness?
Look at those scars, the marks of bygone battles—
    His body's bought him all he does possess.
Perhaps he'll tell how many men he's slaughtered;
    Can you, for gold, touch those hands that confess?

Am I, the priest of Phoebus and the Muses,
    To sing vain verses at a bolted door?
Learn, if you're wise, not what we know, we idlers,
    But battle-lines and wild alarms of war.
Try forming fours instead of forming verses;
    Homer, enlist, and soon inside you'll be.
The power of gold's supreme, and well Jove knew it;
    To get the girl he made himself the fee.
Before the deal the doors were bronze, the tower
    Iron, the father hard, the daughter prim.
But when the cunning lecher came as money,
    She gave the gift required—herself—to him.

Yet when old Saturn had his reign in heaven,
   Deep in the dark Earth kept her wealth secure.
She'd stowed the gold and silver, iron and copper
   Down with the ghosts: no ingots then, for sure.
But she gave better, crops from fields unfurrowed,
   And fruits, and honey from a hollow tree,
And no one scored the soil with sturdy ploughshares,
   And no surveyor marked a boundary.
No dipping oars swept lines across the ocean,
   Man's longest journey ended at the shore.
O human nature, deft for self-destruction!
   Too clever, with such tragedies in store!
What good for you are cities ringed with ramparts,
   What good to give men arms in enmity?
What good the sea—you should have been content with
   The land. Why not a third realm in the sky?
Yes, when you may, you claim the sky too: Bacchus,
   Romulus, and Hercules you deify,
And Caesar too. Not food but gold we dig for;
   For money soldiers shed their blood and fight.
The Senate's shut to poor men; wealth gives honours,
   Wealth makes a solemn judge, a haughty knight.
Well, let them own the lot. Let Courts and Councils
   Bow to them; let them manage peace and war,
As long as our true-loves aren't up for auction,
   And something—that's enough—'s left for the poor.
Now though a girl may match the strait-laced Sabines,
   A man with gifts just rules her like a slave.
But me—on my account she fears her husband,
   The porter locks me out; but if I *gave*,
The two of them would leave the house wide open
   And disappear. O for some god who's just,
To take sure vengeance for a slighted lover,
   And turn that ill-won wealth of theirs to dust!

9

If for Achilles, if for Memnon dead,
    Their mothers grieved, if goddesses can mourn,
Weep, Elegy, and loose your hair forlorn—
    Too truly you are named from sad tears shed.

Tibullus, your own bard, your glory, now
    On the tall pyre, a futile corpse, is burned.
See, Venus' boy his quiver bears upturned,
    With lightless torch, alas, and broken bow.

Look how he goes with drooping wings distressed,
    How the tears fall on his long tousled hair,
How the loud sobs his heaving bosom tear,
    How fierce the fist that beats his naked breast.

Thus mourned he when his brother came to die,
    When from Iulus' halls Aeneas went;
Nor less does Venus this death now lament
    Than when the fierce boar slashed Adonis' thigh.

We bards are classed as holy, heaven's care;
    Divinity, they say, flows in our veins.
But every holy thing brash death profanes;
    There's nothing that his murky clutches spare.

Orpheus' great parents—what did they avail?
    Or song whose magic power the beasts subdued?
To sad reluctant lyre in the wild wood
    'Ah, Linus, Linus' went his father's wail.

And Homer too, whose founts of song inspire
    The Muses' streams on poets' lips for ay,
Sank to Avernus' depths on his last day:
    Verse, verse alone escapes the insatiate pyre.

In poetry the toils of Troy live on,
    And that slow web night's cunning would unwind.
So Nemesis and Delia fame will find,
    Who last and first their poet's worship won.

What use is that Egyptian ritual,
    Those timbrels, these long nights of chastity?
When evil fate dooms good men, may I be
    Forgiven if I've no faith in gods at all!

Live righteously—you die; in prayer take pains—
    Death drags you from the temple to the tomb.
Trust in good verse—Tibullus, look, lies dumb;
    A little urn can hold what now remains.

How could the flames consume you, holy bard,
    And feed upon your heart and have no fear?
The flames that such a crime could ever dare,
    The great gods' golden temples could have charred.

The goddess whom the heights of Eryx throne
    Turned her sad face away, some say she wept.
But better so than had Corcyra kept
    That corpse interred in some mean grave unknown.

For here your mother closed your swimming eyes,
    Here to your ashes the last gifts were borne,
And here your sister came, wild tresses torn,
    To share her sorrowing mother's miseries.

And Nemesis and your first love gave their
    Fond kisses too, both present at the pyre.
'You lived', said Delia, 'while I was your fire:
    I was the lucky one, your love to share.'

But Nemesis, 'Why mourn *my* loss?', she said,
    'His failing hand held *me* when his death came.'
And yet, if aught survives but shade and name,
    Tibullus dwells in some Elysian glade;

And greeting him, their young brows wreathed with bay,
　　Come Calvus and Catullus and you too,
Unless the charge of friendship wronged is true,
　　Gallus, who life and spirit cast away.

Your soul joins theirs, if souls survive at all;
　　You, gracious friend, are numbered with the blest.
Safe in the urn I pray your bones may rest,
　　And earth weigh lightly in your burial.

10

Now comes the yearly festival of Ceres,
　　And my love lies alone in bed at night.
O golden goddess, garlanded with wheatears,
　　Why must your feast inhibit our delight?

The nations of the world extol your bounty,
　　No goddess gives mankind a larger store.
Before you came no shaggy peasant roasted
　　His corn, none knew about a threshing floor.

Oaks, the first oracles, provided acorns;
　　Those were men's food, and herbs and tender leaves.
Ceres first taught the seed to sprout in furrows,
　　She first with sickles cut the coloured sheaves,

Made oxen bow their necks to yokes, the ploughshare
　　Drive furrows through the farmland's ancient heart.
Can *she* rejoice in lovers' tears, her worship
　　Thrive on the agony of nights apart?

She loves the fertile fields, but she's no yokel,
　　Her heart's not wanting in the ways of love,
As witness Crete—(Cretans aren't always liars;
　　Crete was once proud to be the nurse of Jove.

There once was suckled as a little baby
   The mighty ruler of the starry sky.
Her foster son approves her as a witness.)
   Ceres, I think, my charge will not deny.

She saw Iasius below Mount Ida,
   Hunting his quarry with unerring aim;
Saw him—and in her heart the blaze was kindled,
   And to and fro there wrestled love and shame.

Love won, and you could see the hard dry furrows,
   The meagre lean return the seed gave now.
Although the fields were worked with well-aimed mattocks,
   The hard soil broken by the curving plough,

The seed sown evenly across wide acres,
   In vain the cheated farmer made his vow.
Deep in the woods the teeming goddess dallied;
   Her wreath of grain had fallen from her brow.

Only in Crete the year was lush and fertile;
   There all was harvest where her foot was felt.
Ida, the forests' home, was white with wheatfields,
   And in the woodlands boars were reaping spelt.

Law-giver Minos wished for more such seasons;
   Long love for Ceres should have been his plea.
You hated lonely nights, dear golden goddess—
   Why must your feast force lonely nights on me?

Why should I grieve? You've found your darling daughter;
   Second only to Juno does she reign!
A feast day calls for song and wine and women;
   Those are the gifts the lordly gods should gain.

11a

Too much! too long! I'm tried beyond endurance.
　　My heart's worn out; no more, vile Love, no more!
I've got my freedom now, I've shed my shackles;
　　I blush to think I didn't blush before.

I've won the day, and Love lies tamed and trampled;
　　I nerved myself, at last my courage rose.
Just grit your teeth. The pain will prove propitious:
　　One's often better for a bitter dose.

To think _I_ laid my freeborn frame, so often
　　Rejected, on your porch's stony floor!
To think _I_, for some fellow you were fondling,
　　Kept vigil, like a slave, at your locked door!

I watched your lover leave the house exhausted,
　　Discharged from love's campaign as I could see.
But—what was even worse—he saw me waiting:
　　That shame I'd wish on my worst enemy.

When did I not cling constantly beside you,
　　I, comrade, escort, I your lover true?
People liked you because we went together;
　　Our love ensured that many loved you too.

What of your filthy lies, your feckless fibbing,
　　Your perjured oaths designed to damage me?
What of the silent nods of lads at parties,
　　The coded words that signalled secretly?

'She's ill' they said—I rushed off like a madman;
　　Arrived to find my rival found her well.
All this—and things unsaid—have got me hardened.
　　Seek someone else to put up with such hell.

My ship's in port now, garlanded and grateful,
   Unworried by the rising swell at sea.
Don't waste your witching words on me. Your magic's
   Faded—I'm not the fool I used to be!

11b

My fickle heart! Now love and hate are struggling
   This way and that, but love will win, I'm sure.
I'll hate for choice. If not, I'll love unwilling;
   Oxen don't love the yoke, but they endure.

I abhor your wicked ways, I love your body;
   Though you're a bitch, your beauty brings me back.
I can't live either with you or without you;
   I don't know what I want—I'm on the rack.

I wish you were less lovely or less wanton;
   Such loveliness goes ill with villainy.
I loathe your conduct, love you for your beauty—
   Beauty, alas, outweighs depravity.

Oh by the bed that made our bond, by all the
   Gods who have let you take their name in vain,
Your eyes that ravished mine, your face I worshipped
   Like a high goddess, pity my heart's pain!

Be what you may, you shall be mine for ever.
   Just choose then—shall my love be forced or free?
I'd rather winds blew fair, so you who'd force me
   To love unwilling, I'd love willingly.

12

Was there a day when some black crow croaked curses
　　On a soul doomed to love for ever more?
What evil star am I to think has crossed me,
　　What gods against myself are waging war?

Once she was known as mine, and I her only
　　Lover; now I fear many share her heart.
My verse, no doubt, has made her name familiar;
　　That's it—she's prostituted by my art.

And serve me right! I publicized her beauty.
　　If my girl's on the market, just blame me.
I've been the pimp and I've procured the lovers;
　　My hand opened her door, I turned the key.

What verse is worth, I doubt. It's always harmed me,
　　And my success has made men envious.
Though there was Thebes and Troy and Caesar's exploits,
　　Only Corinna fired my genius.

I wish the Muse had balked at my beginnings
　　And Phoebus left me stranded at the start.
Yet poets aren't on oath, you know; I'd rather
　　Less weight were given to my wordy art.

We poets made poor Scylla steal her father's
　　Tress, in her groin made dogs growl rabidly;
We gave feet wings, hair snakes; we mounted Perseus
　　To ride a flying horse to victory.

Tityos, too, we stretched across vast acres,
　　We gave the hound of Hell his faces three,
Made thousand-armed Enceladus hurl lances,
　　Lured heroes with the Sirens' symphony.

We bagged the wild winds in Ulysses' wine-skin,
    Had Tantalus athirst with drink just there,
Set Philomela wailing for poor Itys,
    Made Niobe a rock, the girl a bear,

Got Jove self-changed to birds or gold, or swimming,
    A bull with the princess perched on his back.
Take Proteus too, and dragons' teeth and oxen
    Spewing fierce flames along the furrows' track.

Take Phaethon's sisters weeping tears of amber,
    Ships turned to sea-nymphs to escape the fire,
The sun fleeing the hellish feast of Atreus,
    The blocks of stone led by the magic lyre.

Yes, there's no limit to poetic licence,
    And it's not tied to truths of history.
You should have seen the praise I gave my girl-friend
    Was lies: I'm crushed by your credulity.

13

The orchard town Camillus took, Falerii,
    Was my wife's birthplace; we came there one day.
Juno's chaste feast was being celebrated,
    With games and sacrifice the place was gay;
A feast well worth the visit, though the journey
    Is difficult, a steep and toilsome way.

A grove stands there, ancient and dense and gloomy;
    The place must be a god's, one can be sure.
The faithful offer incense at an altar,
    An artless altar reared in days of yore.

Here, to the sound of flutes and solemn chanting,
    The long procession passes every year
Through streets bedecked, with white Falerian heifers
    From their own fields, while all the people cheer,

With bullocks too whose brows as yet don't threaten,
    Pigs, meaner victims, from their humble sties,
And bell-wethers with horns in spirals; only
    Goats are abhorrent in the goddess' eyes.

Deep in the woods, they say, a goat betrayed her
    And she was found and forced to end her flight.
So now boys make a target of the traitor;
    The goat's the prize of him whose aim is right.

Young men and shy girls go before the goddess,
    Their trailing vestments sweeping the wide street.
The girls' hair is adorned with gold and jewels,
    And stately gowns half-hide their gilded feet.

High on their heads they bear the holy vessels,
    White-robed according to the old Greek rites.
The crowd is hushed as Juno in her golden
    Procession comes behind her acolytes.

The form of the procession comes from Argos.
    On Agamemnon's death Halaesus fled
The murder and his father's wealth and wandered
    Long over land and sea as exile led.

His was the fortune-favoured hand that founded
    Those lofty walls; he taught the ritual
Of Juno to Falerii. May it ever
    Prove a good friend to me and to them all!

14

[Marlow's version modernized]

You're charming—misbehave then—I'll agree
So long as I, poor fool, don't have to see.
My morals don't require you to live chaste,
But just to try to hide it when it's past.
A girl has not done wrong who can deny it;
It's those confessing lose their good names by it.
What madness to reveal night's pranks by day,
And hidden secrets openly betray!
A prostitute performs in privacy
And sees the room is clear and turns the key.
Will you make shipwreck of your honest name
And let the world be witness of the same?
Behave yourself, or play the puritan,
And I shall think you chaste, do what you can.
Do what you do; just say it wasn't done;
In public, too, discretion never shun.

There is a place demands a naughty game;
Fill it with fun, fill it and feel no shame.
But when you're up and dressed, be staid and grave,
And in the bed leave all the faults you have.
Yes, take your clothes off there and don't be shy
Of lying close together, thigh to thigh.
There in your rosy lips my tongue entomb;
Practise a thousand love-games when you come.
There words of loving warmth don't fail to speak,
And with your pastime let the bedstead creak.
But with your dress put on an honest face,
And blush and seem as you were full of grace.
Cheat all, cheat me, so long as I don't see;
Let me enjoy my crass credulity.

Why do I see those notes received and given?
Why both sides of the bed left so uneven,
Your hair that more than sleep has disarrayed,
And on your neck the bites of love displayed?

Before my eyes all but the act I see;
If you won't spare your name, at least spare me.
It's death when you confess what you have done,
And through my veins I feel the cold blood run.
Then you, whom I must love, I hate in vain,
And would be dead, but dead with you remain.
The things you'd hide, I'll never search or sift,
To be deceived I'll value as a gift.
But if I ever catch you in mid-guilt,
And your disgrace is proved up to the hilt,
Deny I've seen what's clear as day, be wise,
And I will trust your words more than my eyes.
It's easy beating one who wants to lose;
Just say 'Not guilty'—they're the words to use.
With those two words there's victory to be had,
So win the judge, although the case is bad.

15

Mother of tender Loves, find a new poet!
    This is the last lap now for Elegy,
The verse I wrote, I, child of the Peligni
    (Nor has the fun I've had dishonoured me),
I, whose knighthood goes back three generations,
    For what that's worth, not new in whirls of war.
Verona claims Catullus, Mantua Virgil;
    From me the Peligni now have fame in store,
The folk who fought with honour for their freedom
    When allied arms caused Rome such dire dismay.
And looking at the walls of stream-fed Sulmo
    And her few fields, some visitor will say:
'To think you could produce so great a poet.
    However small you are, I'll call you great.'
Suave boy and you, the suave boy's Cyprian mother,
    Pluck your gold standards up, my field vacate!
Horned Bacchus with his weightier rod rebukes me;
    A greater field my mighty team must tread.
Goodbye now genial Muse, soft-hearted Elegy,
    My work that will live on when I am dead.

COSMETICS FOR LADIES

Learn, girls, the methods that improve complexions,
    The means by which your looks you may defend.
By cultivation barren acres yielded
    Harvests, and greedy briars met their end.
And cultivation sweetens fruit that's bitter;
    From grafted trees adopted riches grow.
Culture gives pleasure. Lofty halls are panelled
    With gold, and marble hides black soil below.
Fleeces are double-dyed with Tyrian purple,
    Carved ivory to charm us India yields.
In Tatius' time maybe the Sabine women
    Cared less to dress themselves than dress their fields.
Sitting on her high stool the red-faced matron
    With calloused fingers spun her busy thread.
She herself penned the lambs her daughter'd pastured,
    Herself the homely hearth with firewood fed.
But you were born and bred for soft refinement;
    You like your gowns adorned with golden hems;
You like to scent your hair and change your hair-style;
    You like to have your hands ablaze with gems.
And round your neck you wear great Eastern jewels
    With stones so large no ear could take a pair.
That's not bad taste: you need to be attractive
    When men these days are all so debonair.
Your husbands dress up to the nines like ladies,
    A bride has hardly smarter things to wear.

Girls dress to please themselves; smartness can never
    Be wrong; it makes no odds whom they pursue.
Hair's curled deep in the country; though they're hidden
    On Athos, they'll be smart on Athos too.
There's pleasure also in self-satisfaction;
    Their beauty always warms the hearts of girls.
In silent pride of beauty struts the peacock
    And for the praise of men its plumes unfurls.

That's how love should arise, not by the power
  Of plants some frightful sorceress prepares.
And put no trust in herbs or blended juices,
  Nor try the poison-flux of lusting mares.
No snakes are burst by Marsian incantations,
  Nor does a river to its source flow back,
And even though no bronze is banged and beaten,
  The moon will not be shaken from her track.

Your first thought, girls, should be for your behaviour;
  A face will please when character is fine.
Love lasts for character: age ruins beauty
  And looks that charmed are ploughed with many a line.
The time will come when you will loathe your mirror
  And grief a second cause of wrinkles sends.
Goodness suffices and endures for ever;
  On this throughout its years true love depends.

Learn now the ways and means, when sleep has left you,
  Of looking bright and fresh and fair of face.
Take barley brought by sea from Libyan farmlands
  And strip away the chaffy carapace.
Then measure out two pounds of your husked barley
  And beat ten eggs with vetch of the same weight.
When airy draughts have dried this, make a donkey
  Grind it on the rough stone with his slow gait.
Grind with it, too, two ounces of the antlers
  First fallen from a stag that long years lives;
And when it's blended with the mealy powder,
  Sift everything at once in fine-meshed sieves.
Add twelve narcissus bulbs—first skin and pound them
  In a clean marble mortar vigorously,
Then gum and Tuscan seed, of each two ounces,
  With honey of nine times that quantity.
A girl who treats her face with that prescription,
  Smoother than her own mirror will appear.
Likewise roast pallid lupin seeds and with them
  Beans that bring flatulence—you needn't fear.

Weigh out six pounds of each in equal measure,
   Have both of them ground small in slow-turned mills.
Nor let white lead be lacking or red nitre
   Or irises raised on Illyrian hills.
Give them to brawny lads to pound together;
   When crushed, one ounce will be the proper weight.
Freckles are banished by a substance based on
   A sad bird's nest: it's called Alcyonate.
If you enquire the weight that I'm content with,
   It's what at half an ounce will turn the scales.
To make a paste for ease of application
   Add honey that from Attic beehives hails.
Though incense softens gods and angry spirits,
   No need to give it all to altars' fire.
When mixing it with wart-removing nitre
   Four ounces clear of each you will require.
Next add nine ounces of peeled gum and with it
   A cube, not very large, of luscious myrrh,
And when it's all well pounded, sieve it finely;
   Then in the powder honey you must stir.
To perfumed myrrh it's useful to add fennel
   (Five scruples weight of fennel, of myrrh nine),
With dried rose-petals too (a single handful),
   And frankincense and salt from Ammon's shrine.
Roses with salt should weigh the same as incense;
   Then pour some barley-liquor on the lot.
With this cream on your face for quite a short time
   A lovely fresh complexion you'll have got.

I've seen a girl soak poppies in cold water,
   Pound them and rub them on her tender cheeks
. . . .

Weigh out six pounds of each in equal measure,
Have both of them ground small to powder-dust,
Nor be white lead by lacking of red mixt,
Or mixt, rubbed on th' whetstone.
Give them to barren Ceres to pound together,
When ground, one ounce will be the proper weight.
Fresh salt...
...bird's...

I've seen a girl soak poppies in cold water,
Pound them and rub them on her tender cheeks.

THE ART OF LOVE

BOOK ONE

Who in this town knows not the lover's art
Should read this book, and play an expert's part.
It's art that speeds the boat with oars and sails,
Art drives the chariot, art in love prevails.
Automedon was skilled with car and rein,
And Tiphys steered the Argo o'er the main:
For young Love's guide has Venus chosen me,
Love's pilot and Love's charioteer I'll be.
Though he be wild and apt to flout my rule,
He's but a boy, an easy age to school.
From Chiron young Achilles learnt the lyre,
His gentle art subdued that soul of fire.
He who so oft both friends and foes dismayed,
Of one old man, they tell us, was afraid.
Hands that were destined to be Hector's bane
Were held when bidden 'neath the master's cane.
Achilles was his pupil, Love is mine,
Both boys of temper fierce and birth divine.
Yet 'neath the yoke the bullock's neck is bowed,
And the champed bridle frets the charger proud;
So Love shall yield to me, though at my heart
He aim his bow and launch his flaming dart.
The worse he stabs, the fiercer burns his flame,
So much the fitter I to venge the maim.
I'll not pretend to powers by Phoebus given,
Nor warnings uttered by the fowls of heaven,
Nor Clio nor her sisters I espied,
While shepherding on Ascra's mountain side.
Experience prompts my labours. Heed the sage:
With truths, oh Venus! help me fill my page.

Hence, hence, ye signs of wife- and maidenhood,
The ankle-covering skirt, the slender snood!
Of safe intrigues and lawful thefts I rhyme,
Nor can my song be charged with any crime.

To find an object worthy of his suit
Is the first duty of our new recruit:
The next to gain the chosen damsel's 'yea',
The last, to keep her love for many a day.
This is my aim, this course my car shall steer,
This mark my wheels shall touch in mid career.

While you are free with slackened rein to rove,
Choose one whom you can call your only love.
Think not she'll drop before you from the skies:
To find a fitting mistress, use your eyes.
The hunter learns where stags are to be snared,
Learns in what glens the tusky boar is laired;
The fowler knows the woodlands, and the brook
Most live with fish he knows who wields the hook.
So you who're on a lasting love intent
Must learn the spots that damsels most frequent.
No need to set your sails before the wind,
Or journey far the looked-for goal to find.
From swarthy Ind his bride let Perseus bear,
From Hellas let the Trojan steal his fair;
In Rome of lovely women there's no dearth;
Here shall you find the pick of all the earth.
Thick as Methymna's grapes or Gargara's crops
Or fish in seas or birds in greenwood tops,
Thick as the stars the fair abound in Rome;
In her son's city Venus makes her home.
If it's the first still budding years you prize,
A genuine maid is there to greet your eyes,
If youthful prime, a thousand such rejoice
Your heart and make you doubtful of your choice,
If mellow age attracts and riper mind,
Here too, be sure, a goodly throng you'll find.

Do you but saunter gently in the shade,
At summer's height, of Pompey's colonnade,
Or where, twin gifts of son's and mother's hand,
Those halls of rich exotic marble stand.
Nor shun the arcade for its old masters famed,
By Livia founded and from Livia named,
Nor where with falchion drawn fierce Danaus waits,
The while his daughters slay their hapless mates.
Nor miss where Venus for Adonis weeps,
Nor where the Jew his sacred Sabbath keeps.
To white-robed Isis' Memphian shrine recur,
Who makes so many what Jove made of her.
The law-courts too (who'd think it?) suit love's game,
Oft in the noisy courts he lights his flame.
Where hard by Venus' marble fane the spray
Of Appian waters bursts upon the day,
There oft for counsel Cupid sets a snare,
And takes the wary lawyer unaware.
There oft he finds his eloquence has flown,
And he must plead a novel cause—his own;
While Venus from her neighbouring shrine will mock
The advocate translated to the dock.

But the tiered playhouse gives you amplest scope;
There's hunting richer than you dared to hope.
There you shall find a mistress or a toy
To touch but once or be a lasting joy.
As ants that to and fro in endless train
Haste to bring home their wonted load of grain,
As mid their favourite glades and scented leas
O'er flowers and thyme-tops flit the swarming bees,
So to the play the well-dressed bevies throng,
Such wealth of choice as keeps one doubting long.
They come to look and to be looked at too.
Ah! Virtue, it's a fatal spot for you.
With Romulus the scandal first began,
When ravished Sabines cheered his wifeless clan.
No marble then, no awnings were displayed,
No scented boards the golden saffron sprayed.

The Palatine well-wooded lent his green
In simple taste to deck the artless scene.
On tiers of terraced turf the folk reclined,
Rough crowns of leaves their shaggy hair entwined.
They look, and each one marks his chosen fair,
Each in his heart breathes many a silent prayer.
While to the Tuscan piper's homely strain
The player foots it o'er the levelled plain,
Amid the applause (applause was natural then)
The chieftain signals on his waiting men.
Up suddenly with tell-tale shouts they spring,
And hungry hands upon the maidens fling.
As frightened doves before the eagle fly,
As lambkins that the dreaded wolf espy,
So they before the men's wild onset shrink,
And not a cheek retains its wonted pink.
All fear alike, but fear has many a phase;
Some rend their hair, some sit in lost amaze,
One mutely mourns, one vainly 'Mother' cries,
One sobs, one faints, one stays, another flies.
Away the train of captive brides is led,
Many the lovelier for their very dread;
And if one strove her captor to deny,
Clasped to his loving breast he held her high:
'Why spoil those tender eyes with tears?' quoth he,
'Just like your parents you and I shall be.'
Old Romulus the prize for soldiers knew,
For such a prize I'd be a soldier too!
Thus was the fashion started, and the fair
Still find the play a peril and a snare.

Nor miss the ring where high-bred coursers race,
You'll find much vantage in that crowded place.
Not here by sign of hand or nod of head
Need hints be dropped or messages be sped.
Sit next your mistress, none can say you nay,
Press side to side as close as e'er you may;
Thanks to the custom of the crowded bench,
Coy though she be, you're bound to squeeze the wench.

Some opening then for friendly converse seek,
And first on topics of the moment speak.
'Whose team is that?' enquire with earnest air,
And back her fancy, be it whatsoe'er.
Then when the train of images draws near,
For Lady Venus clap and raise a cheer.
And if a speck of dust, as well it may,
Drop on her bosom, flick the speck away,
And if there's none, then flick what isn't there;
Seize any pretext for a show of care.
If on the ground her mantle trail ungirt,
With eager hands uplift it from the dirt.
If she permit it, there and then a sight
Of madam's legs that service will requite.
Then whoso sits behind you, watch and see
Her tender back he prod not with his knee.
Small things please little minds: it profits much
Her cushion to compose with dexterous touch,
With slender fan to waft a breeze or put
The hollow stool beneath her dainty foot.

Such aids to new love, will the Circus bring,
And the sad gladiator's sandy ring.
Love oft in that arena fights a bout,
Then it's the looker-on who's counted out.
While chatting, buying a programme, shaking hands,
Or wagering on the match intent he stands,
He feels the dart, and groaning 'neath the blow
Himself becomes an item in the show.

When Caesar late in mimic warfare staged
The Persian and Athenian fleets engaged,
When youths and maidens came from East and West
And all the world was into Rome compressed,
Who in that throng a sweetheart can have lacked?
What myriads, ah! by alien loves were racked!

Lo! Caesar plans to bring beneath his sway
What's left of earth. Be ours now, far Cathay.
Cheer, shades of Crassus: Parthia shall pay now;
Cheer, standards by barbarian hands laid low.
No boy's emprise, a boy avenger moves
To war, and Captain in his nonage proves.
Count not, you cowards, the birthdays of the great:
A Caesar's valour flowers before its date.
The soul divine outstrips the body's growth,
And chafes beneath the lagging years of sloth.
Hercles with baby hands the serpents slew,
And in his cradle proved Jove's scion true.
How big was Bacchus, who's a stripling yet,
When over Ind his conquering rod was set?
Your father's blessing arms you for the fray,
Armed with his blessing you shall win the day.
That mighty name your prentice hand inspires,
Now Prince of Youth, but one day prince of sires.
Brothers you have, then brothers' wrongs requite.
A father's yours, uphold a father's right.
Your country's sire has armed you and your own:
The foe has robbed a parent of his throne.
Your righteous sword confronts his guilty brand,
And Right and Duty with your banner stand.
May Parthia rue the rout her cause must earn,
And rich with Eastern spoils our prince return!
Bless him, oh Mars and Caesar, heavenly twain,
One God, and one that Godhead shall attain.
Lo! I foresee your triumph; I shall raise
A hymn of thanks and loudly sing your praise.
In words of mine you shall inspire your men,
Words worthy of your spirit might I pen!
I'll tell of shafts from fleeing horses thrown
And Parthian backs to Roman faces shown.
Ah Parthian! how ill-omened is your ruse:
Who flees to win, what's left him if he lose?
Then one great day our darling we'll behold,
Drawn by four snowy steeds and clad in gold.

In front shall walk the chieftains fettered tight,
Lest they take refuge in their wonted flight;
While youths and maids look on in blithe array,
And every heart is gladdened by the day.
And if a damsel ask what chiefs are those,
What towns or hills or streams the pageant shows,
Tell everything she asks and more than that,
And though you know not, give your answers pat.
That's the Euphrates with his crown of reeds,
And that the Tigris with the long grey weeds;
Make these Armenians, that the Danaan Crown
Of Persia, this some Median valley town.
Yonder are generals; add a name or two,
Names that are fitting, though they mayn't be true.

Look too for openings at the festive board,
For wine is not the diner's sole reward.
The head of Bacchus oft, as there he lies,
With soft caresses rosy Cupid plies;
And when the wine his dripping wings besprays,
Weighed down, a captive on the spot he stays.
Quickly indeed he spreads his dewy plumes,
But once bedewed with love, the heart succumbs.
Wine lights the fire of passion in the soul,
Cares melt and vanish in the brimming bowl.
Then laughter comes and poverty shows fight
And frowns and cares and sorrows take to flight.
Then truthfulness, rare comer in our day,
Unlocks the breast and guile is cast away.
There oft men's hearts are ravished by desire,
For Venus in her cups is fire on fire.
Nor trust o'ermuch the treacherous candleshine,
Your eye for beauty's warped by night and wine.
When Paris judged the three and gave the prize
To Venus, there were clear and cloudless skies.
Night hides each fault, each blemish will condone,
The hour can make a beauty of a crone.
To daylight pearls and purple gowns refer;
Of face and limb let day be arbiter.

But why attempt to count the hunting grounds,
Countless as sand, where womanhood abounds?
Why tell of Baiae and her sail-fringed shore,
Her steaming springs with sulphur vapoured o'er;
Returning whence some love-sick wretch exclaimed:
'This water's not so wholesome as it's famed.'
Hard by the Town stands Dian's sylvan fane,
Where priests do murder and assassins reign;
A virgin goddess hating Cupid's dart,
She's damaged, and shall damage, many a heart.

Thus far the Muse, on couplets borne, has mapped
The spots where sweethearts may be found and trapped.
Now by what arts to catch the chosen belle,
A work of highest skill, I'll strive to tell.
Men one and all, lend an attentive ear,
And flock the promised utterance to hear.

First tell yourself all women can be won:
Just spread your nets; the thing's as good as done.
Spring birds and summer crickets shall be mute
And greyhounds flee before the hare's pursuit,
Ere woman spurns a wooer's blandishments;
Even she you'd swear would ne'er consent, consents.
To stolen joys both man and woman thrill;
She hides her yearnings, he dissembles ill.
Could men agree to ask no woman first,
The asker's role perforce would be reversed.
Cow lows to bull across the balmy mead,
The mare still whinnies to the horn-shod steed.
More calm and sober burn the lusts of men,
In lawful bounds our ardours do we pen.
Take Byblis, who with halter unafraid
The price of her incestuous passion paid;
Myrrha, who loved, but in no filial wise,
Her father, prisoned in a tree-trunk lies,
That fragrant tree that from her tears of shame
Distils the perfume that preserves her name.

In Ida's shady valleys once was reared
A snow-white bull, the glory of the herd.
Betwixt his horns one streak of umber thin
Was the sole blemish on his milky skin.
Cnossos' and Cydon's heifers all aflame
To bear the burden of his courtship came.
Pasiphae, longing for a bestial mate,
Eyed the fair cows with jealousy and hate.
Known truth I sing: not even that land of lies,
Crete of the hundred towns, my tale denies.
Herself, it's said, fresh leaves and softest sward
With hands unskilled she gathered for her lord.
She joins the herds nor recks her husband's case,
And Minos to a bull yields pride of place.
Pasiphae, why don that raiment fine?
No gauds can move that paramour of thine.
What use that mirror 'mid the mountain flocks?
What use, fond fool, to smooth your ordered locks?
Yet trust your glass that shows you you're no cow:
How welcome would be horns upon that brow!
Oh! love your spouse and for no stranger lust,
Or sin with your own kind, if sin you must.
She quits her palace and through glades and groves
Like a hag-ridden bacchanal she roves.
How oft she eyed a heifer in despite,
Exclaiming 'Why should *she* my lord delight?
See on the turf she gambols at his feet;
The fool thinks doubtless that she looks so sweet.'
She had her harmless victim, as she spoke,
Torn from the herd and set to bear the yoke,
Or, a sham offering, at the altar felled,
And gloated as her rival's heart she held.
Oft to the Gods her rivals did she vow,
And took their hearts and said 'Go, charm him now!'
And for Europa's lot or Io's prayed,
One the bull's rider, one the heifer-maid;
Till cozened by a wooden cow his seed
He gave her, and the child betrayed its breed.

Had but the Cretan spurned Thyestes' vows,
—How hard to keep one's favours for one's spouse—
The sun in midmost course had never veered,
Nor turned his steeds and back to Dawn careered.
The child who ravished Nisus' golden tress—
About her loins a pack of hell-hounds press.
Escaped from war and tempest Atreus' son
By his accursèd wife to death was done.
Creusa's love-tale who can read dry-eyed—
A mother's hands with children's blood bedyed?
With sightless orbs his fate did Phoenix mourn,
Hippolytus by his maddened steeds was torn.
Why, Phineus, your sons' guiltless eyes despoil?
On your own head that cruelty shall recoil.
By women's lusts were all these horrors wrought,
More fierce than ours and more with madness fraught.
Then doubt not every woman's at your call,
Scarce one will say you 'nay' among them all.
But 'yea' or 'nay', they're by your asking charmed,
And, though you're beaten, you'll retire unharmed.
But why be beaten? All adore new toys,
Despise their own and envy others' joys.
All crops are richer in your neighbour's field,
And next door's cattle give an ampler yield.

First scrape acquaintance with your charmer's maid:
Your path will be the smoother for her aid.
See that her mistress' confidence she shares
And holds the secret of her love affairs.
Her, her with prayers and promises secure;
With her good will your easy triumph's sure.
She'll tell the times with true physician's art
When soft and ripe for capture's madam's heart.
It's ripe for capture when well pleased with life
She's riotous as crops in cornlands rife.
When hearts are free and sorrows gall no more,
Love steals in softly through the open door.
Through years of grief her arms defended Troy;
The troop-filled horse she welcomed in her joy.

Then try her when a rival's roused her spite:
Make it your duty to avenge the slight.
Bid her maid while she plies the morning comb,
Add oar to sail and drive the insult home,
Sigh low and murmur 'neath her breath, 'I doubt
If by yourself you'll ever pay her out.'
Then she should speak of you and plead your case,
Swear frantic love is killing you apace.
But haste, lest sails collapse and breezes die;
Like brittle ice, rage melts as time goes by.
Should one, you ask, seduce the maid as well?
The gravest risks in such adventures dwell.
One's keen, one slacker having shared your sleep,
One takes you for your mistress, one to keep.
The issue's doubtful: even though chance befriend,
The plan's not one that I should recommend.
I lead you not o'er cliff or mountain tip,
Beneath my guidance youth will never trip.
If, while she plays the go-between, you feel
Her looks no less attractive than her zeal,
Secure the mistress first: postpone the maid,
Nor commence lover with a serving-jade.
Of this be warned, if skilled advice prevail
Nor be my words whirled seawards on the gale,
Ne'er make the attempt, or press it to the hilt;
She'll ne'er betray you once she's shared your guilt.
With feathers limed the bird escapes in vain,
Ill fares the boar that bursts the tangling seine.
The fish once hooked hold fast till he's fordone:
Press home the charge, nor leave the field unwon.
Ne'er on her fellow-criminal she'll turn,
And all her mistress says and does you'll learn.
But keep it dark; if dark you keep your spy,
On your beloved you'll always have your eye.

Think not that none need mark the date save he
Who tills the stubborn earth or sails the sea:
Not always should you sow the treacherous grain,
Or trust your frail barque to the azure main,

Nor always is it safe to hunt the fair:
He best succeeds who times his coup with care.
If close at hand's her birthday or the morn
When March is dead, and Venus' month is born,
Or when, the old-time trumpery despised,
The Circus flaunts the wealth that kings have prized
Forbear; it's then the Pleiads utter threats
Of tempest, then the Kid in Ocean sets.
It's best to pause: then whoso trusts the wave
The wreckage of his barque will scarcely save.
But start your venture on that day of woe
That red with Roman blood saw Allia flow,
Or when his seventh day the Syrian Jew
Keeps holy and all business is taboo.
My lady's birthday most of all beware,
Ban any day when giving's in the air.
Dodge as you will, she'll rob you: woman's brain
Discovers ways to fleece an ardent swain.
The jaunty salesman calls while there you sit,
And spreads his wares before the spendthrift chit,
On which she'll bid you cast your expert eye,
Then kiss you and then pester you to buy.
With this she swears for years content she'll stay,
To-day she needs it, it's so cheap to-day.
Allege you're short of funds, and she'll demand
(A pity you can write) your note of hand.
She begs a trifle for her birthday cake,
Gets herself born whene'er there's cash at stake,
Or shams a loss and weeps in blank despair
O'er a dropped earring that was never there.
They borrow oft, but ne'er repay the debt,
You lose your money and no thanks you get.
Ten mouths with tongues in each would ne'er avail
The hellish arts of strumpets to retail.

Let the waxed tablet be a-scouting sent,
Go on ahead and presage your intent,
Your love-like words and soft endearments bear,
And add, whoe'er you be, a humble prayer.

Prayer moved Achilles to restore his child
To Priam: prayer makes even God's anger mild.
Then promise hard: what harm in promising?
There's none too poor to promise anything.
Hope springs eternal in the human breast,
A useful goddess, though a cheat at best.
Give, and you risk dismissal for your pains;
Safe against loss she carries off her gains;
Give not, but e'er on point of giving seem,
Like barren fields that mock the farmer's dream,
Like dice, that eager gamesters still must toss
And go on losing to repair their loss.
This then's your task, your entry free to gain,
She'll ne'er stop giving, lest she's given in vain.
So pen your blarney and despatch your mail
To test her heart and pioneer the trail.
Cydippe, by the apple's message caught,
By her own words to blind consent was wrought.

Be warned, young Rome, to rhetoric pay heed,
Not only some poor prisoner's cause to plead:
Just as the courts, the senate and the crowd,
So woman's heart by eloquence is bowed.
But art must be disguised nor powers displayed,
Nor pages filled with tedious tirade.
Who but a dolt harangues his dainty friend?
A letter oft in bitter hate will end.
Use language plain and speech of common folk,
Yet coaxing, as though in the flesh you spoke.
If it's rejected and returned unread,
Expect she'll read it soon and go ahead.
In time fierce oxen to the yoke submit,
In time the charger learns to bear the bit,
Incessant use an iron ring will wear,
Incessant furrows blunt the curving share.
What's soft as water or than rock more stout?
Yet stoutest rock by water's hollowed out.
Persist and even Penelope you'll bend,
Though captured late, Troy's captured in the end.

Suppose she read, but answer not: don't press,
Just make her keep on reading your tendresse.
She'll want to answer what she's cared to read;
Such things by steps and stages due proceed.
At first perhaps she sends a cold request
That you'll be pleased no longer to molest,
Fears what she asks, and craves the vetoed suit;
Press on: in time you'll reap the sought-for fruit.

Meanwhile if in her litter she repair,
Steal unobserved on the recumbent fair,
And any tiresome eavesdropper to baulk,
With baffling gestures subtly mask your talk.
If idly in the long arcade she stroll,
There linger too and share the idler's role.
Now be at pains to follow, now to lead,
Now mend your pace and now to slacken speed.
Nor round the pillars be ashamed to glide
And cross her path, or saunter side by side.
Nor in the theatre let her waste her charms,
Sit there and see the drama of her arms.
To watch her, to admire her, there's your chance,
And discourse much with gesture and with glance.
Applaud the man who plays the soubrette's part,
And clap whoever shows a lover's heart.
Rise when she rises, while she's seated sit,
And waste your time my lady's whim to fit.

Nor let your hair with curling tongs be coiffed,
Nor make your limbs with caustic pumice soft.
Leave such to those whose frenzied Phrygian glee
Rings in the ears of Mother Cybele.
Man's beauty needs no varnish. Without aid
From hairpins Theseus won the Cretan maid.
On rude Hippolytus was Phaedra set,
Rustic Adonis was a goddess' pet.
Limbs clean and tanned by exercise delight,
And spotless clothes that match the figure right,

With latchets neat, nor tags by rust defaced,
Nor sprawling feet in floppy hides encased.
Nor wear an ill-kempt crop ineptly sheared,
Have expert hands to trim both hair and beard.
Well pared and clean the finger-nails should be,
The nostrils kept from lurking bristles free.
Nor by foul breath from unclean lips exhaled
Nor hircine humours be the nose assailed.
To women of the town leave all the rest,
Or those by lust of male for male possessed.

But Bacchus calls us; he's Love's ally too,
And feeds the flame that once himself he knew.
Wildly the Cretan roamed the unknown sand
Of tiny Dia's billow-beaten strand,
Just as she'd waked, in loose disorder gowned,
Her feet unshod, her saffron hair unbound.
To the deaf waves she cried cruel Theseus' name,
Her tender cheeks bedewed with tears of shame.
She cried and sobbed at once, but sobs and cries
Became her, nor did weeping mar her eyes.
Still with her hands her velvet breast she flailed,
'That traitor's fled, ah! what of me?' she wailed,
'Ah what . . . ?' she wailed, when o'er the sand there comes
The cymbals' clash, the frenzied beat of drums.
With one last scream of fright she swoons away,
No trace of blood her lifeless limbs betray.
Lo! Bacchanals with streaming hair adance,
Lo! Satyrs gay that lead the god's advance,
Lo! Old Silenus, clutching, lest he slip,
His bow-backed ass's mane with drunken grip.
The Nymphs pursued now face him, now recede,
While with a stick the duffer prods his steed.
Head-foremost from his long-eared mount he falls:
'Rise, father, rise', the crew of Satyrs bawls.
And now the god in vine-wreathed car behold,
Curbing his tiger-team with reins of gold.
Then hue and voice and thoughts of Theseus fled,
Thrice sought she flight and thrice held back in dread.

Like cornstalks in the wind she shook with fear,
Like reeds that quiver in the marshy mere.
To whom the god: 'Behold your true-love,' cried,
'Fear not, fair Cretan; you'll be Bacchus' bride.
The sky's your dowry: from the sky look down
And guide the steersman with your Cretan Crown.'
Then, lest his tigers fright her, forth he leapt,
(The sand retained his footprints as he stept).
He clasped her to his breast and off he rode
Resistless: all's so easy for a god.
Then 'Hymen hail!' and 'Bacchus ho!' compete.
Thus god and maid in hallowed union meet.

So if, with Bacchus' gifts before you poured,
You find a damsel next you at the board,
Pray to the Sire of Feasts and Powers of Night
That on your brain the bottle cast no blight.
There many a chance for whispers will occur,
And hints that she can guess are meant for her.
In winy outline on the table spell
Soft nothings telling her that she's your belle:
Or in her eyes with eyes of passion gaze:
Dumb looks can often talk in moving phrase.
The goblet that has touched her dainty lip
Be first to snatch, and where she's sipped it, sip.
Whatever dish she fingers haste to seize,
And, as you seize it, give her hand a squeeze.
To pleasing next her lover give your mind;
He'll be more useful as a friend you'll find.
Give him precedence when the cup goes round,
With your own garland bid his head be crowned.
Help him to each dish first, where'er he sit;
Whate'er he says, be prompt to echo it.
It's sure and proved to use a friend for lure;
Such means are wrong, however proved and sure.
The agent too his part may overact
And look to more than e'er was in his pact.

A canon safe to drink by I'll indite;
Let legs and headpiece function still aright.
Beware of wine-bred quarrels most of all,
Beware of hands too ready for a brawl.
So foolish tippling laid Eurytion low;
Gay frolics best with wine and feasting go.
Dance if you're supple, sing if you've a voice,
Whate'er your talent, use it to rejoice.
But feigning tipsy helps, as being hurts;
Constrain your tongue to artful slips and blurts,
That any naughty word or naughty deed
May seem from o'ermuch drinking to proceed.
'Here's to my love, here's to her bedmate!' cry,
But in your heart 'Deuce take the fellow!' sigh.
But when the party's o'er and guests go out,
Then seize your chance to join her 'mid the rout.
To where she lingers through the scrimmage slip,
Press foot to foot and thigh with fingers nip.
Now, now's the time to speak: begone, fool shame!
Both Love and Luck will help a daring game.
No rules of elocution need I teach:
Do but desire, and nature'll give you speech.
Enact the wooer, play the love-sick youth,
Use all your arts to prove you're speaking truth.
Nor's suasion hard: all think themselves desired;
Even the plainest by herself's admired.
Oft, too, the feigner comes to love in fact,
And lives the part that he'd begun to act.
So, wenches all, look kindly on pretence,
True'll grow the love that did in lies commence.
Now mine her heart with flattery's subtle charge,
As running currents sap the pendent marge.
Nor deem the praise of face and hair unmeet,
Of well-shaped fingers and of tiny feet.
Praise of her charms delights the chastest fair,
And virgins tend their looks with loving care.
Nay, do not Juno and Minerva still
Lament that lost award on Ida's hill?

The peacock spreads his plumes if one applauds,
Watch him in silence, and he'll hide his gauds;
And between races, horses take delight
When necks are patted, manes combed sleek and bright.

Then promise boldly: it's the sex's lure;
And all your gods as witnesses adjure.
High Jove at lovers' faithless oaths does scoff,
And bids the winds to limbo bear them off.
To Juno Jove would break his deadliest vow;
He likes his own example followed now.
Gods have their uses, let's believe they're there;
To the old altars wine and incense bear.
Nor think that in some slumbrous Lotus-land
They dwell apart: be good, for God's at hand.
Pay what you've borrowed, honour virtue's code,
Beware of fraud, nor stain your hands with blood.
Women alone the wise may safely cheat,
And truth's for once more shameful than deceit.
So trick the tricksters; sinners almost all,
Into the toils they've woven let them fall.
Once earth-refreshing rains in Egypt failed,
Nine years of drought, it's said, the land assailed.
Then Thrasius to Busiris came and said
Jove would relent if stranger blood were shed.
To whom the king: 'You be Jove's victim first,
The stranger you to save the land from thirst.'
So Phalaris the brute Perillus bade
Roast in the bull the wretch himself had made.
Each earned his fate; nought fairer than to trice
The death-deviser in his own device.
As liars then by lies are rightly tricked,
Let women feel the hurts that they inflict.

Tears too are helpful, tears will melt a stone;
Wet cheeks at all costs must the fair be shown.
If tears—they come not always at command—
Should fail you, touch your eyes with moistened hand.

With prayers you'll mingle kisses if you're wise;
Though she deny them, take what she denies.
Perhaps she'll first resist and call you rude,
Yet, while resisting, longs to be subdued.
But careful, lest her tender lips be scarred
By snatching, and she cry: 'You kiss too hard.'
Who takes a kiss, but takes not what remains,
Deserves indeed to forfeit all his gains.
How far mere kissing's short of perfect bliss!
Ah! not restraint, but lack of breeding's this.
'Brute force!' you'll say: it's force that women want,
They love refusing what they long to grant.
She who by love's swift onslaught is undone,
Rejoices in the infamy she's won:
Who might have yielded, but retreats intact,
Though feigning joy, is sorry for her act.
Outraged both Phoebe and her sister were,
Yet found their ravishers a charming pair.
Though known the tale, it's well to tell again
The Scyrian maid's amour with Haemon's thane.
It was when the goddess, judged in Ida's glade
First of the three, her fatal bribe had paid,
And Priam welcomed home to Ilion
A bride from distant Hellas for his son.
All swore to venge the injured husband's shame,
And one man's wrong a nation's cause became.
Basely, but yielding to a mother's prayer,
Achilles hid his sex in woman's wear.
What ails you, warrior? Spinning's not your part,
But seeking fame in Pallas' other art.
Why does the hand of Hector's slayer wield
A needle, with a work-box for a shield?
Away with toilsome thread and spindle's dance!
Yours is the hand to hurl the Pelian lance.
There shared the room a maid of royal clan,
Who, when he raped her, found he was a man.
They'd have us think the wench was made unchaste
By force, but force was wholly to her taste.

Oft, 'Stay,' she cried, when forth would fare her lord,
For now he'd changed the distaff for the sword.
Deidamia, who has forced you, say?
Why coax the author of your shame to stay?
While women blush the opening move to make,
What others offer first they gladly take.
The youth with o'ermuch vanity is cursed
Who waits until a woman asks him first.
It's his to open; his to beg for grace;
Hers to list kindly while he pleads his case.
To win her, ask her; asking's all she needs;
Tell why you want her, whence your love proceeds.
Jove humbly on the dames of old would wait,
No woman e'er corrupted Jove the Great.
But if you find Her Highness scorn your sighs,
Retrace your steps and stay your enterprise.
What's gone they covet, what's at hand reject;
Distaste will vanish if your suit be checked.
Nor always all a lover's hopes profess;
Let love be introduced in friendship's dress.
A prudish dame so cozened have I known,
And humble servant into lover grown.

A sickly hue would shame the mariner,
Who tanned by sea and sunshine should appear,
And shame the farmer who by outdoor toil
With plough and ponderous harrow turns the soil;
The athlete too who seeks the crown of bay
It would shame a white complexion to display.
But lovers must be pale: it's love's own hue;
Let others doubt it, it's the mode for you.
Orion pale for Side roamed the wold,
And pale was Daphnis for his Naiad cold.
The ache within let wasting cheeks declare,
Nor scorn a scarf to shroud your glistening hair.
By sleepless nights let youthful limbs be worn,
By cares and pangs of potent passion born.
To gain your hopes look miserable and prove
To all beholders that you are in love.

Shall I lament or warn that faith's a name,
Friendship a word, and right and wrong the same?
Ah! to a comrade never praise your fair:
He trusts your praise and ousts you unaware.
Patroclus never wronged Achilles—true,
Phaedra was chaste, Pirithous, with you.
Pylades' love for Hermione was no more
Than Phoebus or the Twins their sisters bore.
Who still expects such conduct, let him look
For fruits from thistles, honey from the brook.
All love what's base, their pleasures are their end,
All the more pleasing if they hurt a friend.
Ah! not from foes need lovers fear a thrust;
Oh shame! for safety flee from those you trust.
Beware of brothers, kin and comrades dear,
It's they that give the truest cause for fear.

I'd ended, but diverse are women's hearts,
A thousand minds demand a thousand arts.
Not every crop is grown on every soil:
This teems with corn, that favours wine or oil.
As many hearts as faces earth can show,
A myriad natures must the expert know,
And Proteus-like now melt into a stream,
Now tree, now bristly boar, now lion seem.
Some fish are speared, by hooks are others caught,
Some brought to land in trawls with cables taut.
Nor think one method for all ages fit:
Far off the veteran hind will spy the pit.
Who shocks a prude or lectures to a dunce,
Makes the poor wretch distrust herself at once;
And thus, while from a gentleman she shrinks,
Into some low embrace she vilely sinks.

Part of my task is finished, part remains;
Here stay the barque and drop the anchor-chains.

BOOK TWO

A song of triumph sing, and sing again:
The long-sought quarry in the toils is ta'en.
Glad lovers, crown with bay the poet's brow,
To me let Hesiod and Homer bow.
Even so 'neath snowy sails the Trojan bore
His ravished bride from fierce Amyclae's shore,
And such was he who in his conquering car
Brought home Hippodamia from afar.
But patience, youth: our barque mid-ocean ploughs
And distant yet's the haven of our vows.
The damsel to your door I've barely brought,
My art must safeguard what my art has caught.
To keep's no less a virtue than to find;
This comes by luck, but that's the work of mind.
Oh Venus, Love, and Erato, who art
Love's namesake, now, if ever, take my part;
Great is my task, to tell what arts can stay
The flight of Love, that world-wide runaway,
An airy creature with a pair of wings;
It's hard to put restraint upon such things.

With every exit barred by Minos' hand,
A bold escape on wings his prisoner planned.
When Daedalus had pent the monster in,
Half bull, half man, fruit of a mother's sin,
'Just monarch, let my exile end', he prayed,
'In my own country let my bones be laid.
Since in my home a cruel destiny
Forbade me live, there grant me leave to die.
Release my child, if age can earn no ruth,
Or pity age, if you'll not pity youth'.
These words he spoke, but all, and more beside,
Were said in vain: release was still denied.
Whereat quoth he: 'Now, Daedalus, ah now
Your cleverness you have a chance to show!

O'er earth and ocean Minos wields his might,
Nor land nor sea is open to my flight.
The skyey path remains, we'll tempt the skies:
Great Jove, look kindly on my enterprise.
I'll not aspire to reach your starred abode,
To flee a tyrant I've no other road.
I'd swim the Styx, if that way lay escape;
In me shall nature all her laws reshape.'
Woes sharpen wits; whoe'er would think it true
That man could cleave a pathway through the blue?
The oary plumes of birds he sets in line
And binds the fragile texture fast with twine,
Makes firm the ends with wax dissolved in heat,
And now the craftsman's novel work's complete.
With wax and plumes his laughing youngster played
Nor guessed such engines for himself were made.
'These craft shall bear us home,' his father said,
'By aid of these from Minos we'll be sped.
All else he bars, to bar the skies he fails,
The skies are free, the skies my genius scales.
But not by armed Orion steer your way,
Bootes' comrade, nor Callisto's ray.
I'll pilot you; behind me wing your flight;
Thy task's to follow; I shall guide you right.
For if through heaven's ether towards the sun
We mount, beneath his rays the wax will run,
And if too near the sea our pinions scud,
The airy plumes will sodden in the flood.
Fly midway, child; of breezes too beware,
And trim your sails to catch the favouring air.'
He fits the gear thus warning, and explains
Its working, as a bird her fledglings trains.
Then his own pinions binding on his back
With trembling limbs he tests the novel track.
A parting kiss he gives his son so dear,
Nor could a father's cheeks resist a tear.
A low-browed hill that rose above the plain
Upon their venture launched the luckless twain.

Still Daedalus maintains his steadfast poise,
Sways his own wings and turns to watch the boy's.
Now feels the lad his novel journey's thrill,
He casts off fear and flies with daring skill.
These one who fished with quivering rod espied;
Straight from his fingers dropped the task he plied.
Left Samos lay, with Naxos in the rear,
And Paros and the isle to Phoebus dear;
To right Astypalaea's fishy deeps,
Lebynthos and Calymne's wooded steeps,
When all with boyhood's recklessness afire
The youngster soars aloft and leaves his sire.
He nears the sun, the waxen bonds dissolve,
Nor buoyant on the breeze his arms revolve.
Aghast he scans the deep from heaven's height,
And darkness surges o'er his stricken sight.
The wax gives out, the naked limbs contort,
He flutters, clutching vainly for support,
He drops, and dropping, 'Father, Father,' shrieks,
'I'm lost'; the green flood chokes him as he speaks.
'Icarus,' wails his sire, a sire no more,
'Where's Icarus? Oh whither do you soar?
Ah Icarus!' He sees the wave-tossed plumes.
Earth has his bones: the sea his name assumes.

A mortal's wings not Minos could restrain,
A wingèd god I purpose to enchain.
Deluded he who tries the wizard's craft
And wrests from brow of foal the magic draught.
No sorcerous herbs can conjure love to stay,
No Marsian enchanter's witching lay.
Could spells bind love, Ulysses had been tied
To Circe, Jason to his Colchian bride.
With philtres pale the fair are dosed in vain;
The philtre works fell madness in the brain.
Avaunt black arts! For love it's charm you need,
Charm that nor face nor form alone can breed.
Though fair as Nireus, old-time Homer's flame,
Or Hylas, ravished to the Naiads' shame,

To keep your love nor gasp to find her fled,
With grace of body join a mind well-bred.
Beauty's a frail possession; with the years
It fades, and as it grows it disappears.
Nor violet nor cupped lily always blows,
The shiny thorn survives its vanished rose.
You too, fair boy, your locks will soon be grey,
Soon o'er your flesh will wrinkles plough their way.
Let Beauty rest on Mind's foundation sure,
Unto the grave will Mind alone endure.
With liberal studies to enrich your soul
And master both the tongues must be your goal.
Ulysses shone in speech but looks he lacked,
Yet Ocean's nymphs by love of him were racked.
How oft Calypso mourned his haste to quit,
And vowed the sea for rowing was unfit;
And o'er and o'er she'd ask of Troy's travail:
In different words, he'd tell the same old tale.
They paced the beach; there too the lovely sprite
Begged for the tale of Rhesus' gory plight.
With slender cane (a cane perchance he bore)
He traced the story on the crumbling shore.
'Here's Troy', he said, and built a wall of sand,
'This can be Simois, here my camp shall stand;
This field' (he drew one) 'Dolon's life-blood dyed,
While on Achilles' steeds intent he spied.
Here camped the Thracian leader, by this track
That night I brought the captured chargers back.'
There came a sudden wave while yet he drew,
Swamped Troy and Rhesus' camp and Rhesus too.
Then said the goddess, 'See what mighty names
Your trusted ocean for its victims claims.'
Ware then, whoe'er you be, the treacherous grace
Of flesh, or boast of something more than face.

A wise forbearance specially captivates:
Ill tempers lead to bitter feuds and hates.
We hate the hawk that wars through all its days,
We hate the wolf on timid flocks that preys.

But none against the gentle swallow plots,
And turtle-doves live safely in their cotes.
Away with strife and war of tongues accurst,
On gentle words must tender love be nursed.
Let spouse from spouse be sundered by disputes,
Think life a series of contested suits:
Leave wives to quarrel; strife's the marriage dower,
A mistress must be cooed to by the hour.
No law prescribes one bed for you to share,
Love plays the part of law in your affair.
With flatteries soft and words that charm the ear
Approach, and make her glad when you appear.
Not to the rich these rules of love I preach:
He who can give needs nothing I can teach.
'Here's something for you' is the soul of wit,
And all my arts of pleasing yield to it.
The poor man's bard am I, who loved as such,
Fine words I gave, for presents cost too much.
The poor must love discreetly, fear to chide,
Put up with much the rich would ne'er abide.
Once in a pet I pulled my charmer's hair,
A pet that cost me several days, I swear.
She vowed I'd torn her frock—it wasn't the case—
And made me buy another in its place.
But shun your master's faults, you men of sense,
And ware the dire results of my offence.
War with the Parthian, with the dainty fair
Peace, smiles and all that makes for love declare.

But if your suit nor grace nor favour find
Submit and suffer: soon she'll grow more kind.
By patience you'll induce the bough to curve,
You will but break it if you strain your nerve.
By patience over rivers you can swim;
Who fights the current ne'er will gain the brim.
To patience pards and Libyan lions bow;
Slowly the rustic trains his ox to plough.
Arcadian Atalanta's cruel mood
—None harder known—a lover's faith subdued.

His plight and her ill treatment, runs the tale,
Oft did Milanion in the woods bewail,
Oft at her bidding bore the huntsman's gear,
Oft stabbed the savage boar with deadly spear,
Felt too Hylaeus' arrows to his rue—
Another's arrows better still he knew.
I bid you hoist no gear upon your back,
Or fully armed to mount the woodland track,
Or bare your breast before the levelled dart;
Mild are my precepts and discreet my art.
Yield to resistance, yielding wins the day,
Just play whatever part she bids you play.
Damn what she damns, whate'er she praises, praise,
Echo alike her 'yeses' and her 'nays'.
Laugh when she laughs, cry promptly when she cries,
Let her give orders to your lips and eyes.
If with the numbered ivories she play,
Take the first throw, and throw the game away.
At knucklebones ne'er make her pay her loss,
The luckless deuce yourself contrive to toss;
And when the raiding chessmen take the field,
Your champion to his crystal foe must yield.
Yourself must rear her sunshade's outspread shroud,
Yourself must clear her passage through the crowd.
Quick, set a stool beneath her couch and put
The slipper on or off her slender foot.
Oft, though yourself be shivering, she'll demand
That at your breast you warm her chilly hand;
Nor deem it base (you'll like it, though it were)
In freeborn hands her looking-glass to bear.
Who, when his step-dame tired of plaguing, gained
The heavens that he'd erst himself sustained,
Even he once held a workbox, so it's said,
'Mid Lydian maids, and wrought the wool to thread.
A woman's rule the great Tirynthian bore;
And who are you to shirk the bonds he wore?
For meeting you in Town she names a date,
Then be there early and remain there late.

She wants you elsewhere; putting all aside,
Run, let no traffic stay you in your stride.
When from the rout returning home to bed
She calls her lackey, you appear instead.
Or to her country cot she bids you hail—
Love hates a laggard—walk if transport fail,
And let not storms nor Dog-star's parching heat,
Nor highways white with snowdrifts check your feet.

Love is a warfare: sluggards be dismissed,
No faint-heart 'neath this banner may enlist.
Storms, darkness, anguish, weary trails you'll find
On love's campaign, and toil of every kind.
Oft will the rainclouds empty on your head,
Oft on bare earth you'll make your chilly bed.
Apollo in a humble cabin lay,
And grazed the lord of Pherae's flocks, they say.
Who dares disdain what Phoebus deigned to do?
Put off your pride, who'd have your love stay true.
If safe and level access be denied
And gates are barred and bolted fast inside,
Into the courtyard take a dizzy leap,
Or softly through an upper casement creep.
To know you've run such risks on her behoof
Will glad your mistress: it's love's surest proof.
For Hero oft Leander felt no whim,
To show his love he took his nightly swim.

Nor think it shameful in their several grades
To court the lackeys and the chambermaids.
Greet each—it costs you nothing—by their names,
Grasp humblest hands to further highest aims.
Grudge not the lackey—it won't be much to pay—
Who begs a trifle on St Fortune's day,
Nor grudge the housemaid on the day the Gaul
By matrons' robes was cozened to his fall.
Gain all the staff, but make especially yours
The keepers of the house- and bedroom-doors.

No need your substance on the fair to waste:
Give little, but that little in good taste.
When fields are ripe and laden branches bend,
A basketful of rustic dainties send.
Say they're a present from your country seat,
Although you bought them in a West-End street.
Send grapes and chestnuts, loved long since, I trow,
By Amaryllis, for she'd scorn them now.
Likewise a pigeon and a quail or so
Will serve to prove you still the faithful beau.
Thus would-be heirs on childless dotards trade:
Curse those who thus the giver's name degrade!
No use to bid you send a lover's ode;
Scant honour ah! on poetry's bestowed.
Poems are praised, but it's for cash they itch;
A savage even is welcomed if he's rich.
This truly is the Golden Age; for gold
High place is purchased, love is bought and sold.
Came Homer's self with all the Nine in tow,
If empty-handed, out would Homer go.
Still, there are cultured women here and there,
And some not cultured, but who wish they were.
Write verse to either; read with melting voice
The poorest verse its hearer will rejoice.
So burn the midnight oil; whiche'er she be,
Your ode may reckon as a trifling fee.

Then, what yourself you deem it wise to do,
Contrive to make your charmer beg of you.
You've promised (say) his freedom to a slave:
That favour from your mistress make him crave.
Some prisoned drudge you pardon of your grace:
Grant her the boon you'd give in any case.
The gain is yours, the credit she can keep;
Let her play Lady Bountiful: it's cheap.

Who hopes to keep his loved one on the hooks
Must make her think he's ravished by her looks.
If she's in silk, her taste in silks admire,
In Tyrian colours, praise the gowns of Tyre,

In gold, herself's more precious far than gold,
If tweed's her choice, her choice of tweed uphold.
In négligé, exclaim she burns and thrills,
But add in anxious tones, 'Beware of chills.'
If hair be parted, praise the parting neat,
If curled with tongs, a curly head looks sweet.
Her dancing limbs, her singing voice adore,
And say you're sorry when the piece is o'er.
Even her embraces, her voluptuous ways,
Her nightly joys must have their meed of praise.
Though hard as grim Medusa's be her mood,
She'll melt and soften when she's wisely wooed.
Ware only lest the trickster she descry,
Nor let your features give your words the lie.
Guile helps when hidden, brings disgrace when caught,
And ruins faith for ever, as it ought.

Oft in the lovely days of Autumntide
When full of wine the grape to purple's dyed,
When languid heat takes turn with chilly rime,
The body droops beneath the changeful clime.
Please God she's scatheless, but if sick she lies
And feels the bale of insalubrious skies,
Then prove your love's devotion, then plant deep
The seed that soon in sicklefuls you'll reap.
Repelled not by the humours of the ill,
Be yours the hand to tend her all she will.
Show her you're weeping, nor from kisses shrink,
Nay, give her parching lips your tears to drink.
Pray much, but all out loud, and when she seems
Disposed to listen, tell of lucky dreams.
Call in the crone with trembling hand to spread
Sulphur and egg for cleansing room and bed.
All this a sweet devotion will display;
Thus many into wills have found their way.
But curb your kindly fussing and forbear
To plague your patient with excessive care;
Nor bid her starve, nor give her bitter juice
To swallow; that your rival can produce.

The breeze, howe'er, that sped you from the shore,
The open seas once gained, will serve no more.
Young wayward love must thrive by exercise,
He'll soon grow stronger, if your nurture's wise.
Yon fearsome bull's the calf you used to stroke,
A sapling once this canopy of oak.
The baby stream by flowing gathers force,
And garners many waters in its course.
There's nought like usage; get her used to you;
Shrink from no boredom with this end in view.
Ne'er out of hearing, ne'er be out of sight,
Show her your features both by day and night.
But when you feel more certain you'll be missed
And, though you're gone, her care for you'll persist,
Give her a rest: the earth when rested yields
Her best, and rains are drunk by arid fields.
The love of Phyllis for Demophoon,
Cool in his presence, blazed up when he'd gone.
Ulysses' absence moved his lady's grief,
Laodamia loved her absent chief.
But stay not long, for passions cool apace,
Loves fade with absence, new ones take their place.
Afraid of lonely nights, her spouse away,
Safe in her guest's warm bosom, Helen lay.
What folly, Menelaus, forth to wend,
Beneath one rooftree leaving wife and friend!
Mad! Trust the hawk your timid doves to guard!
Trust to the mountain wolf the well-stocked yard!
Blameless is Helen, and her lover too:
He did what you or anyone would do.
The means you offered made them misbehave;
What did the wench but take the hint you gave?
What should she do? No spouse, a guest well-bred,
The awful loneness of an empty bed—
Helen's acquitted; bring her spouse to book:
What his complaisance offered her, she took.

But not so fierce the tawny boar's attack
With flashing tusk dispels the rabid pack,
Not lioness to her young ones giving suck
Or tiny asp a careless foot hath struck,
As raves the wench, her cheeks with passion red,
Who finds a rival in her lover's bed.
With fire and sword, all dignity forgot,
She storms like one to Bacchic frenzy wrought.
By Jason wronged, his savage Colchian spouse
On her own babes avenged the outraged vows.
That swallow too, a guilty mother see,
Behold her breast not yet from blood-marks free.
Thus firm and lasting loves have been undone;
Such fearful risks no prudent man will run.
Not that I'd doom you to a single flame:
Preserve us! this a wife could hardly claim.
Indulge, but o'er your lapses draw a veil,
Nor of your peccadilloes boast the tale.
Give nought another wench may recognize,
Have no time-table for your gallantries.
Lest in her own haunts she should come on you,
Appoint for each a different rendezvous.
Before you write inspect your tablets well;
Oft more is read than e'er you meant to tell.
Love outraged flies to arms and shoots his dart,
And smarting makes you feel the self-same smart.
While with one love was Atreus' son content,
She too was chaste. He sinned and virtue went.
She'd heard how with his bands and bays arrayed
In vain had Chryses for his daughter prayed;
She'd heard what grief the stol'n Briseis racked
And what base quarrels did the war protract.
All this she'd heard; she *saw* Cassandra's face—
Captor by captive conquered—such disgrace!
Then took Aegisthus to her heart and bed,
And on her false lord wreaked a vengeance dread.

But if your secret's known despite your care,
Known though it be, deny the whole affair.
Nor be subdued, nor more than usual fond;
These with a guilty conscience correspond.
But—peace depends on't—give your loins free play,
And let your passion chase her doubts away.
Some recommend a dose of savory,
That herb of evil—poison rank, say I—
Mix pepper with sharp nettle-seed or brew
In mellow wine the saffron fever-few.
Not thus she'd have you spurred to her delights,
That Goddess throned on Eryx' wooded heights.
White onions from Alcathous' Grecian town,
The plant of love that's in your garden grown,
Eggs, honey of Hymettus—these will suit,
Or kernels of the pointed pine-tree's fruit.

Why to black arts, wise Erato, descend?
On the inside my wheels must round the bend.
Whom late I bade to keep your lapses hid,
Turn and confess your secrets now I bid.
Nor dub me fickle. Never sailor finds
His galleon wafted by unchanging winds;
Now West, now South she speeds before the gale,
Now South, now West the breeze that fills her sail.
Behold the charioteer with reins astream!
Anon with skill he checks his eager team.
A tame devotion oft is ill repaid;
No rival in the offing, love will fade.
Oft hearts, when all goes well, are puffed with pride,
Nor their good fortune tranquilly abide.
As when a fire that gradually dies
Deep hidden 'neath the whitening ashes lies,
But at a pinch of sulphur wakes once more
Its vanished flames and blazes as before,
So hearts that lulled in careless torpor drowse
Need a sharp spur their passions to arouse.
Make her uneasy, stir the tepid fires,
Let her grow livid when your guilt transpires.

Oh thrice, oh times unnumbered, is he blessed,
By whose deceits a woman is distressed:
Whose sins, when her unwilling ears they reach,
Bereave the stricken wretch of hue and speech.
Be mine the hair a termagant may rend,
Mine the soft cheeks on which her nails descend,
I, at whose sight she weeps and glares askant,
I, whom she longs to live without, but can't.
'How long?' you ask. Check soon the wild discourse,
Nor give her anger time to gather force.
Round her white neck your arms proceed to fling,
Into your bosom take the weeping thing;
Kiss her, caress her, though she weep and weep:
This way comes peace, and anger's put to sleep.
When in full cry, on war she's plainly bent,
Propose adjourning bedward; she'll relent.
There Concord dwells and weapons are forsworn,
There too, believe me, is forgiveness born.
Doves that have quarrelled join their bills anew,
And soft endearments to each other coo.

At first the world in shapeless chaos surged;
Earth, sky, and ocean into one were merged.
Into its parts the welter then was riven,
Sea circled land and earth was topped by heaven.
Beasts colonized the forest, fowls the air,
In running streams the fishes found a lair.
Mankind began to range the wilds at length,
A thing of untaught mind and brutish strength.
Wood-folk, on plants they lived, on foliage slept,
And long unknown to one another kept.
Soft joys, it's said, the savage mood allayed,
When once a man had chanced upon a maid.
No teacher there to show them what to do:
His joyous function love untutored knew.
Birds have their sweethearts, 'neath the water's spate
To share her joys the fish will find a mate,
Hind follows hart, and snake with snake's enwound,
While dog and bitch are in love's union bound.

Ewes love the ram's and cows the bull's amours,
Her odorous buck the snub-nosed goat endures,
Mad with desire the mare pursues her lord
To distant pastures far beyond the ford.
Then treat your Fury with this potent balm:
This way alone her raging spite will calm.
To this will all Machaon's drugs give place:
Thus will the sinner be restored to grace.

While thus I sang, I looked and there behold!
Was Phoebus fingering his harp of gold.
Bays in his hand, his sacred locks with bays
Encrowned, the Prophet stood before my gaze.
'Professor of love's wanton art,' he spake,
'Come, your disciples to my temple take;
Whereon the words renowned throughout our sphere
That counsel you to know yourself appear.
Who knows himself, alone will wisely love,
And best to suit his talents plan each move.
Whom nature's dowered with looks his looks must air,
Whose skin is white recline with shoulders bare.
From silence mute must witty talkers shrink,
Skilled singers sing, and expert drinkers drink.
But wits must ne'er with lectures intersperse
Their talk, nor poets read their crazy verse.'
Thus counselled Phoebus: hark to Phoebus' rede,
For on those lips divine is truth indeed.
To come to earth, who loves in prudent wise,
Will with my teaching win the sought-for prize.

Not every furrow yields a rich largesse,
Nor breezes always help the barque's distress.
More pains than pleasures will the lover find,
To suffer much his heart must be resigned.
Thick as the fruit on grey-green olive-trees,
As hares on Athos or on Hybla bees,
Or shells on shores, so love with pains is heaped:
The shafts that strike us are in poison steeped.

They'll say she's out, whom you may see inside;
Believe she's out, and that your eyes have lied.
The promised night you'll find the bolts are shot:
Just meekly in the dusty roadway squat;
To hear perhaps her false maid's scornful tone,
'Why won't that fellow leave our gate alone?'
Fondle the doorposts of the cruel fair
And suppliant hang there roses from your hair.
Enter if bidden, but if banned submit;
To be a nuisance shames a man of wit.
'There's no escaping from him', she'll exclaim,
Why let her? Feelings don't remain the same.
Nor be ashamed to pocket from your sweet
A curse or blow, or kiss her tender feet.

But higher themes inspire me; why waste time
On trifles? Heed you well my lofty rhyme.
Hard is our task, but virtue's always hard,
And still our path with obstacles is barred.
Bear with your rival; that way victory lies,
Thus even on Jove's own hill you'll win the prize.
Not man indeed, but Sacred Oaks impart
This, the profoundest precept of my art.
She ogles, let her; writes, ne'er ask to whom;
Where, whence she pleases, let her go and come.
This husbands to their lawful wives concede,
When kindly slumber plays his part at need.
Such heights of art I own I cannot reach,
Nor (how to help it?) practise what I preach.
What? see my mistress winked at to my face,
And bear it, nor go raving o'er the place?
Her husband kissed her once, I call to mind:
I damned that kiss; my love's the savage kind.
Oft has this weakness harmed me. Wiser then
Oneself to introduce the other men.
But nescience is best: ignore her slips,
Nor force the base confession from her lips.
So, youth, ne'er catch your loved one at her sin:
Let her play false and think you're taken in.

Love grows unmasked. Who share a sorry case,
Persist in what has brought them to disgrace.
Throughout the skies a far-famed tale has fared,
How Mars and Venus were by Vulcan snared.
Our Sire with raging love for Venus burned,
And Lord of War was into wooer turned.
Nor Venus, kindliest sprite, to his appeal
Proved for an instant coy or difficile.
Oft at her husband's legs the wanton jeered,
Oft at the hands his fiery trade had seared.
To Mars in graceful mimicry she'd ape
Her spouse, and charm enhanced her lovely shape.
To keep their commerce secret first they used,
A blush of shame their guilty hearts suffused.
The Sun (for who can e'er escape the Sun?)
Revealed to Vulcan what his spouse had done.
Ill precedent, oh Sun! demand a fee
For silence rather; she'll give readily.
Around the bed and o'er it Vulcan weaves
A magic net-work that no eye perceives;
Then feigns a trip to Lemnos. Come the pair
To bed, and trapped lie naked in the snare.
He calls the Gods; the captives are on view,
Venus, it's thought, her tears can scarce subdue.
Nor can they hide their faces, no, nor e'en
Employ their hands their privy parts to screen.
Then one who laughed, 'Most valiant Mars,' quoth he,
'If your chains irk you, hand them o'er to me.'
The prisoners scarce are freed by Neptune's grace:
Venus retires to Paphos, Mars to Thrace;
All to this purpose, that of shame well rid
They now do frankly what before they hid.
Ah, Vulcan, oft in rage you now admit
Your act was foolish and regret your wit.
This I forbid you; Venus too, once tricked,
Forbids you what she suffered, to inflict
Set you no traps for rivals: not for you
To intercept the secret billet-doux.

Leave those such methods, if they think them right,
Whom holy matrimony's bonds unite.
No lawless sport is this, once more I claim;
No matron's skirt shall figure in my game.

Who'd dare to blab abroad of Ceres' rites
Or the great truths that Samothrace indites?
Though keeping silence no great credit wins,
Yet babbling secrets is the worst of sins.
It's well that tell-tale Tantalus should clutch,
Parched in his pool, at fruits that flee his touch.
Venus especially bids you ne'er to broach
Her secrets: ware, you chatterers, nor approach.
For though no coffered sacraments are hers,
Nor clashing cymbals craze her worshippers,
But in her ritual freely all indulge,
Yet none would care that ritual to divulge.
Nay, when she doffs her garments, Venus too
Half stoops, her left hand curtaining the view.
Beasts everywhere and openly unite:
Maids oft avert their faces at the sight.
Locked bedrooms suit the joys we humans steal
And coverlets the parts of shame conceal,
And if not darkness, still a twilight blurred
And something less than open day's preferred.
Even when no rooftree countered rain and sun,
Even when the oak still housed and fed in one,
In woods and caves, not daylight, lovers met;
Such store by shame those simple tribesmen set.
But now we advertise the nights we make,
And pay good money just for boasting's sake.
Yes, you must sample every wench you see,
To tell the quidnuncs, 'She too favoured me,'
Nor e'er lack girls at whom to point for such,
Smirching with scandal every name you touch.
Worse still, concocting stories, as some do,
Of wholesale rape, which they'd deny if true.
Failing the body they assault the name,
And though the body's pure, defile the fame.

Then go, loathed watchman, shut your lady's door,
Bar the stout posts with locks and bolts galore!
What's safe when name-debauchers are at large
To make the world believe a baseless charge?
I even of true intrigues but rarely tell;
The seal of silence guards those secrets well.

Ne'er cast a woman's defects in her face:
Dissembling oft were wise in such a case.
He who on swift-winged feet was borne aloft
Ne'er at Andromeda's complexion scoffed.
Andromache, too tall to common eyes,
Hector alone pronounced of moderate size.
Use cures distaste, much comfort time will bring,
But new-born love will notice everything.
New grafted in the green the tender spray
Shook by the slightest breeze will break away,
Inured by time will face the storm, and grown
Enrich the tree with treasures not its own.
Mere time will banish all the body's flaws,
And what was blemish cease to give you pause.
From ox-hide unaccustomed nostrils blench;
Tamed by long usage they ignore the stench.
Names too can gloze o'er defects: call her dark
Whose skin Illyrian pitch would scarcely mark,
Be Tow-heads, Cross-eyes, Bags-o'-Bones half-dead
Minervas, Venuses and Sylphs instead;
Let fat be buxom, undersized petite,
And ill behind the nearest good retreat.

Nor ask her age, nor probe her year of birth,
—This it's the censor's duty to unearth—
More so if her bloom's gone and, past her day,
Already from her hair she plucks the grey.
Much profit this or later ages yield:
Sow it, you lovers, it's a fruitful field.
Work hard while years and strength permit: anon
With stealthy tread will bent old age creep on.

Cleave furrows with the plough or seas with oars,
Gird on your armour for the cruel wars;
Or spend on woman loins and strength and zest:
This too is warfare, this is manhood's test.
The older too are adepts in affaires;
That practice which alone perfects is theirs.
With taste they mend the ravages of time,
Contriving still to look not past their prime.
They'll pay a thousand love-games at your whim,
So many postures ne'er did artist limn.
They need no spur to passion: in love's rite
Should man and woman equally delight.
I hate a union that exhausts not both:
To fondle boys it's this that makes me loth.
I hate a wench who gives because she's bound,
While coldly thinking of the wool she's wound;
I like not joy bestowed in duty's fee,
I'll have no woman dutiful to me.
I like to hear a voice of rapture shrill,
That bids me linger and prolong the thrill,
To see the wild-eyed creature, as she cowers
And droops and bids me touch her not for hours.
Such joys to youthful natures ne'er arrive
That come so readily at thirty-five.
Raw liquor let impatient youngsters swill,
My glass the old ancestral brand shall fill.
Not till it's grown the plane withstands the sun,
By new-sprung lawns are naked feet fordone.
Hermione to Helen, my good sir,
Or Gorge to her mother d'you prefer?
Whoe'er aspires to charms of riper date
Earns a rich guerdon if he will but wait.

Two lovers to their privy couch repair:
To pass the bolted door, my Muse, forbear.
Without your aid will gushing words be shed,
Nor the left hand lie idle on the bed,
While fingers find their function in those parts
Wherein in secret Cupid plies his darts.

Thus with his spouse bold Hector played of yore
And proved his worth for something else than war;
Thus great Achilles with his captive maid,
When on the couch his war-worn limbs he laid,
And you, Briseis, let yourself be stroked
By hands that still in Trojan blood were soaked.
You jade, did you this very thing enjoy,
That conquering fingers with your limbs should toy?
Love's climax never should be rushed, I say,
But worked up softly, lingering all the way.
The parts a woman loves to have caressed
Once found, caress, though modesty protest.
You'll see her eyes lit up with trembling gleams,
As sunlight glitters in pellucid streams;
Then plaintive tones and loving murmurs rise
And playful words and softly sounding sighs.
But ne'er must you with fuller sail outpace
Your consort, nor she beat you in the race:
Together reach the goal: it's rapture's height
When man and woman in collapse unite.
This course observe when ample time avails,
Nor fear the furtive episode curtails.
When danger threatens, best with all your force
To ply the oar, to spur the willing horse.

My task is done. Ye grateful lovers shed
The meed of myrtle on my scented head.
As 'mid the Greeks leech Podalirius shone,
Nestor the sage, the whip Automedon,
Ajax in arms, Calchas in prophecy,
In might Achilles, such in love am I.
Honour the bard, you men: my praise proclaim,
Let all the earth re-echo with my name.
As Vulcan armed Achilles, you by me
Are armed: thus armed shall triumph even as he.
Who with my sword an Amazon shall smite
'*Pupil of Ovid*' on your trophies write.

Lo! Now the fair ones for a textbook ask:
Your case shall be my pen's ensuing task.

BOOK THREE

Greeks have I armed 'gainst Amazons to stand,
Remains to arm Penthesilea's band.
Fair be the field, and to the cause success
That Venus and her world-wide flyer bless.
For men-at-arms are unarmed maids no match,
A sorry triumph that for men to snatch.
Some voice will ask 'Why give the serpent gall,
Why the fierce she-wolf in the fold install?'
Lay not a handful's crimes on all the race,
But on its merits judge each woman's case.
Though Helen outraged Atreus' second son,
While by her sister was the first undone,
Though Oecles' son by Eriphyl's misdeeds
Was whirled to hell alive by living steeds,
Yet to her lord Penelope was true
Through ten years' war, and ten years' wandering too.
Think of Phylacides and her they say
Followed her spouse and died before her day.
For Pheres' son Alcestis gave her life
And in the husband's hearse was borne the wife.
'Oh take me, Capaneus, to share your pyre',
Evadne cried and leapt upon the fire.
Nay, Virtue's self takes woman's name and guise;
Of course she's pleasing in her sex's eyes.
Not for such minds, howe'er, my art is meant;
With smaller sails my barque will be content.
Light loves shall be my teaching's sole concern,
How to be loved from me shall woman learn.
It's not with fire and sword that women arm;
Through these I rarely see men come to harm.
Men oft deceive, less often womankind,
They're seldom charged with perfidy, you'll find.
False Jason took to bed another bride,
And cast the mother of his babes aside.

For aught that Theseus cared, his spouse left lone
Had fed the sea-birds on a shore unknown.
Who asks why one way's known as 'Nineways' hears
How woods o'er Phyllis shed their leaves for tears.
Though famed as pious, Dido's guest supplied
Both sword and motive for her suicide.
This damned you all: in love you had no tact;
Art keeps love constant; it was art you lacked:
And still you'd lack it, but before my sight
Stood Venus' self and bade me teach you right.
'Poor sex,' she said, 'why treat them in such sort?
An unarmed mob to be an army's sport!
Two books to make men expert have been writ,
It's our turn now to profit by your wit.
Who first reviled the bride from Therapnae
Soon sang her praises in a happier key.
You'll ne'er (I know you) hurt the dainty fair,
Throughout your life you'll look for favour there.'
A myrtle leaf and berries as she spake
—For myrtle wreathed her hair—she bade me take;
I took and felt her power; serener glowed
The heavens and my spirit shed its load.
While she inspires me, learn the code, you dames,
That law, propriety and right proclaims.
Remember first that age must come some day,
And let no moment idly slip away.
While yet you can, while life is at its spring
—Years fleet like running water—have your fling.
The wave that's past its course can ne'er retrace,
The hour that's gone you never can replace.
Use well your time; time slides along so fast,
The next state's ne'er the equal of the last.
I've seen those shrivelled weeds a violet bed,
From yonder thorn a wreath has graced my head.
The time will come when you, who now deny
Your swain, a cold lone hag at night will lie,
Nor have your gate in midnight riot torn,
Nor find your steps with roses strewn at morn.

How soon, alas, in wrinkles sags the flesh,
Flees from the cheek its old complexion fresh,
And hairs you swear have been from girlhood white
O'er all your head will spring up overnight.
Snakes shed their dotage with their filmy sloughs,
The roebuck's youth survives the horns he doffs:
Man's glories fade and help avails him not:
Pluck then the flower, which left will merely rot.
Youth, lastly, is curtailed by childbirth's toil:
Perpetual harvesting exhausts the soil.
Nor Moon for him of Latmos blushes red,
Nor Dawn for ravished Cephalus hangs her head:
Though Venus mourns Adonis to this day,
Aeneas and Harmonia, whence come they?
Copy the goddesses, you earthly fry,
Nor your delights to hungry men deny.
If you're deceived, what's lost? Your all's intact;
Your stock, though thousands share it, can't contract.
With use will iron wear and stone decay:
Your store is safe; it will not waste away.
Who can object to lighting flare from flare?
Who the vast Ocean's water wants to spare?
When man by cautious woman is refused,
She just wastes water which she might have used.
No, don't be whores; just banish from your thought
Vain fears of cost: your giving costs you nought.

Now, though with stronger winds I'll speed anon,
While yet in port light airs shall waft me on.
I start with care of body: glebe and vine
Well cared-for yield rich crops and bounteous wine.
Beauty's a gift of God. How few can boast
Of beauty? It's a gift denied to most.
Looks come by art: looks vanish with neglect,
Yes, though the charms of Venus they reflect.
Women of old ne'er groomed themselves it's true,
But in those days the men were ungroomed too.
Andromache wore woollens all her life;
Small wonder in a hard-bit soldier's wife.

Would Ajax' spouse come near him smartly dressed,
With seven ox-hides covering his chest?
Once life was rude and plain; now golden-paved,
Rome holds the treasures of a world enslaved.
The old and modern Capitols compare;
Built for two different Jupiters, you'd swear.
The Senate-house, fit home of high debate,
Was wattle-built when Tatius ruled the state,
And ploughmen's oxen grazed on Palatine
Where glitter now the palace and the shrine.
The good old days indeed! I am, thanks be,
This age's child: it's just the age for me;
Not because pliant gold from earth is wrought,
Not because pearls from distant coasts are brought,
Not that from hills their marble hearts we hew,
While piles encroach upon the ocean's blue:
It's that we've learnt refinement, and our days
Inherit not our grandsires' boorish ways.

Don't have your ears with costly baubles hung
From emerald seas by dusky Indians wrung;
Nor stagger forth in cloth of gold: display
That's meant to catch us scares us oft away.
By chic we're charmed; no rebel curl should show;
A finger's touch, and looks will come or go.
Nor in one only mode may heads be dressed,
Consult your glass for what becomes you best.
A simple parting suits an oval face,
—Laodamia such coiffure did grace—
A round one needs a dainty cluster posed
Above the brow, that leaves the ears disclosed.
One o'er her shoulders should her tresses fling
Like tuneful Phoebus when he sweeps the string,
One braid her hair, as Dian's wont to do
When girt her startled quarry to pursue.
This head a lavish flow of hair demands,
That must be prisoned in restraining bands,
This one delights in combs of tortoiseshell,
That one affects a wave-like fall and swell.

No more the acorns on the oak you'll count
Or beasts on Alps or bees on Hybla's mount,
Than I can count the fashions that prevail,
While every day adds new ones to the tale.
Even tangles can be charming; oft you'd vow
The hair's been slept in that's been combed but now.
Art apes the artless. Thus did Hercles see
And fall in love with captive Iole,
Thus into Bacchus' chariot lifted safe
'Mid cheering Satyrs looked the Cretan waif.
How nature does the fairer sex befriend,
That gives them means their damaged charms to mend!
We wretched men grow bald, and spoiled by age
Our tresses fall like leaves when tempests rage.
A woman tints the grey with Dutch shampoo
And thus improves by art on nature's hue;
A woman flaunts in yards of purchased curls;
Failing her own, she buys another girl's,
Buys unashamed: they're sold without disguise
'Neath Hercles' and the Muses' very eyes.
What now of dress? Put rich brocades aside
And stuffs in Tyrian purple double-dyed.
Now that of cheaper colours there's no lack,
It's mad to bear one's fortune on one's back.
There's blue of skies, of skies without a stain,
No warm south-westers bringing threat of rain,
Gold that recalls the fleece whereon it's said
Phrixus and Helle from fierce Ino fled,
The green of waves, from waves that take its name
(Methinks such garments clothe the Naiads' shame).
Here's saffron too (in robes of saffron bright
The dewy Morning yokes her team of light),
Pale rose and Paphian myrtle swell the list,
Plumage of cranes, and purple amethyst,
Your chestnuts, Amaryllis, almonds too,
And wax to fabrics gives its name and hue.
Rich as earth's new-born flowers in balmy spring,
When vine-buds swell and winter's gloom takes wing,

So rich, nay richer, is the choice of dyes:
But all become not: let your choice be wise.
Black suits a blonde; Briseis favoured black,
Thus robed she trod her captor's bivouac.
White suits brunettes; Andromeda looked best
In white; in white Seriphos saw her dressed.

How nearly had I warned you to beware
Lest armpits smell or legs be rough with hair!
But it's no squaws from Caucasus I teach
Or Mysian dwellers on Caicus' beach;
As well to bid you wash your face each day,
Nor leave your teeth to blacken and decay.
You've learnt how rouge can play complexion's part,
And lacking blood to blush with, blush by art,
By art the eyebrow's wilted tips replace,
While dainty patches hide the natural face,
And shameless lids have lines of Kohl applied
Or saffron grown by Cydnus' river-side.
A little guide to make-up have I writ,
Though small in bulk, in labour infinite;
There too may cures for damaged looks be learned:
My art's no laggard where your need's concerned.
But let no lover find the table strown
With paintpots: beauty's aids should ne'er be shown.
A face besmeared with dregs, whose drippings light
On the warm bosom, is a loathsome sight.
How vile, though brought from Athens, smells the grease
Extracted from a sheep's unwashen fleece!
Using deer's marrow publicly's not wise,
Nor cleaning teeth in public I advise.
All this gives beauty, but it's ugly viewing,
Much that delights when done disgusts when doing.
The works by which laborious Myron's known
Were once unmeaning lumps of ponderous stone.
To make a ring, first crush the shining ore;
That frock of yours was dirty fleece before,
From rough-hewn rock was wrought the statue fair,
A Venus nude who wrings her spray-drenched hair.

You too were best seen in the finished state,
We'll think you're sleeping while you titivate.
Whence comes your blush is no concern of mine;
Shut fast your door. Why show the crude design?
There's much it's best from human ken to hide,
Most things would shock us could we look inside.
Those golden trappings on the stage displayed,
See with how thin a leaf the wood's o'erlaid,
But till they're done, the crowd are kept apart:
So turn the men out ere the prinking start.
No harm, though, if beneath the comb they see
Your tresses o'er your shoulders rippling free.
But then, if ever, ware of spiteful fits,
Nor keep on pulling the coiffure to bits,
Or bullying the maid; an odious trick
To scratch her face or give her arm a prick.
Her mistress' head she'll curse at every touch,
While blood and tears the hated curls besmutch.
But guard your door, whose hair is in decline,
Or have it dressed in Bona Dea's shrine.
Once unexpectedly announced was I,
In haste my hostess donned her curls awry.
May foes deserve to feel such cruel shame,
May such disgrace befall some Parthian dame!
Hideous a bull dishorned, a lawn that's bare,
A plant sans foliage, and a head sans hair.

No Semele nor Leda need I teach,
Nor her the false bull haled from Sidon's beach,
Nor Helen whom her spouse did well to claim,
As well the Trojan did to keep his flame.
To me the common run of plain and fair,
But mostly plain, for tutoring repair.
A beauty needs no lessons from the schools
In right of her own natural gifts she rules.
The sailor takes his ease when ocean sleeps,
When seas are high a constant watch he keeps
But faultless forms are rare: as best you may,
Disguise the faults and foibles of your clay.

If short, lest standing you be thought to sit,
Sit, or your inches to the couch commit,
While, lest one take your measure as you lie,
Throw o'er your feet a shawl to cheat the eye.
If lean, a gown of ample cut select
That from the shoulders downward flows unchecked.
Bright patterns best with sallow skins comport,
Dark ones to Egypt's fabric should resort.
In snow-white shoes let ugly feet be cased,
From skinny legs the cross-bands ne'er unlaced.
If shoulder-blades be high, let pads be low,
Round a flat chest a big-cupped bra should go.
Make sparing use of gesture while you chat
Whose nails are scrubby or whose fingers fat.
Talk not when empty if your breath offend,
And always keep your distance from your friend.
If teeth be big, or black, or set askew,
To laugh would be a fatal thing to do.

Who'd think that even laughing must be taught?
By this means too is fascination sought.
Just ope the mouth, just dimple either side,
Just let the lips to show the teeth divide;
Nor strain your lungs with laughter undeterred;
Let something soft and feminine be heard.
One will distort her face with hideous leers,
Another's laughter you'd mistake for tears.
Another gives a cackle harsh and shrill,
As brays some poor old she-ass at the mill.
Where will art end? To weep with grace and ease
They learn, and blubber when and how they please.
More—letters cheated of their rightful sound
And tongues that lisp to order may be found.
It's winsome o'er occasional words to halt,
And faultless lips are schooled to be at fault.
Pay heed to all this: all is for your good;
Learn how to bear yourselves as woman should.
By carriage—it's no little part of charm—
The unknown male is lured or takes alarm.

One sways her hips, to air with studied pose
Her flowing gown, and points her stately toes;
Another, like a farmer's red-cheeked mate,
Walks with great strides and straddles in her gait.
But here, as in so many things, between
Clumping and mincing find the happy mean.
But on the left, where shoulder joins to arm,
A glimpse of bareness gives an added charm,
To blondes especially: when I light on this
That peep of shoulder I feel bound to kiss.

The Sirens were sea-fairies, who by force
Of song could stay the swiftest vessel's course.
Ulysses nigh broke loose upon the sound,
His comrades' ears, we're told, in wax were bound.
Learn singing, fair ones. Song's a thing of grace;
Voice oft's a better procuress than face.
Airs from the marble theatre repeat,
Or ditties danced with light Egyptian beat.
No woman trained according to my will
Should lack the art to handle lyre and quill.
By Orpheus' lute were beasts and boulders led,
And streams of Hell and hound with triple head.
Stones leapt to build new ramparts at the song
Of him who justly venged his mother's wrong.
How the mute dolphin felt a voice's spell
The legend of Arion's lyre will tell.
Teach too your hands in unison to smite
The merry harp designed for our delight.

Next you must con Callimachus's page,
The bard of Cos, and Teos' vinous sage,
And Sappho whom all wantonness inspires,
And him whose cunning slaves outwit his sires.
Nor some of sweet Propertius' songs omit,
Nor some by Gallus or Tibullus writ,
Nor Varro's tale how Phrixus' sister rued
The far-famed fleece with flock of gold endued;

Nor how—the noblest lay in Latin tongue—
High Rome from fugitive Aeneas sprung.
And with those names shall mine perchance be classed,
Nor all I've writ on Lethe's stream be cast.
'Read', one will say, 'that work in polished vein,
Wherein our master schools the sexes twain,
Or choose a piece to read in winning tone
From the three books by name of Love-Tales known,
Or an Epistle tunefully recite,
A novel form that he did first indite.'
Oh grant this, Phoebus, grant it, powers divine
Of poesy, horned Bacchus and the Nine!

Of course I'd have a wench in dancing skilled,
To sway the bidden limb when cups are filled.
The ballet troupe's the darling of the boards,
So great the charm their supple grace affords.
I blush to urge such trifles as to know
How dice are tossed, the value of the throw,
Now three to cast, now judge with apt resource
Which side to challenge, which to reinforce;
To guide with wary skill the chessmen's fight,
When foemen twain o'erpower the single knight,
And caught without his queen the king must face
The foe and oft his eager steps retrace;
Or from an opened bag pour balls that glide,
And pick one out, disturbing none beside.
A game there is marked out in slender zones
As many as the fleeting year has moons:
A smaller board with three a side is manned,
And victory's his who first aligns his band.
Practise all pastimes; not to play would shame
A wench: love's oft engendered at a game.
But dicing skill's a little thing to ask,
To keep one's temper is a graver task.
We're reckless then by zest itself betrayed,
And o'er a game the naked soul's displayed.
Wrath shows his ugly head, and greed of gain
And brawls and quarrels and distressful pain;

Reproaches fly, the air resounds with cries,
And each invokes his outraged deities;
Debts are forsworn and honour disappears,
Nay, cheeks I've often seen bedewed with tears.
God save you from such infamies as these
Who hope a man of any kind to please.

Such games with woman's weaker clay comport:
Richer are men's materials for sport.
Theirs the swift ball, the hoop, the lance to fling,
And arms and horses circling in a ring.
No sportsground's yours, nor do your bodies know
Calm Tiber's streams or Maiden's icy flow.
But Pompey's Porch you may and must frequent,
When August blazes in the firmament.
Repair to bay-crowned Phoebus' palace-shrine,
Who sank the barques of Egypt 'neath the brine,
Or the arcades by Caesar's spouse begun,
His sister and his laurelled sailor son.
Haunt the Egyptian heifer's censered fane,
Let the three theatres observe you plain,
Visit the Ring that gouts of blood besmear,
Watch round the goal the burning wheels career.
What's hid's unknown, and what's unknown's unsought;
A pretty face sans witness profits nought.
Though Thamyras and Amoebeus you excel,
An unknown singer wields no powerful spell.
Had Venus by Apelles ne'er been limned,
Sunk 'neath the Ocean she'd remain unhymned.
What seeks the sacred poet else than fame?
Of all our labours it's the cherished aim.
Once for the poet gods and kings took heed
And ancient singers earned a lavish meed;
In reverence high was held the name of bard,
Honour and oft great wealth was his reward.
The nursling of Calabria's mountain race,
Ennius, next great Scipio earned a place.
But now we scorn the bays, and say he shirks
Who in the Muses' service wakes and works.

It's fame he works for: who'd know Homer's name
Were his immortal Iliad lost to fame?
Who'd know of Danae, had she always stayed
Pent in her prison, an obscure old maid?
There's profit, beauties, in the crowded street;
Oft o'er the threshold set your roving feet.
The wolf to gain one victim stalks the herds,
On flocks of fledglings swoops the king of birds.
A beauty too in public must be seen,
Out of so many, one perchance she'll glean.
Intent to please she'll linger everywhere
And to her looks devote assiduous care.
Chance is almighty: keep your hook at work,
In the least likely pool a fish will lurk.
Oft while hounds vainly scour the wooded crag,
Into the toils undriven walks the stag.
What could Andromeda have hoped for less,
Than to look winning in her sore duress?
Friends oft are made at funerals; tears unchecked
And hair dishevelled have a good effect.

But shun those handsome elegants professed
Who keep their hair immaculately dressed.
What they tell you they've told to scores beside,
And nowhere long their vagrant loves abide.
What use a man who's smoother-skinned than you
And peradventure has more lovers too?
Believe me, doubters all: had Troy believed
Cassandra's warnings, she'd have stood reprieved:
Some will besiege you with a courtship feigned,
To rob you foully once their footing's gained.
But nor by hair with glistening perfume wet
Nor latchets neatly in their creases set,
Nor by a suit of finest texture weaved
And rings on every finger be deceived.
The smartest dandy of them all may be
A rogue enamoured of your finery.
'Stop thief!' will often cry the plundered fair,
'Stop thief!' re-echoes loud through all the Square,

While Venus from her gold-emblazoned hall,
Her nymphs around her, calmly views the brawl.
To some names too known infamy belongs,
Scores on their conscience have a woman's wrongs;
Learn to be cautious from another's fate,
Let no false lover pass within your gate.
Trust, maids of Athens, Theseus' oaths no more:
The gods he swears by he's forsworn before.
You too, Demophoon, heir to Theseus' guilt,
Your honour went when Phyllis called you jilt.
For promises be promises exchanged,
For cash bestow your favours as arranged.
Well might she steal the horns from Io's shrine
Or quench the sleepless Vestal fires divine,
Or give her husband spurge with hemlock brayed,
Who'd cheat a man of joys for which he's paid.

But let me now come closer to my theme,
Draw rein, my Muse, nor headlong plunge your team.
The fir-wood tablet comes to spy the land:
See that its message reach a trusty hand.
Read it with care, and from its language judge
If its appeal be *cri-de-cœur* or fudge.
Before you answer wait a day or more,
Love's spurred by waiting if it's quickly o'er.
Vouchsafe no easy promise to his prayer
Nor yet reject it with a ruthless air;
Blend hopes with fears; but hopes must grow more bright
And fears diminish every time you write.
Write in a cultured but colloquial way;
Men like the common style of every day.
Oft has a letter spurred a doubting youth,
And comely looks been damned by words uncouth.
But since, though lacking wedlock's honoured ties,
You're just as keen to wipe your masters' eyes,
Let maid or lackey pen your billets-doux,
Nor trust your tokens to a hand that's new.
Who keeps such tokens plays a traitor's game,
But wields a weapon fierce as Etna's flame

Through this I've seen a woman blanched with fear
Tormented and enslaved for many a year.
To counter trick with trick I hold no harm,
The law permits one 'gainst the armed to arm.
One hand must practise penning many styles,
—A plague on those who make me teach such wiles!—
There's risk in writing save on wax well rased,
Lest on one block two messages be traced.
E'er to your lover as a wench refer,
And in your letters speak of 'him' as 'her'.

Let me from small to greater themes proceed
And 'neath a spread of swelling canvas speed.
For looks it's vital ugly moods to ban,
Wrath's for the brute beast, tranquil peace for man.
Rage puffs the cheeks; the veins empurpled rise,
Fiercer than Gorgon's glances flash the eyes.
'Begone vile flute! you're worth not such grimace,'
Cried Pallas in the water spying her face.
So if in rage your mirrors you were shown,
Scarce one would know her features for her own.
Beauty is spoilt by arrogance no less:
Love must be lured by looks of tenderness.
Trust one who knows, we hate a haughty air,
Hate's oft implanted by a silent stare.
To glance with glance and smile with smile reply,
Return his signal if he catch your eye.
This by-play ended, Cupid drops his game,
And from his quiver draws the shafts that maim.
Gloom too we hate: Tecmessa's Ajax' choice;
Gay sparks like us in merry hearts rejoice.
Nor you, Tecmessa, nor Andromache
I'd ever ask to come and live with me.
But for your babes that prove it, I'd have said
That neither ever shared her husband's bed.
Do you supose, that melancholy dame
Called Ajax 'pet', or other coaxing name?

From great to small I'll argue by your grace
And boldly quote the high commander's case,
Who wisely trusts to each in his degree
The company, the flag, the cavalry.
So you for what we're fitted each the most
Judge, and assign to each his proper post.
The rich can give, the lawyer help at need,
The orator a client's cause can plead,
We poets nought but poems can bestow,
But we're the best of lovers here below.
By us the fair one's charms are far proclaimed,
Through us are Nemesis and Cynthia famed.
From East to West Lycoris' tale is sung
And my Corinna's name's on many a tongue.
Guile too in poet's nature hath no part;
Our characters are moulded by our art.
No lust of place or riches weighs us down,
We love our shady couch and spurn the town.
But quickly caught, by passions strong we're burnt,
Too well the lesson of true love we've learnt.
Our hearts are softened by our gentle trade,
And by our calling is our conduct swayed.
Be kind, ye fair, to the poetic choir
Whom Muses love and deities inspire.
God's in us and with heaven we discourse,
In springs divine our instinct has its source.
It's sin to look for payment from the bard,
A sin, alas, that women ne'er regard.
But hide your thought, nor barefaced greed display;
New love espies the trap and runs away.

No horseman with the self-same bit would ride
The colt new-broken and the hack well-tried,
Nor by the self-same method will you cage
Both callow youth and sober-minded age.
Yon raw recruit, in Love's campaigns untaught,
Who stands upon your threshold newly caught,
Must know and cling to you, to you alone:
Let lofty fences round that crop be thrown.

Keep rivals off: alone your victory's sure;
Nor thrones nor love in partnership endure.
Your veteran woos with quiet self-command,
Submits to much that no recruit will stand;
He never breaks or burns the door or seeks
To use his nails to scratch his darling's cheeks,
Tears his own garments, tears the lady's dress,
Draws floods of tears by snatching out a tress.
To amorous young hotheads leave such tricks;
Our friend will calmly bear the sharpest pricks.
He burns, alack, as slow as sodden hay,
As timber fresh-cut on the lofty brae.
This love's the stabler, that more richly sweet,
But briefer; haste to pluck the fruits that fleet.

Betrayal! Gates opened to the foe by me!
Let me continue true to treachery!
Love thrives not long on easy faring: mix
With amorous delights occasional kicks.
Leave him outside to cry 'Oh heartless door!'
Let him beseech you much and threaten more.
Jaded by sweets we need a pungent whet;
Ships perish oft by favouring gales o'erset.
It's this that makes a wife beloved so ill;
Her husband comes to her whene'er he will.
Closed doors, a porter's rasping 'not at home'—
And you, Sir Locked-out, too to love succumb.
Now drop the foils, with rapiers fight it out;
With my own weapons I'll be met no doubt.
The youth you're snaring or have lately snared
Must think your chamber by none else is shared,
But later scent, competing for your bed,
A rival: drop such arts and love goes dead.
At fall of gate the courser shows his pace
When he has peers to follow and outrace.
By perfidy are deadest fires relit;
I only love when jilted, I admit.
No overt cause for jealousy disclose,
Just hint there's more, poor devil, than he knows,

Or spur him on with myths of dreadful spies
Or cruel husband's ever-watchful eyes.
Joy without danger loses half its charm,
Though free as Thais, simulate alarm.
Open the window, not the simpler door,
Your features oozing fear at every pore.
A well-drilled maid must up and cry 'We're trapped!'
In any hole the trembling gallant's clapped.
But with these terrors mingle calm delights,
Lest overrated he should deem your nights.

I'd nigh omitted how to dodge the eye
Of cunning lover or of watchful spy.
A wife must fear her lord, a prisoner's life
Is lawful, right and proper for a wife:
But an ex-housemaid kept 'neath lock and key!
Who'd bear it? Learn my ritual and be free.
Though all the eyes of Argus on you pry,
You can outwit them if you really try.
What gaoler can ensure you'll never write,
When in your bath for hours you're out of sight,
When letters an accomplice can convey
'Neath her deep bodice snugly tucked away,
Or can secrete a packet in her shoe,
Or in her stocking hide the billet-doux?
Such tricks foreseen, for paper she'll devote
Her back, and on her skin will bear your note.
It's safe and secret with new milk to write,
A touch of coal-dust brings the words to light.
Likewise the moisture from a flax-stalk dripped
On the clean page will trace an unseen script.
Acrisius strictly pent his daughter in,
Yet was made grandsire by that daughter's sin.
What use a spy when theatres abound,
When you are free to haunt the racing-ground,
Or with your rattle sit at Isis' feet,
And where no groom may follow, can retreat,
When the male eye from Bona Dea's rites
Is banned, save such as she herself invites,

When, while the lackey guards your clothes outside,
The baths much scope for furtive joys provide,
When you can find at need an ailing friend
Who, though she ail, her bed's prepared to lend,
When picklocks show how we can pick—and choose,
Nor doors alone for exit you can use?
By Bacchus too the gaoler's watch is lulled,
Even though the grape on Spanish hills be culled.
Then there are drugs that woo to heavy sleep,
And vanquished eyes in dark oblivion steep.
What's more your maid may coax the wretch away
And keep him long with blandishments in play.
But why these tricks and petty rules prescribe,
When spies are open to the smallest bribe?
Both gods and men, believe me, yield to pelf,
And offerings soothe the wrath of Jove himself.
No less than fools, the wise to bribes succumb,
The bribe once swallowed, either will be dumb.
But strive to buy your gaoler once for all:
Who's fallen once, again is like to fall.
I once complained that we must fear our friends;
Not to men only that complaint extends.
Trust, and your joys to others will accrue,
The hare you've started others will pursue.
She, who's so keen to offer room and bed—
Be sure I've oft enjoyed her in your stead.
Nor keep a too attractive waiting-maid,
For me her mistress' part she's often played.

Madman, why naked plunge into the fight,
Why turn informer to your own despite?
Bird guides not fowler to her hiding-place,
Nor stag instructs the hated hound in pace.
A fig for self! my task I'll carry through,
And for my own doom arm the Lemnian crew.
Make us believe we're loved—it's simply done;
Wishers are quick to think their wishes won.
With loving looks your gallant contemplate,
Sigh deep and ask him why he comes so late,

Then cry, and o'er a rival feign despair,
And with your nails his cheeks proceed to tear.
Convinced at last, to pity he'll react,
And say 'By love of me the creature's racked.'
A fop especially and his mirror's slave
Will think that o'er him goddesses can rave.
But by no wrongs whate'er be overwrought,
Nor, hearing of a rival, go distraught,
Nor believe lightly: Procris' case will show
What dire results from light belief can flow.

Hard by Hymettus' gaily flowered mount
Mid soft green turf there springs a sacred fount,
Girt with low trees, the sward with arbute laid,
Bay, rosemary and dark myrtle scent the glade,
While dense-leaved box abounds and clover fine
And fragile tamarisk and graceful pine.
This wealth of leaves, these grassy surfaces
Dance to the Zephyrs' soft refreshing breeze.
Here Cephalus, hounds and servants left behind,
Tired and in love with quiet, oft reclined.
'Come, wanton air, to cool my sweltering heat,
Come nestle to my bosom,' he'd repeat.
Some busy-body whispered word for word
In the shy ear of Procris what he'd heard.
At the word 'air', some fancied rival's name,
She swooned and dumb with sudden shock became.
She paled, as pale by early winter nipped
Late leaves in vineyards of their clusters stripped,
Or quinces ripe on bending branches hung,
Or cornels yet too sour for human tongue.
Revived, she rent her harmless cheeks and tore
The airy shift that o'er her breast she wore,
Then swiftly down the ways with hair unbraced
Mad as a thyrsus-stricken Maenad raced.
Nearing the spot, within the vale she stayed
Her maids and boldly stole into the glade.
What was your purpose, lurking there possessed,
What madness, Procris, burnt within your breast?

Soon, did you think she'd come, this Air unknown,
And to your very eyes the shame be shown?
Sorry you came now, lest you find him out,
Now happy, tossing between fear and doubt.
All proves it; place and name and witness too,
And love's conviction that its fears are true.
At sight of limb-prints on the turf impressed
A quicker heart-beat shook her pulsing breast.
Now had the shadows to their shortest drawn,
And equidistant were both eve and dawn,
When Hermes' offspring, Cephalus, sought the glade
And at the spring his burning forehead sprayed.
Fearful sat Procris. On the wonted bed
Reclined, 'Come Zephyr, come sweet air', he said.
Oh joy! the error of the name was plain,
And sense and native hue returned again.
She rose, and rushing to embrace her spouse
With eager limbs pushed through the barring boughs.
Supposing he heard game, with youthful heat,
Weapon in hand, he started to his feet.
What are you at? Don't throw! No quarry's here:
Alas your lady's stricken by your spear.
She cried 'Ay me! You've pierced a loving heart,
Cephalus wounds me always in that part.
Untimely, but dishonoured not, I die:
For this more lightly on me earth shall lie.
Into that suspect air my spirit flies,
I faint; oh hand beloved, close my eyes.'
On his sad breast his lady's form inert
He propped, and bathed with tears the cruel hurt;
Her reckless spirit slowly ebbed and passed,
Caught on her ill-starred lover's lips at last.

But back to work and cut digression short,
That we may bring the weary barque to port.
You're longing I should take you out to dine,
There too you're anxious for advice of mine.
Come late, and pose by lamplight at the door;
Suspense, the pander, makes us want you more.

Though plain, you'll look superb to drunken eyes;
Night of itself all blemish will disguise.
Mind table-manners: eat with finger-tips,
Nor smear a greasy hand all o'er your lips.
Sup before setting forth, or cease while still
Short of repletion: eat not quite your fill.
Were Helen gorging seen by Priam's son,
He'd say disgusted 'A fool's prize I've won.'
Drinking is more becoming to the fair:
Cupid and Bacchus make a well-matched pair;
Provided heads be stout, and foot and brain
And eyes that see not double stand the strain.
A dead-drunk woman is a hideous sight;
She's anybody's sport, and serve her right.
To fall asleep at table's risky too:
In sleep may happen much that you might rue.

The rest I blushed to tell, but Venus smiled,
'What makes you blush concerns us most, my child.'
Know each your person: there's no single norm
For all: let posture to physique conform.
Recline face upwards, you who're fair of face,
Display your back, whose back's your chiefest grace.
Well-shapen legs on shoulders should be laid;
Milanion thus with Atalanta's played.
Who's short should ride a-cockhorse: Hector's bride
Was far too tall to sit her horse astride.
Whom the long hip-line graces, on the bed
Should kneel and slightly backward bend her head,
While youthful thighs and faultless breasts demand
That you lie slantwise and your lover stand.
Nor think the Maenad's fashion misbeseems:
Fling back your neck and loose your locks in streams.
You too, whose belly childbirth's furrowed out,
Like the swift Parthian, wheel your steed about.
Love's modes are legion: easiest and best
Betwixt the right side and the back to rest.
But truths as great as e'er horned Ammon told
Or Phoebus' tripods, let my muse unfold.

Trust, if aught else, the art I've practised long:
Your faith shall find its warrant in my song.
Thrill, woman, to your depths with passion racked,
That both alike may revel in the act.
Let ceaseless coos and gurglings soft be heard
Amid your play and many a naughty word.
You too, whose nature feels no sexual joys,
Feign ecstasy with much delusive noise.
Poor wretch in whom that organ's numbed and chill
Which man and woman equally should thrill!
Ware only lest you give yourself away:
With looks and movements make convincing play;
Your bliss by voice and panting breath proclaim
And secret signs from parts I blush to name.
Nor dun the lover whom you've just enjoyed,
Your prayer—you must expect it—will be void:
Nor let your windows light up all the room;
Much of your body best were left in gloom.

The game is o'er. It's time for your descent,
You swans whose necks beneath my yoke have bent.
As once your brothers, now, my scholars fair,
'*Pupils of Ovid*' let your spoils declare.

THE CURES FOR LOVE

When Cupid read the title of this volume,
  'It's war on me', he cried, 'I see it's war.'
Please, Cupid, don't hold me, your poet, guilty,
  Who at your side so long your standard bore.
I'm not like Diomede who hurt your mother
  (And Mars' steeds bore her back to Heaven above).
Others may cool, but I'm in love for ever;
  If you ask what I'm at, I'm still in love.
Besides, I've taught the art and craft to win you;
  It's science now where impulse ruled of yore.
Sweet boy, I've not betrayed you or my talent
  And no new Muse unweaves work done before.
Good luck to any lover who likes loving;
  Let him rejoice and sail before the wind.
But if some minx has got him in her clutches,
  Succour and safety in my art he'll find.
Why should a lover knot a noose and dangle
  Aloft from a high beam, a tragic weight?
Why plunge a sword-blade in his breast? This bloodshed
  Is yours, peace-lover, and it earns you hate.
Let him who'll die of love unless he ends it,
  End it; then you shall be the death of none.
You are a boy; you're only fit for playing;
  A kindly reign bests suits your years: play on.
You could have waged your wars with naked arrows,
  But fatal blood your weapons never draw.
Your stepfather may fight with spear and broadsword
  And triumph in the carnage caked with gore;
You, use your mother's arts: they're used in safety:
  Through them no parent finds herself bereft.
Get doors burst open by nocturnal brawlers;
  Let many a garland on the step be left.
Get young men and shy girls to meet in secret,
  By hook or crook a watchful husband cheat.

Have lovers coax or curse a dogged doorpost
    And sing a doleful ditty in the street.
Tears will suffice, with no death to reproach you;
    Your torch should not be set to greedy pyres.
Then golden Love waved jewelled wings and answered:
    'Complete', he said, 'the work your heart desires.'

You fellows who've been cheated, take my precepts,
    You whom your love has totally betrayed;
Learn to be cured of love from him who taught it;
    The hand that gave the wound will now bring aid.
The same soil nurtures healing herbs and harmful,
    The nettle's often neighbour to the rose.
Achilles' spear that once had wounded Telephus
    Gave succour to the wound and cured his woes.
(What I tell men take also as intended
    For girls; we issue arms to either side.
And if this part or that does not concern you,
    Good lessons all the same may be applied.)
It's a sound plan to quench a fire. Don't harbour
    A heart to its infirmities enslaved.
Phyllis would have retrod, with me for tutor,
    The path she trod nine times—her young life saved.
Nor from the tower's top would dying Dido
    Have watched the Trojan vessels put to sea,
Nor would a mother's vengeance on her husband
    Have steeled her heart to slay their progeny.
Had Tereus used my art when Philomela
    Pleased him—no crime, no bird-change price to pay.
Give me Pasiphae, she'll drop her bull-love;
    Or Phaedra, Phaedra's lust will fade away;
Or Paris, Menelaus will keep Helen,
    The Greeks won't win, unconquered Troy will stay.
If traitress Scylla could have read my treatise,
    King Nisus' head would have its purple tress.
With me in charge, men, curb the cares that kill you,
    With me in charge let ship and crew progress.

When you learnt love, you had to read your Ovid,
   And Ovid likewise now you ought to read.
Yes, I'm the Emancipator; I'll free hearts from
   Slavery: count your blessings now you're freed.
As I begin, I beg your laurel's favour,
   Phoebus, first fount of physic and of song.
Support alike the poet and physician;
   Within your guardianship they both belong.

While time permits and you've still no strong feelings,
   Stop at the start, if you've the least unease.
Check your horse straightaway, and while they're recent
   Destroy the baleful seeds of the disease.
Time creates strength, time makes the young grapes ripen,
   Builds the strong wheatcrop from the tiny blade.
The slip at first so small when it was planted
   Becomes a broad tree giving strollers shade.
A hand could then extract it from the topsoil,
   Now it stands huge in all its strength arrayed.
Take a hard look at what it is you're loving;
   Free your neck from the yoke before it's galled.
Scotch the first start. Procrastination lets a
   Disease gain strength; too late the doctor's called.
So hurry! Don't postpone it till tomorrow.
   If you're not ready now, you'll be less then.
All love's a fraud and fattens on deferment.
   Freedom tomorrow! Put it off again!
Few rivers start, you know, from giant sources,
   By tributaries most are multiplied.
Had Myrrha known at once the crime she purposed,
   She'd not have needed bark her face to hide.
I've seen a wound that prompt care could have mended
   Wait and be damaged by a long delay.
But since it's fun to pick the fruit of Venus,
   We say tomorrow's better than today.
Meanwhile the evil tree drives its roots deeper,
   And flames into our vitals worm their way.

But if the time's been missed for early treatment,
  And in the captive heart love's long installed,
A greater task is left: I'll not abandon
  The invalid now, late though I've been called.
The septic foot that tortured Philoctetes
  He should have amputated long ago;
Yet he was cured, they say, and then years later
  Dealt the great Trojan war the final blow.
I who have just made haste to halt first symptoms,
  Now bring slow succour at a later stage.
Either one tries to douse a fire first starting
  Or waits till it's died down and spent its rage.
While frenzy's in full flow, give way to frenzy;
  Impetuosity is hard to face.
A man's a fool who swims against the current
  When crossing slantways he can reach the place.
A mind that won't be touched and can't be tackled
  Will hate advice and expertise reject.
I'd best approach him when he'll let me handle
  His wounds and treat the truth with due respect.
Who in his senses would forbid a mother
  To weep at her son's grave? That's not the best
Place for advice. When tears are done and heartbreak
  Is sated, words may ease a soul distressed.
The doctor's art is largely one of timing:
  Timed right wine helps, timed wrong the malady
Is worse. Indeed denial may inflame it,
  If your approach is not judged properly.
So when you judge you're ready for my treatment
  Take my advice: shun leisure from the start.
Leisure breeds love, and guards the love it's breeding;
  It's leisure feeds the sweet bane in your heart.
Take away leisure—Cupid's bow is broken,
  His torch is scorned and sheds no light around.
As planes love wine and poplars purling water
  And rushes of the lakeside marshy ground,
Venus loves leisure. To finish love keep busy;
  Love yields to business: busy—safe and sound.

But indolence and sleep too long unchallenged
   And dice and drink and hangovers remove
(Though no wound's made) a man's whole moral fibre;
   To hearts unwary in slips wily Love.
Sloth's that boy's quarry; he hates busy people;
   So give an idle mind a job to do.
There are the lawcourts, friends to be defended,
   Civilian battles bringing fame for you.
Or you can undertake the manly duties
   Of bloody Mars: then lovegames say goodbye.
The fleeing Parthian now, a great new triumph,
   On his own steppes sees Caesar's soldiery.
Conquer both bows, the Parthian's and Cupid's;
   Home to your Country's gods twin trophies take.
As soon as Diomede had wounded Venus
   She let her lover battle for her sake.
You ask what caused the adultery of Aegisthus;
   The reason's ready: he was indolent.
Others were fighting Troy's long lagging battles,
   Her soldiery the whole of Greece had sent.
Had he had war in mind—no war at Argos;
   Or lawcourt business—there was none of that.
He *could* make love, and did: better than nothing.
   So comes and so still stays Love's little brat.

There's pleasure too in country life and farming;
   There's no care will not yield to country cares.
Bid oxen bow their necks beneath the burden
   To wound the hard soil with the curving shares;
Then when you've turned your ploughland, sow the seed-corn
   For rich return with interest from your fields.
See how the weight of apples bends the branches,
   The tree can hardly hold the fruit it yields.
See the sheep grazing in the lush green meadows,
   See the streams purling merrily along.
And look, the goats are making for the hillside;
   They'll bring back bursting udders for their young.

The shepherd plays a ditty on his pan-pipes
  With watchful dogs to keep him company,
And over there the woods are loud with lowings—
  Her calf has strayed, a cow's in misery.
Think of the swarms that fly off when you smoke them
  To take the combs and clear the wicker hives.
Autumn gives fruit and summer's gay with harvest;
  A fire cheers winter; spring with blossoms thrives.
At the due time the peasant picks his vintage
  And under his bare feet the juice will flow.
At the due time he cuts his hay and binds it,
  And gleaning then the wide-toothed rakes will go.
You can plant cuttings in your watered garden
  And *you* can guide the runnels rippling down.
There's grafting now: one branch adopts another;
  Let the tree stand with foliage not its own.
When once the mind finds comfort in such pleasures,
  Love's failed and off on flagging wings he's flown.

Or take up hunting. Many a time has Venus
  Slunk off in shame and Phoebus' sister's won.
Now spread your nets across the leafy hillside,
  Now after leaping hares let beagles run,
Or frighten the shy deer with strings of feathers,
  Or with your spear's sharp point bring down a boar.
You'll be tired out and sleep by girls untroubled,
  And rich deep slumber will your frame restore.
A less taxing pursuit, but real, is catching
  Birds with a net or lime, a humble prize,
Or set a little bait to hide a fish-hook
  And greedy fishes to their cost surprise.
This way or that, till you've unlearnt your passion,
  You've got to keep the wool pulled over your eyes.

There's travel too. Though you're held fast in bondage,
  Start a long journey and go right away.
You'll weep; your girl-friend's name will often haunt you,
  And on the road you'll linger and delay.

The less you want to go, the more keep going;
   Force those reluctant feet of yours to flee.
Don't pray for rain or let a foreign Sabbath
   Check you or Allia's catastrophe.
Don't ask how many miles you've done, how many
   Remain; don't feign delays to stay nearby.
Don't count the hours or look back at Rome's skyline.
   Just fly: safe from their foes the Parthians fly.

People may call my precepts tough. It's true they're
   Tough: to get well much pain you'll have to feel.
Often, when ill, I've had to swallow bitter
   Doses and been denied a decent meal.
To cure your body fire and steel you'll suffer
   And drink no water to relieve your thirst.
To heal your mind, what would you not put up with?
   But then the value of the mind comes first.
My treatment's most distressing at the outset;
   To get through the first stage is your prime need.
You see how first yokes chafe new-broken bullocks
   And how a new girth galls a swift young steed.
To leave your hearth and home you may be sorry,
   But leave you will; then back you'll want to go.
It won't be hearth and home but love that calls you,
   Disguising with grand words the guilt you know.
When once you've left, you'll find a hundred comforts:
   The lengthy journey, comrades, countryside.
And don't rely on distance; stay away till
   The fire has lost its force, the flame has died.
For if you hurry back with mind unbuttressed
   Love will renew the fight, his fierce flame burn.
For all your absence that whole time will do you
   Damage—hungry and thirsty you'll return.

If a man thinks he can be helped by magic
   And herbs of Thessaly, the choice is his.
That's the old way of witchcraft; my Apollo
   Gives harm-free help in holy harmonies.

With me for guide there'll be no spirits summoned,
   No witch's wicked spells will split the ground,
No crops will cross from one field to another,
   No sudden pallor dim the sun's bright round.
As usual the Tiber will flow seawards,
   As usual the moon will ride at night.
No spells unspelled will ease a heart of heartache,
   No pungent sulphur fumes put Love to flight.
What use, Medea, were the herbs of Phasis,
   When in your father's home you wished to stay?
What, Circe, did your magic plants avail you,
   When the breeze bore Ulysses' barque away?
You did your best to keep your guest from going:
   He spread his sails, determined to depart.
You did your best to fend the fierce flame from you:
   Love settled long in your reluctant heart.
You had the power to change men to a thousand
   Shapes, but no power to change your own heart's laws.
When your Ulysses was about to leave you,
   It's said with these fair words you made him pause:
'I don't pray now, what I first used to hope for,
   I well recall, that you would marry me—
But I'm a goddess, I'm the great Sun's daughter,
   And worthy thus, I thought, your wife to be.
I beg you, not such haste. I ask a favour,
   A little time; what less could be my prayer?
You see the waves are rough, you've cause to fear them;
   The wind will serve you better when it's fair.
What cause have you for flight? No new Troy rises
   Here, no one calls allies to arms again.
Here's love and peace, where I alone am wounded,
   And over this whole country you shall reign.'
Even as she spoke Ulysses was unmooring;
   Away his sails—her words—the breezes bore.
Circe, aflame, resorted to her magic,
   But that made love no feebler than before.

So put no trust in spells or witchcraft, all who
   Look to my art for help in an amour.
If some strong reason keeps you in Rome's city,
   The world's great mistress, learn my city lore.

He's his best champion who's burst the shackles
   That galled his heart, and suffered once for all.
Though courage of that kind just makes *me* marvel;
   He'll not need my advice, I think, at all.
But you who find it hard to unlearn your loving,
   Who can't and wish you could, on me must call.
Keep thinking what your wicked girl's been doing;
   Before your eyes set every loss you've had.
'There's this and that and still she wants more plunder;
   I've had to sell my house, it got so bad.
She swore to me and, swearing, just deceived me,
   Letting me lie so often at her door!
She dotes on others, finds my love offensive,
   And gives a salesman nights I get no more.'
Let all these things embitter your whole being;
   Brood over them, seek seeds of hatred here.
I want you to be eloquent about them;
   Just suffer—you'll be fluent, never fear.
Not long ago a certain girl had hooked me;
   She didn't suit, our tastes were not the same:
Like Podalirius my own drugs cured me,
   The doctor sick! I grant it to my shame.
It helped to harp on my girl-friend's shortcomings;
   That often made me better, as I learnt.
'Those legs of hers', I used to say, 'how ugly.'
   And yet in fact, to tell the truth, they weren't.
'Those arms of hers', I'd say, 'by no means pretty.'
   And yet in fact, to tell the truth, they were.
'How short she is!'—she wasn't. 'How demanding!'
   For those demands I chiefly hated her.
The bad too's neighbour to the good, so virtue
   Often gets blamed for vice when misapplied.
Decry, as best you can, your girl's attractions
   And let your judgement fall on the wrong side.

She's buxom, call her fat; she's dark, a negress;
  Her figure's slender, say she's lank and lean.
And you can call her pert, if she's not naive,
  And if she's well-behaved, naive you mean.
Then too whatever talent the girl's short of
  Keeping coaxing her to demonstrate its charms.
If she's no voice, insist upon her singing,
  And make her dance if she can't move her arms.
Her accent's bad? Keep her in conversation;
  She hasn't learnt to play? Call for the lyre.
She waddles? Make her walk. Her breast's a bulging
  Bust? See she wears no brassiere to tie her.
Her teeth are bad? Say what will set her laughing;
  Or set her weeping, if she's got weak eyes.
It will help too to pay a sudden visit,
  Early, before she's put on her disguise.
Dress sweeps us off our feet: in gold and jewels
  All's hid; the girl herself's her smallest part.
Among so much you wonder what you're loving;
  Love's armour thus deceives the eyes and heart.
Come unannounced: you're safe, she's caught defenceless;
  Victim of her defects the poor girl falls.
(But it's not safe to overtrust this precept;
  For artless beauty many men enthralls.)
So go to see her face (and have no scruples)
  When on her cheeks she's smearing dope and drugs.
You'll find a thousand colours, pots and boxes,
  And ointments dripping down on her warm dugs,
Greases that more than once have turned my stomach,
  Stinking as foul as Phineus' filthy fugs.

Now for the *act* we'll give you our prescription:
  All passion must be driven clear away.
There's much in this that I'm ashamed to mention;
  You must imagine more than my words say.
For lately people have attacked my poems;
  They blame my Muse as bawdy and immoral.
So long as I give fun and I'm world-famous,
  If one or two decry me, I shan't quarrel.

Envy decries the genius of Homer;
 From Homer Zoilus' fame (who's he?) proceeds;
And sacrilegious tongues have torn the poet
 Who Trojan gods to Rome from ruin leads.
Envy strikes at the peaks: the storm winds batter
 Summits: to strike the peaks Jove's fierce bolt flies.
But anyone offended by my freedom—
 Judge matter by the metre, if you're wise.
Hexameters are right for wars and battles;
 For love's delights what place there can one see?
The tragic style is grand; rage suits its buskins;
 And daily life's the stuff of comedy.
For fighting foes unsheath the sharp iambic,
 Either swift-footed or with last foot lame.
Let charming Elegy hymn quivered Cupids
 And at her pleasure play her sprightly game.
Callimachus's verse can't suit Achilles,
 Cydippe's not for Homer's epic song.
Thais played as Andromache—who'd stand it?
 Andromache as Thais—just as wrong.
But Thais is my business—fun unfettered;
 I'm not concerned with wives; Thais for me.
If my Muse matches my light-hearted matter,
 I've won; the accusation's false and she goes free.
So burst, devouring Envy! My fame's great now,
 And, going as it started, will grow more.
You go too fast. If I but live, you'll rue it;
 My head's got many poems still in store.
I find fame fun the more I find I'm famous—
 The climb's ahead, my panting steeds won't stay.
Now Elegy owes *me* as much (she admits it)
 As epic owes to Virgil's noble lay.

We've answered Envy. Pull the reins in harder
 And on your proper circuit, poet, steer.
Well then, when you want bed and young men's business
 And night's appointed time is drawing near,
For fear of your girl's charms if you come brimming,
 With someone else you'd better have first go.

Find someone else in whom your first fresh pleasure
　　May spend itself; the next one will come slow.
Love delayed's best; in sunshine shade is welcome,
　　In thirst a drink, in cold the sun's warm glow.

Now this I blush to say. Choose a position
　　You think's least good, least charming for the act.
And that's not hard: girls face the stark truth rarely,
　　And think they never fail to charm in fact.
Then too make sure the windows are wide open;
　　Her parts thus in broad daylight you should eye.
As soon as passion's past the post and finished
　　And down exhausted brain and body lie,
And in disgust you wish you'd never touched a
　　Girl and think you'll not touch a girl for long,
Then make a note of each and every blemish
　　And fix your eyes on everything that's wrong.
Perhaps this may be called small stuff, and rightly,
　　But when things don't help singly, many may.
A bulky bull's a tiny viper's victim,
　　A small hound often brings a boar to bay.
Just fight with numbers; gather all my precepts
　　In one; from many a great pile will spring.
There are so many styles, so many postures,
　　I see no need to detail everything.
The sort of act that won't offend your feelings
　　Another well may judge a shameful sport.
The private parts displayed may shock some fellow
　　And in mid-purpose stop his passion short,
Or when a woman rises from love's business,
　　Stains on the bedclothes may his love abort.

If things like that upset you, you're just playing,
　　Your heart breathed on by torches barely warm.
Should that Boy strain the bow he bends more strongly,
　　You'll seek robuster help to heal the harm.

What if a man lurks while a girl's most private,
  And sees what decency forbids to see?
God forbid *I* should give advice of that sort;
  It might do good, but done it should not be.
I recommend you have a pair of girl-friends
  (For having more it takes a man who's braver);
Then each love saps the vigour of the other
  And to and fro the fissured feelings waver.
Great rivers are reduced by many channels;
  When fuel is dispersed the flame will die.
One anchor's not enough to hold a warship,
  One hook is not enough when water's high.
A man who's long arranged two consolations
  Has long stood victor on the heights above;
But you, whose folly trusted in one girl-friend,
  Must now at least procure another love.
Minos gave up Pasiphae for Procris,
  Idaea forced Phineus' first wife away,
Callirhoe made sure Alcmaeon's love for
  His dear Alphesiboea didn't stay.
Oenone all her life would have kept Paris
  But for that pretty Spartan paramour,
And Procne's beauty would have charmed King Tereus
  Had not her sister's beauty charmed him more.

But why waste time on instances that tire me?
  Old love's lost always when the new appears.
A mother mourns less for one son of many
  Than when she cries 'My only son!' in tears.
Don't think I'm framing you new rules to follow.
  (Would the idea were mine, with fame for me.)
Why, Agamemnon saw it. He commanded
  The whole of Greece, so what did he not see?
He loved Chryseis, conqueror loving captive;
  Her foolish father wept in false alarm.
Why tears, old killjoy? They're both doing nicely.
  Your tactless fuss just does your daughter harm.

When Calchas bade her be restored (Achilles
    Protecting him) and home again she came,
'There's one' said Atreus' son 'whose beauty matches,
    And save one syllable her name's the same.
Her, if he's wise, Achilles will hand over,
    Or else, well, he shall learn the power I've got.
If any of you Greeks impugns my action,
    My strong hand on the sceptre's worth a lot.
For if I'm king and no girl sleeps beside me,
    Then let Thersites sit upon my throne.'
He had her, ample solace for the first one,
    The new love thrusting in, the old love gone.
So take another flame like Agamemnon,
    And as the road forks let love split in two.
You ask where you can find one? Read my textbook;
    Your ship will soon be full of girls for you.

If my precepts have value, if Apollo
    Through me gives mortals any good advice,
Though you, poor chap, are scorching inside Etna,
    Beguile your girl, appear as cold as ice.
Pretend you're well, so she won't notice if you're
    Wretched; and laugh when you should want to weep.
(Not that I'd have you break off in mid-passion;
    My marching orders really aren't that steep.)
Feign what you're not; pretend the frenzy's finished;
    Thus what you've feigned and faked in fact you'll be.
To shun a drink I've often shammed I'm sleeping,
    And while I shammed, sleep won the victory.
A shamming lover, duped himself, I've laughed at—
    A fowler in his own decoy secured.
Love comes by habit, habit too unlearns it;
    If one can feign one's cured, one will be cured.
She's bid you come: come on the night appointed.
    You've come; the door is bolted; never mind.
Spare the shut door your insults or endearments,
    And don't place on the step your poor behind.

Tomorrow dawns. Don't make a fuss or grumble;
    Your face must show no sign that you're upset.
She'll drop her pride when she observes your coolness;
    That bonus too from my technique you'll get.
But fool yourself too. Set no date to finish
    Loving; a horse will often fight the rein.
Don't think about the prize: unthought you'll land it;
    A bird avoids a net that shows too plain.

Don't let her be too smug, don't let her scorn you.
    Take courage, courage makes her yield to you.
Her door is open? Pass it, though she calls you.
    She gives a date: doubt if that date will do.
It's easy to endure, if, when endurance
    Fails, one can get an easy girl straightway.
How could you call my precepts hard to handle?
    You see it's now a pander's part I play.
Hearts vary, so our techniques too we'll vary;
    For countless ailments there'll be countless cures.
A surgeon's blade will hardly heal some bodies,
    For many herbal treatment help ensures.
Your're soft, perhaps, can't leave, held fast in bondage,
    Foot on your neck, cruel Love stands over you.
Cease struggling. Use the wind and sail before it.
    And where the waves call let your oars go too.
You've got to slake that burning thirst that kills you.
    We grant leave: you may drink from mid-stream now.
But drink even more than heart and stomach crave for
    Until you're choking with the overflow.
Go on, enjoy your girl unchecked, untrammelled,
    Let her fill every night, fill every day.
Get glutted by the virus; glut means finish.
    Though you could do without her, you should stay
Till you're stuffed full and love succumbs to surfeit,
    The house offends, you're glad to get away.
Love also lingers long when mistrust feeds it.
    If you want love to cease, cease being afraid.

If you fear she's not yours and someone's filched her,
    Your cure's almost beyond Machaon's aid.
A mother of two sons loves most the soldier
    She fears may not return from his crusade.

Beside the Colline Gate there stands a temple,
    A venerable shrine in Venus' name.
There dwells Lethean Love, who heals the heartsick
    And quenches in cold water his fierce flame.
It's there forgetfulness young fellows pray for
    And any girl a heartless man has caught.
These words he spoke to me, if it was Cupid
    And not a dream—a dream in truth I thought:
'You who now cause, now cure, the pangs of passion,
    Ovid, to your instructions add one more.
If each man's mind's fixed on his woes, love's finished;
    Woes, more or less, for all God holds in store.
A man who dreads his quarterly repayments
    About the whole sum owed should agonize;
And he whose father's hard, though all else prospers,
    Must keep that hard old man before his eyes.
Another's living with a wife ill-dowered;
    Let him believe his spouse blocks his career.
On your estate you have a fertile vineyard,
    Fine grapes just swelling: scorching you should fear.
Your ship is homeward bound: brood on seas always
    Hostile, your wreckage littered on the shore.
A soldier son, a marriageable daughter—
    Worries! Who hasn't worries by the score?
Paris, upon your brothers' deaths you should have
    Pondered, so you could hate your paramour.'
Still speaking, from my sleep the boyish vision
    Vanished, if sleep it was. What shall I do?
Our ship's lost Palinurus in mid-ocean,
    And paths uncharted I must now pursue.

Shun lonely places, lovers. Lonely places
    Are harmful; in a crowd you're more secure.
You have no need of privacy; in private
    Obsessions grow, a crowd makes succour sure.

If you're alone, you'll mope. Your girl, abandoned,
　Before your eyes in flesh and blood will loom.
Thus night is sadder than the hours of sunshine,
　With no companions to relieve your gloom.
Don't keep your door shut, don't shun conversation,
　Nor in the dark your tearful self conceal.
Always have Pylades to help Orestes;
　Here too the worth of friendship will be real.
What but the lonely woods destroyed poor Phyllis?
　The cause of death is clear: no friend at hand.
With hair dishevelled, off she went, as in their
　Biennial rites streams out a Bacchic band.
Sometimes she gazed at the wide sea before her,
　Sometimes lay down exhausted on the sand.
To the unhearing waves she cried 'O faithless
　Demophoon'; sobs let her say no more.
There was a narrow path all overshadowed
　By which she often walked down to the shore.
The ninth time now, poor soul: 'On his head be it!'
　She said and at her sash, death-pale, she gazed,
Then at the boughs, in doubt and hardly daring,
　And to her throat in fear her fingers raised.
How sad you were alone just then, poor Phyllis!
　The woods would not have mourned, their leaves all gone.
So, girl-hurt men and men-hurt girls, take warning
　From Phyllis not to spend too long alone.

A young man once did all my Muse commanded,
　The haven of his safety now was nigh.
Then he relapsed—he'd met some eager lovers;
　Love took again the weapons he'd laid by.
If you're in love, and don't want love, shun contact;
　Contagion often injures cattle too.
Eyes that look close at wounds themselves are wounded;
　Infection also injury will do.
Not seldom water from a nearby river
　Will seep apace into a parching plot.
Love seeps unseen, if you're not quit of lovers;
　When love's the business we're a clever lot.

One man was cured already; contact doomed him:
  He met his girl and couldn't stand the strain.
My art had no success: the scar, unstable,
  Reopened, the old wound was back again.
To fight a fire next door's no easy matter;
  To leave the neighbourhood is safe and sound.
Don't stroll in the same colonnade as she does,
  Or cultivate the self-same social round.
What good is it when memories rekindle
  A cold heart? Better find a world that's new.
(When dinner's served, restraint's hard if you're hungry,
  And spouting water whets a huge thirst too.
It's hard to hold a bull who's seen a heifer,
  A charger whinnies when a mare's in view.)
That done, if you're at last to reach your haven,
  It's not enough to leave the girl. Goodbye
To sister, mother, nurse who knows her secrets,
  And all who share her life and company.
Don't let her slave come, or her maid with humble
  Greetings on her behalf and tears not true.
And don't ask what she's doing, though you long to;
  Stand firm! To hold your tongue will profit you.
You too who tell the world why your love ended
  And have so much against your girl to say,
Stop moaning! You'll best get revenge by silence;
  So from your longings she'll just fade away.
Better keep mum than say you've stopped. A man who
  Too often says he isn't *is* in love.
A fire's put out more surely by slow quenching
  Than quick: if you stop slowly, safe you'll prove.
A flash flood's deeper than a year-round river,
  But one is brief, the other always there.
Let love die by degrees and gently vanish,
  Dissolving without trace into thin air.
But it's a crime to hate your late-loved girl-friend;
  That bad way out it takes a brute to go.
Indifference is enough: who ends love hating,
  Loves still or finds it hard to end his woe.

When man and woman, lately linked, start fighting,
    That's bad: such cases make even lawyers frown.
Men accuse girls—yet love them: with no contest,
    No longer kept on call, away Love's flown.
I had a client once—wife in a litter;
    'Get out!' he cried, all set to have her bailed.
His threats were savage, every word just bristling;
    His wife got out, he saw the girl, words failed.
Hands fell, and from his hands the double tablets;
    'You win'—he's in her arms and she's prevailed.
A friendly separation's more becoming
    And safe: don't go from bed to litigate.
Tell her to keep your gifts without a lawsuit:
    Small losses are outweighed when gains are great.
But if some accident brings you together,
    Keep in your mind my weapons crystal clear.
Now you need weapons; here, brave heart, is battle;
    Your lance must overcome Penthesilea.
Recall her oaths forsworn, recall your rival,
    And that hard step where love was forced to lie.
Don't comb your hair because you're going to meet her,
    Don't wear your toga loose to catch her eye.
She's someone else's now, so take no trouble,
    To you just one of many passing by.

I'll tell you what particularly hinders
    Our efforts—each from his own case can see.
We hope we're loved: that's why we cease so slowly;
    Self-flatterers, a credulous lot are we.
And don't think words (for what is more deceptive?)
    Have weight or the eternal gods on high.
And be on guard that women's tears don't move you;
    Those eyes of theirs have been well trained to cry.
Unnumbered arts assail a lover's feelings
    As waves on every side pound rocks at sea.
Don't spell out why you want a separation,
    Or say what pains you; nurse it secretly.

Don't list her faults—she'll whitewash them. You'll weaken
  Your own good case and help to make hers strong.
Silence is strength: a man who piles reproaches
  On his girl-friend demands to be proved wrong.
I wouldn't dare steal arrows like Ulysses,
  Or seize the torch of Love and quench its glow,
Nor would I clip the Boy-god's gleaming pinions
  Or by my art unstring his sacred bow.
It's sound advice I sing, so heed the singer.
  Apollo, bless my strains, come, healing, here!
Apollo's here, lyre sounding, quiver rattling;
  I know him by his signs: Apollo's here.
Compare a fleece dyed in the vats of Sparta
  With Tyrian purple: ugly it will be.
Compare your girls too with the reigning beauties:
  You'll start to be ashamed of what you see.
To Paris either might have seemed a beauty,
  But, judged beside them, Venus won the day.
And not looks only; judge their minds and manners,
  So long as love won't lead the judge astray.

My next point's small, but many have found it useful,
  Small though it is, and I myself was one.
Take care you don't reread your charmer's letters;
  Rereading letters stirs a heart of stone.
Put them all on the flames (you'll hate to do it)
  And say 'This now shall be my passion's pyre.'
Althaea's brand burnt absent Meleager:
  Shall you fear giving false words to the fire?
Remove her portraits too. Why let wax faces
  Upset you? Thus Laodamia died.
And places often hurt, cause pain and sorrow;
  Avoid a place that knew you side by side.
'Here she was, here she lay; this was her bedroom.
  Here she gave me her joys night after night.'
Reminders rub love raw, the wound's reopened,
  Weak minds are hurt by lapses very slight.

If you touch embers, almost dead, with sulphur,
    They'll live, the tiniest fire immense will grow.
So, if you don't shun what rekindles passion,
    The flame, from nothing, fierce anew will glow.
Caphereus and the false fires lit for vengeance—
    The Greek ships must have wished they'd not sailed near.
When Scylla's passed the cautious sailor's happy;
    Beware, yourself, of places once too dear.
Make this your Syrtes, shun these Thunder Mountains;
    The sea she sucked Charybdis spews back here.

Some things there are no one can get to order,
    But, happening by chance, much good proceeds.
Ruin Phaedra's wealth—Neptune will spare his grandson,
    And Grandpa's bull won't terrify his steeds.
Make Minos' queen poor, she'd have loved more wisely:
    The luxury of love on riches feeds.
Why did no one court Hecale, no one Irus?
    Because he was a beggar, she was poor.
Poverty lacks the means to feed its passion,
    Though being poor's not worth all that for sure.
But well worthwhile you'll find not to indulge in
    The theatre till love's clean gone from you.
The flutes and lyres and zithers undermine one,
    The voices and the ballet-dancers too.
The dancers there are always playing lovers,
    The charms of what you shun the actor shows.
I speak against the grain: don't touch love-poets;
    For my gifts too—what sacrilege!—that goes.
Avoid Callimachus: he's no love-hater;
    Philetas too does harm and him you'll ban.
Sappho, I'm certain, groomed me for my girl-friend,
    Anacreon made me no puritan.
Who can have read unscathed Tibullus' poems,
    Or his whose theme was Cynthia alone?
Who could rise strict and stern from reading Gallus?
    Something like that's in poems of my own.

Unless Apollo, our patron, tricks his poet,
  The prime cause of our ills is rivalry.
Don't let yourself imagine any rival;
  Alone in her own bed believe she'll lie.
Orestes loved Hermione the keener,
  Because she had another by her side.
Why, Menelaus, moan? You went off wifeless
  To Crete, and dawdled there without your bride.
You didn't miss your wife till Paris took her;
  Another fellow's love made yours grow hot.
What riled Achilles when he lost Briseis
  Was just the pleasure Agamemnon got.
And riled with reason, take my word. He got it,
  And had he not, a shameful slug he'd be.
I would have done the same, and I'm no wiser:
  Of their fine feud the fairest fruit was she.
He swore upon his sceptre he'd not touched her,
  Deeming his sceptre was no deity.
May the Gods give you power to pass the door of
  Your former girl-friend, may your feet avail.
It's time to spur your horse into a gallop;
  Make up your mind, be brave, and you won't fail.
Imagine that's the lair of Lotus-eaters
  And Sirens: row now, row, and set full sail.
The fellow too whose rivalry once galled you
  I'd have you cease to think an enemy.
Though you still hate the man, at least don't cut him;
  As soon as you can kiss him, cured you'll be.

There's diet too; I'll end my doctor's duties
  By telling what to shun and what pursue.
All onions, whether native or imported
  From Africa or Greece much harm will do.
It's right no less to avoid salacious rocket
  And anything that may our love promote.
Much better to eat rue that sharpens eyesight
  And anything that is love's antidote.

You ask for my advice on wine and drinking?
   You'll get your quittance sooner than you'd think:
Wine leads the heart to love unless your senses
   Are sunk and stupefied by too much drink.
By wind a fire is fed, by wind extinguished;
   Light breezes fan the flames, gusts blow them out.
So either be blind drunk or stick to water;
   If you're halfway, you're doomed beyond a doubt.

My task is done; garland the weary vessel;
   I've reached the port for which I sailed so long.
You'll pay your vows anon to Apollo's poet,
   Cured now, both man and woman, by my song.

EXPLANATORY NOTES

The numeration follows that of the Latin text, which in the main is that of E. J. Kenney, with the readings of other editors occasionally preferred.

Details of mythological characters mentioned or alluded to more than once will as a rule be found at their first occurrence, which may be located by means of the Index.

AMORES

BOOK I

Preface

1 *five slim volumes*: issued separately at intervals and now collected in this reduced format. See Introd. p. xiii.

I

1 *in solemn metre*: hexameters, the metre of epic.

A tale of arms . . .: 'like the Aeneid', as is hinted by the words *arma* (the first word of this line and of Virgil's epic) and *bella* (*Aeneid* vii. 41, in the second proem), as also by the pattern of vowels in the first half of the verse, which echoes that of the corresponding half-line of the Aeneid. At ii. 1. 11–16 we learn the subject, a Gigantomachy. None of this is to be taken literally: see Introd. p. xiv.

4 *filched one foot away*: sc. from every other verse, to give a pentameter. See Introd. p. xiv.

5–16 Fanciful variations on a traditional idea, that the gods did not trespass on each other's provinces: e.g. *Metamorphoses* iii. 336–7 'since no god / Has right to undo what any god has done', xiv. 784–5.

7, 8 *Pallas*: Minerva (Athene).

10 *the warrior Virgin*: Diana (Artemis).

15 *Is all the world then yours?*: the answer, as the instructed reader would know, was Yes. In the most primitive form of his genealogy Eros was a mighty cosmic power (Hesiod, *Theogony* 120–2; Plato, *Symposium* 178b), and in his more familiar

mythological guise he was feared by all the gods, Zeus (Jupiter) included.

20 *No boy*: Catullus and Tibullus exploited the theme of (male) homosexual love, as it had been exploited by Callimachus and other Greek epigrammatists. Propertius ignored it, and Ovid explicitly rejected it at *Ars* ii. 683–4.

27 *So in six beats . . .*: so Coleridge, after Schiller: 'In the hexameter rises the fountain's silvery column; / In the pentameter aye falling in melody back.'

29 *myrtle of the sea*: myrtle was associated with Venus, who was born from the sea. Aphrodite: Greek *aphros* 'foam'.

2

1 *What can it be . . .*: false naïvety. The sleepless lover was a hackneyed theme.

23 *your mother's doves*: the dove was a type of amorous devotion (cf. ii. 6. 56) and a favourite lover's gift. In Sappho's famous ode (1 Lobel–Page) Aphrodite's chariot is drawn by sparrows (proverbial for lechery), but Apuleius, in his charming picture of Venus' aerial progress (*Metamorphoses* vi. 6) follows Ovid.

24 *Your stepfather*: Mars, Venus' lover and god of war, naturally an expert on the proper conduct of triumphs. Some take the reference to be to her husband Vulcan (Hephaestus), artificer-in-ordinary to Olympus; but Ovid elsewhere explicitly identifies Mars as Cupid's stepfather (ii. 9. 47–8, *Remedia* 27–8), and the joke is taken up by Apuleius (*Metamorphoses* v. 30. 1).

31-2 *Good Sense . . . Modesty*: *Mens Bona . . . Pudor*; Propertius in his rejection of Cynthia appeals to Mens Bona (iii. 23. 19), who had a temple at Rome, as did Pudicitia. Roman religion readily accommodated such personified abstractions.

34 *the triumph song*: the traditional cry *Io Triumphe*.

35 *Endearments, Madness, Wanderings*: *Blanditiae . . . Errorque Furorque*, the irrational counterparts to the prisoners of ll. 31–2.

47 *So Bacchus marked . . .*: Bacchus (Dionysus) was the other god who represented the power of unreason, but the comparison is also pictorial, for this is how he is figured in art: cf. i. 3. 11–12 n.

51 *your kinsman Caesar*: Augustus; his adoptive family, the *gens Iulia*, traced its descent from Iulus, son of Aeneas and grandson of Venus. Whether he relished this compliment if it came to his notice may be doubted. In view of the ruthlessness of his rise to power and the fact that the standing epithet of both Cupid and Venus in Latin poetry is *saeuus* 'cruel' (cf. e.g. i. 1. 5) it is tempting to suspect irony. Cf. i. 8. 41-2, ii. 16. 13, *Ars* i. 74 nn.

3

8 *from a knight*: cf. iii. 15. 3-6.

11-12 *his nine / Companions and the inventor of the vine*: the Muses and Bacchus, source of poetic inspiration.

15 *acrobat*: *desultor*; his act was to jump from one horse to another in mid-gallop.

17 *the Sisters*: the Fates (*Parcae*); Clotho held the distaff, Lachesis span the thread of life, Atropos—'the blind Fury with th' abhorred shears'—cut it.

19 *a happy subject*: *materies* 'matter', a technical and unpoetical word: see Introd. p. xv.

20 *verse . . . worthy of its source*: an allusion to what was evidently an influential verse of Gallus: see Introd. p. xv.

21-4 *Io . . . Leda . . . Europa*: all victims of Jupiter's lust and on the face of it not the most apposite of illustrations. Io was turned by Juno into a cow and pursued by a gadfly (*Metamorphoses* i. 568-749); Leda was bedded by Jupiter in the shape of a swan (ibid. vi. 109), Europa abducted by him in the a shape of a bull (ibid. ii. 836-75, vi. 103-7).

4

1 *Your husband*: *uir tuus*; the opening words, now that the literary preliminaries are completed and the compact between the poet and the (unnamed) girl signed and sealed, plunge us *in medias res*—the eternal triangle is in full swing. *uir* is ambiguous= both 'husband' and 'protector', 'lover'.

5 *will snuggle*: traditionally Roman women sat at table while their husbands reclined. Cicero (*Epistulae ad familiares* ix. 26. 2) thought a breach of this custom worth noting; in the beau monde of Augustan Rome it was clearly a dead letter, but it is

interesting to note that Apuleius describes a provincial worthy as still following it (*Metamorphoses* i. 22. 7). On the opportunities afforded by the dinner-table cf. *Ars* i. 229 ff.

8 *Hippodamia*: Pirithous, king of the Lapiths, invited the Centaurs (half men, half horses) to his wedding with Hippodamia (Hippodame). The ensuing battle royal was a favourite subject in Greek art; Ovid treated it at length and with every extravagance his fancy could devise at *Metamorphoses* xii. 210–535. This Hippodamia is distinct from the daughter of Oenomaus (iii. 2. 15–16 n.).

40 *I'll say 'they're mine'*: here and elsewhere in the context the phraseology has a legal flavour. Ovid makes a more extensive use of legal metaphor than any other Roman poet—oddly, in view of his expressed distaste for the official career.

52 *lace the brew*: by adding unmixed wine (*merum*). Wine was generally drunk diluted with water.

62 *To his cruel door*: a classic situation, to be duly exploited in i. 6.

5

1 *mid-time of the day*: when the gods were apt to be abroad and the prudent stayed indoors. Corinna's coming is treated as a divine epiphany; compare Catullus on Lesbia: 'My radiant goddess came to me there soft-footed' (68. 70). Cf. below, 4, 9 nn.

2 *upon a bed*: the Latin is *medio . . . toro* 'in the middle of the bed', with a play on *mediam . . . horam* 'middle hour (of the day)' in l. 1. It was the proper time for an assignation, but the cast was incomplete; cf. ii. 10. 17–18.

4 *such light*: compare the apparition of Apollo Lycius to the Argonauts 'at the moment when it is not quite light nor altogether dark' (Apollonius, *Argonautica* ii. 669–70).

9 *In came Corinna*: *ecce, Corinna uenit*; the suddenness of her appearance (*ecce*='lo!') suggests something superhuman. This is the first mention of her name: see Introd. p. xv.

10–11 *Lais . . . Semiramis*: a famous courtesan of Corinth and a legendary queen of Assyria. On the ambiguous status of the elegiac mistress see Introd. p. xvii, and cf. i. 4. 1 n. on *uir*.

23 *Why detail more?*: sensuous as all this is, it follows the rules of a classical *ecphrasis* (formal description) in proceeding systemati-

cally from the top downwards—the favoured direction, though the reverse occurs. Corinna is treated like a beautiful statue or picture displayed for the appraisal of the connoisseur (cf. i. 7. 13–18, 51–2 nn.). The breaking off of the enumeration before it is complete is also a deliberate stroke of art characteristic of such descriptions. Cf. l. 25 'And next—all know!' (*cetera quis nescit?*).

26 *Jove send me*: the Latin is *proueniant* 'may there be produced' (cf. *prouentus* 'crop', 'harvest'). These are the first-fruits of the deal struck in i. 3.

6

1 *Porter!*: the scene is instantly set; this is the vigil of the locked-out lover, a familiar theme in Greek and Latin literature. *you're chained*: the doorkeeper was usually a slave and was often chained to his post.

16 *You wield the bolt*: as in English, *fulmen*=both 'thunderbolt' and 'doorbolt'. The conceit is treated more elaborately at ii. 1. 15–20.

24 *The night is slipping by; unbolt the door*: a recurring refrain (ll. 32, 40, 48, 56). The device, not unusual in other genres, is found here for the first (and almost the only) time in elegy. Ovid's readers would be reminded of the refrains in the songs of the lovers in Theocritus' second Idyll and Virgil's eighth Eclogue.

26 *drink slaves' water*: Trimalchio, announcing his intention of freeing his slaves in his will, says 'soon they will taste the water of freedom' (Petronius, *Satyricon* 71. 1). Cf. 1 Kgs. 22: 27 'feed him with the bread of affliction, and with water of affliction'.

38 *garland*: worn by diners, drinkers, and revellers as 'the ancient equivalent of evening dress'. See below, 68 n.

47 *I'd love to wear those shackles*: an echo of the story of Aphrodite and Ares (Venus and Mars) as told in Homer and again, presently, by Ovid: see *Ars* ii. 561–90 and nn.

53 *Boreas . . . Orithyia*: the rape of Orithyia by the North Wind was a subject much favoured by Attic vase-painters; Ovid tells the story at *Metamorphoses* vi. 675–721.

57 *sword . . . flame*: violence was often threatened and sometimes employed on these occasions: see Horace's Ode i. 25 to Lydia

'The young men don't bang on your windows as much as they did . . .', and cf. the inventory of weapons dedicated by him at Odes iii. 26. 6-8. In the absence of street-lighting a torch would in any case be carried on moonless nights by the nocturnal passenger.

65 *on frosty axles*: like the Sun and the Dawn (i. 13. 2), the Morning Star (Lucifer) is imagined as driving a chariot.

68 *Let it lie*: the use of the garland as a lover's calling-card is a common theme.

7

4 *My mad hands hurt her*: violent treatment of a girl by her lover is a recurrent theme from Menander's comedy *Perikeiromene* (She who is shorn) onwards; the novelist Chariton takes the motif to extremes when he makes the plot of his book turn on a kick in the stomach delivered by the jealous Chaereas to his wife Callirhoe. At *Ars* ii. 167-76 the lover is expressly warned of the dangers of losing his temper. Here, however, Ovid shows how such a happening can be artistic grist to the poet's mill.

7-8 *Ajax . . . laid them low*: in his mad rage at not being awarded the arms of Achilles (*Metamorphoses* xiii. 1-398). The best-known version of the story was that in Sophocles' play *Ajax*.

9 *Orestes . . . sought a bow*: when pursued by the Furies for killing his mother Clytemnestra in revenge for her murder of his father Agamemnon. The detail of the bow is mentioned by Euripides in his play *Orestes* (268).

13-18 *Atalanta . . . Ariadne . . . Cassandra*: the pictorial quality of the comparisons suggest that by reducing the girl to this state Ovid has created a work of art: Ariadne in particular was a subject much favoured by painters. The reservation in Cassandra's case only serves to draw attention to the ploy. Cf. below, 52 n. On Atalanta see *Ars* ii. 185 n.

15 *False Theseus*: see *Ars* i. 525-64.

18 *In chaste Minerva's shrine*: where she had taken refuge from the victorious Greeks, being priestess of Athene. See *Ars* iii. 440 n.

30 *my loved one*: in the Latin *domina* 'mistress'; with legalistic wit Ovid exploits the ambiguity. To strike a fellow-citizen would have been bad enough; how much worse for a lover, traditionally figured as the slave of the beloved (cf. e.g. i. 3. 5

'one who . . . would slave for you') to raise his hand against his mistress.

31 *Diomede's crime*: he wounded Aphrodite (Venus) when she was fighting for the Trojans (Homer, *Iliad* v. 330 ff.).

32 *He first*: 'It was a widespread conviction in antiquity that all arts and artefacts must have been invented by somebody . . . In particular, imprecations on an inventor were a common theme' (R. G. M. Nisbet and Margaret Hubbard on Horace, *Odes* i. 3. 12). See *Ars* i. 101 n. on Romulus, and cf. further e.g. ii. 3. 3-4, ii. 11. 1-6, ii. 14. 5-6, al.

52 *Like marble*: now she reminds him of a statue—his creation again.

60 *It was my blood*: a hyperbolical variation on an old theme, that the souls of lovers migrate into the beloved. Cf. e.g. Plutarch's *Amatorius* (759d), where the saying is attributed, of all people, to Cato. Ovid exploits it in the stories of Narcissus (*Metamorphoses* iii. 473) and Ceyx and Alcyone (xi. 388). Cf. ii. 13. 15-16.

68 *put it back in place*: the sitting is over (13-18, 52 nn.) and the model may come off the throne, relax, and join in admiring the work of art—the poem—which she has helped to produce, exactly as agreed in i. 3.

8

3 *speaks for itself*: Dipsas='thirsty'. Cf. i. 15. 25-6, iii. 9. 4 nn.

5 *Circe*: the witch-goddess, daughter of the Sun and aunt of Medea.

7-8 *The flux . . . The whirling wheel*: love-charms. On hippomanes cf. Virgil, *Georgics* iii. 280-4 'Whereupon a clammy fluid, which herdsmen call / Correctly "hippomanes" [mares' madness], oozes from out their groin— / Hippomanes, by wicked stepmothers much sought after / And mixed with herbs and malignant cantrips to brew a spell' (tr. C. Day Lewis). The words *torto . . . rhombo* are commonly taken to refer to the magic wheel which the Greeks called *iynx*; but *rhombus* in Greek identifies a lozenge-shaped object which was whirled round on the end of a cord to produce a whirring noise, like the 'bull-roarer' of the Australian aborigines (so *Oxford Latin Dictionary* under *rhombus* 1). For a full description of the two instruments see A. S. F. Gow's commentary on Theocritus ii.

17, 30. Ovid's language is in fact ambiguous; and a reference to rotation would inevitably recall the *iynx* in Theocritus and the repeated refrain 'Magic wheel, bring that man to my house.'

13 *she flies*: as a screech-owl (*bubo* or *strix*); so Pamphile in Apuleius' novel (iii. 21. 6).

15 *double pupils*: Pliny reports that certain tribes who were credited with the evil eye were equipped in this manner (*Natural History* vii. 16-17).

19 *a marriage*: *thalamos . . . pudicos* 'chaste (marriage)-chambers'— chaste in a Pickwickian-elegiac sense. The poet-lover feels entitled to expect fidelity (at least in principle) from the girl even if she is married or otherwise the property of somebody else; cf. i. 4. 1 n. on *uir*.

29-30 *Mars . . . Venus*: an astrological variation on the philosophical opposition between Strife and Love as cosmic powers, familiar from Lucretius' sensuous tableau (*De Rerum Natura*, i. 31-40). Venus is now in a sign of the Zodiac which favours her influence, one of her 'houses' (see A. E. Housman, *Classical Papers* ed. J. Diggle and F. R. D. Goodyear, iii (1972), p. 909 n. 1.).

39 *Tatius . . . frumpish Sabines*: a traditional exemplar, cf. ii. 4. 15, iii. 8. 61, *Medicamina* 11 n. Titus Tatius was a legendary figure who became joint ruler of Rome with Romulus in the aftermath of the Rape of the Sabines (see *Ars* i. 101-32).

41-2 *Today . . . it's Venus' reign*: another variation of their opposition (above, 29-30 n.). 'Her son' is Aeneas, who did not in fact found Rome; it is tempting, given the reference to foreign conquests, to suspect an allusion to the pervasive identification of Aeneas with Augustus in the Aeneid. If so, Ovid was playing with fire: cf. i. 2. 51, *Ars* i. 60 nn.

45-6 *A matron . . . may be shed*: i.e. a forbidding frown may be a mask for wanton behaviour. The (rather odd) image is from shaking out the folds of a garment.

47-8 *Penelope . . . great horny bow*: not even the great archetype of marital chastity is exempt from Dipsas' (Ovid's) cynical and lascivious wit. The famous test of the stringing of Ulysses' bow (Homer, *Odyssey* xxi) was really an expedient for assessing the virility of the suitors.

59–60 *golden . . . gilded*: the point seems to be that the poet cannot claim divine precedent for his poverty; he ought to be doing better for himself.

64 *A whitened foot*: the feet of slaves exposed for sale were whitened with chalk.

65 *busts*: of ancestors, displayed in the atrium.

74 *Isis' day*: a recurrent cause of complaint by the elegiac lover; see ii. 13. 17–18, iii. 9. 33–4, iii. 10.

86 *a deaf divinity*: *Ars* i. 635 n.

100 *the Sacred Way*: the Via Sacra was the old road through the Forum to the Capitol; it contained goldsmiths' and jewellers' shops (cf. *Ars* ii. 266).

9

1 *Lovers are soldiers*: a common conceit, extensively exploited in i. 2 and ii. 12. Here it is stated and systematically developed in the manner of a rhetorical set-piece.

2 *Atticus*: not securely identified (Syme, 72). Only three of the *Amores* are addressed to contemporary individuals (ii. 10. 1, ii. 18. 3 nn.); Syme (6–7, 73–5) argues that none of these three poems can have been in the 'first edition'. It is noteworthy that the collection lacks a dedicatee: Introd. p. xiii f.

23 *Thracian Rhesus*: a Trojan ally; see *Ars* ii. 130, 135 nn.

33 *Briseis*: it was when she was taken from him by Agamemnon that Achilles withdrew from the war and 'sulked in his tent'.

36 *gave him his casque*: the parting of Hector and Andromache is one of the most celebrated and moving episodes of the Iliad (vi. 369–502); this detail is Ovid's addition (cf. *Heroides* xiii. 139–40).

37 *Cassandra*: allotted to Agamemnon as war-booty; cf. i. 7. 18 n.

39 *the blacksmith's meshes*: i. 6. 47 n.

10

1 *You were like . . .*: i.e. this was how I thought of you, vulnerable to abduction. Ovid can be seen playing with his readers' expectations. His *qualis . . qualis . . . qualis . . . talis* exactly reproduces the words of Propertius at the beginning of

his elegy i. 3, where the sleeping Cynthia is compared successively with Ariadne, Andromeda, and a Bacchante. However, when the apodosis to Ovid's comparisons is reached, the point turns out to be quite different: not, as in Propertius, how she looked, but how she behaved.

3 *Leda*: i. 3. 21–4 n.

5 *Amymone*: raped by Neptune.

7 *the bull, the eagle*: Jupiter's disguises when he carried off Europa (i. 3. 21–4 n.) and Ganymede (*Metamorphoses* x. 155–61) respectively.

15 *a naked boy*: so represented in art and literature, but the equation of nakedness with innocence appears to be Ovid's idea.

49–50 *Tarpeia*: she gave her name to the rock from which traitors were thrown. Her price for opening the gates of Rome to the Sabines was what they wore on their arms: instead of their bracelets (*armillae*) they piled their shields (*arma*) on her and crushed her. The story was told by Livy (i. 11) and Propertius (iv. 4).

52 *Alcamaeon's sword*: he killed his mother Eriphyle for sending his father Amphiaraus to his death in the expedition of the Seven against Thebes. She was bribed by Polynices with a golden necklace. Cf. *Ars* iii. 13 n.

56 *Alcinous*: king of the Phaeacians; the riches of his palace and orchard as described by Homer (*Odyssey* vii. 112–32) were proverbial.

11

14 *incised*: by the stylus. For ordinary correspondence and other day-to-day needs wax tablets were favoured, since the writing could be erased and the surface reused as often as required. Cf. i. 12. 27 n.

12

10 *notorious*: because bitter.

11 *to make you ruddy*: the wax was generally coloured black.

27 *double*: they were hinged together in book form with the written surfaces inwards.

13

1 *her ancient husband*: Tithonus; she obtained immortality for him but forgot to ask for eternal youth as well. Cf. the Sibyl, *Metamorphoses* xiv. 134-9.

3-4 *Your Memnon's / Birds*: her son Memnon was killed by Achilles before Troy. The legend here alluded to, that birds sprung from his ashes fought an annual battle over his grave on the anniversary of his death, seems to be peculiar to Ovid: see *Metamorphoses* xiii. 576-622.

30 *trip your steeds*: this is like *Metamorphoses* ii. 133, 167, where the chariot of the Sun is spoken of as having scored a track across the sky.

31 *was black*: his father Tithonus was Ethiopian.

36 *no tale . . . of greater shame*: 'She was one of the most predatory of goddesses; besides Tithonus and Cephalus she also carried off Orion (*Od.* 5. 121) and Cleitus (*Od.* 15.250)' (M. L. West on Hesiod, *Theogony* 986-91). By now Tithonus was incommunicado: 'When hateful old age oppressed him and he could no longer move . . . she put him in a room and shut the doors. There he babbles ceaselessly, and there is no strength in him any more' (*Homeric Hymn to Aphrodite* 233-8).

39 *Cephalus*: the story of his abduction by Aurora is told by Ovid at *Metamorphoses* vii. 700-13.

40 *Run slow, run slow, you steeds of night*: *lente currite, noctis equi*; quoted by Marlowe's Faustus as he awaits the summons to Hell.

43 *Endymion*: she put him to sleep for ever so that she could visit him whenever she wished.

46 *Made one night into two*: when in the guise of her husband Amphitryon he begat Heracles (Hercules) on Alcmene; the story is the subject of Plautus' play *Amphitruo*.

14

12 *when one peels the bark*: a curiously specific comparison for Ovid. The tree meant 'is probably our *Juniperus oxycedrus*: its bark separates in long strips . . . The colour meant is auburn' (Guy Lee *ad loc.*, on the authority of Mr Humphrey Gilbert-Carter). As Ovid had in fact been to the Troad on the then

equivalent of the Grand Tour, the detail may well stem from observation on the spot.

16 *was always safe*: cf. *Ars* iii. 239 n.

21 *like a Bacchante*: a pictorial image also exploited by Propertius (i. 10. 1 n.); both poets would have known the famous description of the sleeping Maenads in Euripides' *Bacchae* (683–6).

34 *the famous picture*: Apelles' celebrated painting of Aphrodite (Venus) Anadyomene, showing the goddess arising from her native ocean; the model was by some identified as the celebrated courtesan Phryne. The picture had been brought to Rome by Augustus and installed in the temple of Divus Julius (Caesar); by the time of Nero its condition had deteriorated badly and it was replaced with a copy (M. Robertson, *A history of Greek art* (Cambridge, 1975)), i. 493–4). Cf. *Ars* iii. 223–4, 401–2.

45 *captured tresses*: we may infer that blonde wigs were in demand among (predominantly dark) Roman women. Cf. *Ars* iii. 163–4.

49 *some Sygambrian*: the Sygambri had put up a particularly stiff resistance against Drusus in 12–11 BC (*Cambridge Ancient History²* (1952), 363).

55–6 *Make up your face . . . with home-grown hair*: she has duly provided the material for another poem, and there is no need for further histrionics; subject and poet can now relax. Cf. i. 7. 13–18, 51–2 nn.

15

1 *Devouring Envy*: cf. *Remedia* 389, where the same phrase (*Liuor edax*) recurs. Ovid's readers were intended to recall the dialogue between Envy (Phthonos) and Apollo in the second Hymn of Callimachus, which ends with the god dismissing him with a kick (107) before delivering his justification of the Callimachean poetics.

3–8 The elegiac poet-lover's traditional repudiation of military service and public life: Introd. p. xi. Ovid's model is the first Ode of Horace's first Book, in which however the list of rejected alternatives, the so-called 'priamel' (preamble), takes up almost the entire poem. Contrast the (tactical) volte-face at *Remedia* 151–210 (see n.).

9–30 It is instructive to analyse this list of poets singled out for
    approval by genre and language:

    Epic: Homer; Ennius, Varro of Atax, Virgil.
    Tragedy: Sophocles; Accius.
    Comedy: Menander.
    Didactic: Hesiod, Aratus; Lucretius, Virgil.
    Elegy: Callimachus; Gallus, Tibullus.
    Bucolic: Virgil.

Such lists generally excluded living writers; that would account, if
    this poem was written before 8 BC, for the omission of Horace
    and Propertius, who duly figure in the autobiographical *Tristia*
    iv. 10, which dates from Ovid's exile; on Propertius see
    further *Ars* iii. 333 n. Even so, it is surprising to find no
    mention of lyric poetry, whether monodic (Sappho, Alcaeus)
    or choral (Pindar); and one might have expected Catullus to
    figure, as he does at iii. 9. 62 (see n.) and iii. 15. 7, though not
    at *Ars* iii. 329 ff.

    Most of the poets actually mentioned are obvious candidates
for inclusion and require no special comment. Clearly the list
could not be exhaustive; in selecting *Sophocles* to represent
Greek tragedy Ovid may have been influenced by metrical
considerations as much as anything, since Eurīpǐdēs is intract-
able in dactylic verse. For the special pre-eminence claimed for
Callimachus cf. Introd. p. xiv. His polished artistry (*arte ualet*) is
contrasted with Ennius's lack of art (*arte carens*); this may pass
muster on a superficial view, but Ennius, though his verse
inevitably appears rough-hewn when compared with the high
finish of Augustan poetry, had in truth introduced Greek
standards and conceptions of technique to Italy and thereby
originated the literary tradition of which Ovid saw himself as a
representative (see A. S. Gratwick, 'Ennius the Hellenistic
poet', *Cambridge History of Classical Literature* i (1982) 66–75).
Aratus' reputation is apt to seem surprising to a modern reader,
but his astronomical and meteorological poem *Phaenomena*
(Appearances) was translated into Latin no fewer than four
times: by *Varro* of Atax (included in the catalogue for his
Argonautica (below, 21 n.)), Cicero, Germanicus, and Avienius.
Accius survives only in fragments; he is praised by Quintilian
(*Institutio Oratoria* x. 1. 97), in terms which recall Ovid's
verdict on Ennius, as unpolished but powerful (cf. below,
14 n.). It is significant that the list ends with *Gallus*, the first
Roman elegist and founder of the genre in which Ovid is
writing: see iii. 9. 64 n., Introd. p. xv. Compare the list (based
on a rather different premiss) at *Ars* iii. 329–48.

14 *art . . . genius*: the standard antithesis in ancient critical writing
between technique (*ars*) and innate ability (*ingenium*). Ovid
applies it in reverse to Ennius at *Tristia* ii. 424 'great in genius,
unformed (*rudis*) in art'.

16 *sun and moon*: i.e. so long as men were interested in astronomy.
In antiquity people, especially farmers and sailors, had good
practical reasons to watch the heavens.

21 *Varro*: of Atax, to be distinguished from Cicero's friend, the
polymath M. Terentius Varro. That Ovid, like Virgil, had
read him critically, emerges from an anecdote preserved by the
Elder Seneca in his *Controversiae* (vii. 1. 27): of Varro's
successful rendering of Apollonius, *Argonautica* iii. 749–50
Ovid is supposed to have remarked that it would have been
improved if the line *omnia noctis erant placida composta quiete* 'all
things were at rest in the peaceful calm of night' had ended at
erant, giving the sense 'all things were night's'.

26 *As long as Rome's the conquered globe's great head*: this echoes both
Virgil's prophecy of immortality for the Aeneid (ix. 446–9)
and Horace's claim that he will survive through his poetry 'so
long as the pontiff shall ascend the Capitol with the silent
Vestal' (*Odes* iii. 30. 8–9). Such allusions lend authority to
Ovid's own claim to poetical immortality. In the word 'head'
there is an allusion to the tradition that the Capitol was so
called because a human skull (*caput*) had been found there and
interpreted as an omen of world domination (Livy i. 55. 6, v.
54. 7). On this and other etymological plays in the *Amores* see
McKeown, i. 45 ff. and cf. iii. 9. 4 n.

30 *Lycoris*: her real name was Cytheris and she was an actress; as
usual with such pseudonyms her poetic name was metrically
equivalent to her real one. She was associated with Gallus by
Virgil in the tenth Eclogue: 'I have a song for Gallus—short,
but such as Lycoris herself may read' (2–3); and the Qaṣr
Ibrîm fragments (Introd. p. xii) include a reference to her
'delinquency', *nequitia*, the word used by Ovid of his own
elegies in the introductory poems of Books II and III (ii. 1. 2,
iii. 1. 17).

34 *Tagus*: the Tejo in Spain, famous for its gold.

36 *Castalian spring*: a fountain on Mt Parnassus at Delphi, seat
of Apollo's chief oracle.

37 *myrtle*: i. 1. 29 n.

42 *Shall still survive*: *uiuam*, the last word of the much more elaborate coda of the *Metamorphoses* (xv. 871–9). The affirmation is taken up again in the final couplet of the *Amores* (iii. 15. 20).

BOOK II

I

1 *stream-fed Sulmo*: cf. ii. 16. 1–2. More than once in his exile in the barren and featureless Dobruja Ovid refers wistfully to the waters of his native countryside.

2 *my naughtiness*: *nequitiae . . . meae*; cf. i. 15. 30 n.

3 *Prudes, keep off*: *procul hinc, procul este, seueri*; a disrespectful parody of the words of Virgil's Sibyl, *procul, o procul este, profani* (*Aeneid* vi. 258) and, lurking behind them, Callimachus' warning in his Hymn to Apollo (2. 2). In this context, however, the underlying allusion is rather to Horace's injunction as poet-priest (*Musarum sacerdos*) to the common herd to keep its distance as he inaugurates the third book of his Odes: *odi profanum uulgus et arceo*. Horace wrote for girls and boys, *uirginibus puerisque*, Ovid for grown-ups—who, however, include susceptible girls, *non frigida uirgo* (5). Cf. i. 15. 3–8, iii. 8. 23–4 nn.

11–12 *Heaven's wars . . . Giants*: the rebellion of the Giants was by Ovid's time a hackneyed theme and taboo to Callimachean sensibilities, and it is not to be imagined that he had actually embarked on any such poem. Cf. i. 1. 1 n. and Introd. p. xiv.

13 *Earth's fell revenge*: the poets commonly confused or conflated the three generations of the children of Ge or Gaia (Earth) by Uranus (Heaven). (i) The three hundred-handed monsters Gyges or Gyes, Cottys, and Briareus, punished for their insolent behaviour by being buried. Earth then incited (ii) the Titans to rebel against their father. (This, properly speaking, was her 'fell revenge'.) The senior Titan Cronus castrated Uranus; the blood from his severed genitals fell on the Earth and engendered (iii) the Giants. They attempted to dethrone Zeus (Jupiter), who had meanwhile deposed his father Cronus, piling Ossa on Olympus and Pelion on Ossa in their assault on heaven. Cf. *Metamorphoses* i. 151–62.

20 *a stronger bolt*: i. 6. 16 n.

23 *Verses*: Ovid plays on two senses of *carmen*, 'poem' and 'magic spell'. Cf. i. 8. 9–18.

29–32 Heroic subject-matter gets the elegiac poet-lover nowhere. The point had been previously developed by Propertius (i. 7, 9); Ovid exploits it by identifying girl and subject (cf. i. 3. 19 n.). She comes 'in person, Herself the payment' in a double sense.

30 *either son of Atreus*: Agamemnon and Menelaus.

31 *he who spent . . . wandering*: Ulysses (Odysseus).

32 *dragged along*: behind Achilles' chariot.

2

1 *Bagoas*: a common name for eunuchs, being the Persian word for the thing (Pliny, *Natural History* xiii. 41).

4 *Danaids*: this was the portico of the temple of Apollo on the Palatine, built by Augustus and dedicated in 28 BC; it was decorated with statues of Danaus and his fifty daughters. It is recommended, with other porticoes, as a lovers' hunting-ground at *Ars*. i. 73–4 (see n.).

23–4 *She comes back late . . .*: it is unlikely that these lines are Ovid's.

25 *in Isis' temple*: another favoured spot for pick-ups and assignations (*Ars* i. 77–8, iii. 393–4, 635–6). Cf. ii. 13. 7–8 n.

44 *Tantalus*: he was punished for divulging the secrets of the gods by being immersed in a pool of water which receded when he tried to drink, under a tree which withdrew when he tried to eat its fruits. Cf. iii. 7. 45–6.

45 *Io*: i. 3. 21–4 n. Juno set the hundred-eyed Argus to guard her after her metamorphosis; Mercury lulled him to sleep and killed him at Jupiter's orders (*Metamorphoses* i. 667–723). Cf. ii. 6. 55 n., iii. 4. 19–20.

3

3 *He who was first . . .*: i. 7. 32 n.

4

15 *the rigid Sabines*: i. 8. 39 n.

19 *Callimachus*: i. 15. 9–30, 14 nn.

32 *Hippolytus*: a type of chastity; he was devoted to the service of the virgin huntress Artemis (Diana). See ii. 18. 24, *Ars* i. 338 n.

42 *Leda*: i. 3. 21–4 n. This is quintessential Ovid. Traditionally the women of the mythical and heroic past were fair; he makes Leda a brunette for pictorial effect and for the contrast with Aurora. Cf. *Ars* iii. 189–91 n.

5

30 *My legal claim*: i. 4. 40 n.

35 *Tithonus' wife*: i. 13. 1 n.

40 *a Lydian woman*: this is borrowed from a famous Homeric simile, in which the comparison is with blood welling from a wound in Menelaus' thigh (*Iliad* iv. 141–7); the comparison with a blush is borrowed from Virgil's description of Lavinia (*Aeneid* xii. 64–9), itself indebted to the same passage of Homer.

41 *or one or other*: another reminder that the poet, having created this tableau, is at liberty to retouch it as he sees fit; cf. i. 7. 13–18, 52 nn.

6

Epitaphs on pets in the Greek Anthology include several on birds (see A. S. F. Gow and D. L. Page, *The Greek Anthology. Hellenistic Epigrams*, Cambridge 1965, i. 90–1). In Latin the most famous example is Catullus' much-discussed lament over Lesbia's *passer* (Poem 2). Ovid's poem is a full-dress parody of a formal dirge or epicedion. Cf. iii. 9 headn.

7–10 *Tereus . . . Philomela . . . Itys*: Tereus, king of Thrace, raped his sister-in-law Philomela and cut out her tongue out to silence her. In revenge her sister Procne killed Itys, her own son by Tereus, and served up his flesh to his father at dinner. All three were changed into birds: Tereus into a hoopoe, Procne into a swallow, and Philomela into a nightingale. The story is told by Ovid at length at *Metamorphoses* vi. 412–674.

15 *Pylades . . . Orestes*: proverbial for friendship. It was Pylades who nerved Orestes to murder his mother (i. 7. 9 n.) and accompanied him on the expiatory quest for the statue of the Tauric Artemis which is the subject of Euripides' tragedy *Iphigenia in Tauris* and Gluck's opera *Iphigénie en Tauride*.

35 *Minerva's pet aversion*: Minerva (Athene) punished her for tale-bearing (*Metamorphoses* ii. 547–65).

41 *Thersites*: an ugly trouble-maker, beaten by Odysseus (Ulysses) for his loud-mouthed presumption (Homer, *Iliad* ii. 211–77). *Protesilaus*: the first Greek ashore at Troy, killed as he landed.

54 *Phoenix*: its miraculously repeated death and rebirth are described by Ovid at *Metamorphoses* xv. 392–407. Its appearances in Elysium must by definition be both infrequent and intermittent.

55 *Juno's peacock*: cf. *Ars* i. 627. She embellished its tail with the hundred eyes of the murdered Argus (ii. 2. 45 n.).

7

3 *in the gods*: iii. 2. 3 n.

17 *Cypassis*: 'Kilty' (A. G. Lee). The *kypassis* was a short-skirted garment worn by Greeks, both men and women. In this case Ovid had no need of stratagems (iii. 2. 25–6) to get a sight of her legs. Cf. *Ars* i. 31–2 n.

8

14 *shall I think wrong for me?*: the idea and the illustrations are lifted from Horace, *Odes* ii. 4. 1–12. The allusion ironically under-pins the message: 'need I remind you that we have it on no less an authority than that of Horace . . .?'; cf. ii. 9. 19–22 n. Cassandra has been exploited before (i. 7. 13–18 and nn.).

20 *Waft that white lie*: *Ars* i. 635 n.

9a

1 *Cupid . . . indignation*: text and meaning of this verse are uncertain.

7 *Telephus*: he was told by an oracle that his wound could be cured only by the giver of it. Achilles healed it with rust from his spear. Cf. *Remedia* 47–8.

18 *a huddle of thatched huts*: in 1948 the remains of three huts of the Iron Age (8th century BC) were discovered on the Palatine, dating from the earliest settlement on the site. The so-called cottage of Romulus (*casa Romuli*) was still to be seen on the Palatine in Ovid's day: see Frazer's commentary on Ovid, *Fasti* i. 199. The Augustan poets liked to contrast Rome's contemporary splendour with her rural origins; Ovid's readers would have remembered Evander's guided tour of Aeneas over the future site of the City (Virgil, *Aeneid* viii. 337–69). In

due time the wheel came full circle and cattle once more lowed in the Forum, now the Campo Vaccino. Cf. *Ars* i. 103−8, iii. 113−20.

19−22 These comparisons are adapted from Propertius (ii. 25. 5−8) and were to be re-adapted by Ovid himself with bitter irony in his exile (*Tristia* iv. 8. 17−24).

22 *wooden foils*: the *rudis*, traditionally presented to a gladiator on retirement.

9b

48 *Stepfather*: i. 2. 24 n.

10

1 *Graecinus*: C. Pomponius Graecinus, a distinguished figure, later consul: Syme, 74−5.

11

1 *first taught*: 1. 7. 32 n. That the invention of seafaring represented an impious encroachment on the natural order was a poetic commonplace. In beginning his send-off to Corinna with such sentiments Ovid was taking a leaf from Horace's book. In *Odes* i. 3 Horace combines, as Ovid does here, two poetical types, the *propempticon* or formal send-off, and the stock diatribe against inventiveness: cf. especially ll. 9 ff. 'He had a heart sheathed in oak and triple brass, who first launched a fragile ship on the rough sea . . .'. Ovid also alludes in these opening lines to the beginnings of Catullus' *Peleus and Thetis* (64) and Euripides' *Medea*, the latter doubly familiar to Roman readers from Ennius' adaptation. All this imparts authority to his (self-interested) denunciation of sea-travel.

3 *clashing cliffs*: the Symplegades, rocks which snapped shut on passing ships. The alliteration reproduces the *concurrentes . . . cautes* of the Latin.

10 *the balmy south, the icy north*: et gelidum Borean egelidumque Notum. This is one of the three verses that were the subject of an anecdote told by the elder Seneca (*Controversiae* ii. 2. 12): Ovid allowed his friends to choose any three verses for removal from his poems, provided that he might stipulate for the retention of any three chosen by him. The two lists were identical. Seneca identified two of the lines, this one and *Ars* ii. 24 *semibouemque uirum semiuirumque bouem*; a possible candidate

for the third place is iii. 4. 40 *Romulus Iliades Iliadesque Remus*.
Ovid is supposed to have been fond of the saying that a face is
more attractive if it has some blemish on it (Seneca, ibid.); cf.
iii. 1. 10 n.

12 *unjust*: because it does not differentiate between the deserving
and the undeserving.

18 *Scylla . . . Charybdis*: the twin hazards of the straits of Messina:
'Scylla infests the right-hand coast, the left / Restless
Charybdis; one grasps passing ships / And sucks them down
to spew them up again; / The other's ringed below her hell-
black waist / With raging dogs' (*Met.* xiii. 730–3, a summary
of Homer, *Odyssey* xii. 73–126). Cf. ii. 16. 23–6.

19–20 *the Thunder Mountains*: Ceraunia in Epirus.
Syrtes: sandbanks off the coast of North Africa.

27 *Triton*: a seagod, son of Poseidon (Neptune) and Amphitrite,
who raised or abated storms by blowing his horn.

29 *the sons of Leda*: the Dioscuri, Castor and Pollux, invoked by
Horace at *Odes* i. 3. 2 (cf. above, 1 n.). They were sometimes
identified with the constellation Gemini (the Twins), but the
reference here is more probably to St Elmo's Fire 'a dull blue
glare . . . that appears on the masts and rigging of ships . . .
associated with the Dioscuri and regarded as a propitious
omen during a storm' (Nisbet and Hubbard, *A commentary on
Horace: Odes Book 1*, Oxford 1970, ad loc., qq. v.).

36 *their father*: Nereus.

44 *my goddess*: literally 'my gods', *nostros . . . deos*; a reference to
the Lares and Penates? or to the ship's figurehead?

56 *his steeds*: i. 6. 65 n.

12

10 *Atreus' son*: Agamemnon, supreme commander of the Greeks.

19 *A woman*: 1. 4. 7 n.

21 *A woman*: Lavinia, daughter of Latinus, who promised her to
Aeneas, overruling the claims of Turnus.

23 *The women*: the Sabines, carried off at the instigation of
Romulus (see *Ars* i. 101–32 n.). The reference here is to the
subsequent war, resolved by the dramatic mediation of the
(now Roman) wives and mothers: Livy i. 13. 1–6, Ovid, *Fasti*
iii. 201–28.

13

2 *Corinna lies*: the words of the Latin pick up those of the same
line of the preceding elegy, with the name of Corinna
occupying the same place in the verse. The responsibility
tentatively claimed by Ovid for Corinna's condition in line 5
below is thus implied here to be directly attributable to the
conquest triumphantly celebrated in poem 12. Irony is clearly
at work—but who or what is the target? The theme of poems
13 and 14, abortion, is alien to the carefully circumscribed
fantasy world of Roman elegy and strikes a note of unexampled
realism. Unwanted pregnancies must have been a recurrent
hazard of the Roman demi-monde, and abortion was widely
practised in all classes of society; but the subject—unlike, for
instance, death, so prominent a topic in the elegies of
Propertius—resists either humorous treatment or romantic-
ization. The unfeeling tone of both poems and the abrupt
transitions of mood from 12 to 13 and again from 14 to the
lascivious daydreaming of 15 suggest that Ovid's intention
was satirical. The placing of the two poems and the sly allusion
in this verse back to the extravagantly macho poem 12 point to
an ironical presentation of a typically masculine attitude. To
take the poems at face value entails attributing to Ovid, not
only a lapse of taste, not in itself an unthinkable contingency,
but also a breach of *literary* propriety.

7-8 *Isis*: she was especially worshipped by women: cf. ii. 2. 25 n.
Paraetonium, Memphis, Pharos, Canopus: such lists are common
in prayers and invocations. Ovid is more concerned with the
sound and general effect of the names than with their specific
associations. Compare *Met*. ix. 684-94, where the dog-headed
Anubis, the bull-god Apis, and Isis' husband Osiris are
similarly listed.

11 *sistrums*: the sistrum was a metal rattle, a prominent feature of
the cult.

15 *on her—and me*: i. 7. 60 n.

17 *She's often sat . . .*: i. 8. 74 n.

18 *Where the priests wet your laurel's greenery*: sc. with their blood,
as they gash themselves in frenzy; but text and interpretation
are uncertain.

21 *Ilithyia*: (Greek) goddess of childbirth; Ovid's words (*laborantes
utero*) echo those of Horace's Ode to Diana (iii. 22. 2) and thus

allusively imply the common identification of Ilithyia with
Artemis (Diana).

14

5 *She who first . . .*: i. 7. 32 n.

8 *the tragic sand*: cf. *Ars* i. 164; her rash action is compared
allusively (and rather oddly) to a gladiatorial combat.

11 *someone for throwing*: another Deucalion and Pyrrha. They were
the sole survivors of the Great Flood and repopulated the earth
in obedience to the oracle of Themis by throwing stones over
their shoulders, which turned into people (*Met.* i. 313–415).

14 *her womb's due weight*: Achilles; see ii. 17. 17 n.

15 *her twin freight*: Romulus and Remus; iii. 6. 45–82 n.

18 *without its Caesars*: cf. i. 2. 51 n.

29 *Medea*: she murdered her children by Jason in revenge for his
supplanting her by Iole; cf. *Ars* i. 336, iii. 33–4, *Remedia* 59–60;
Heroides 12.

30 *Itys*: ii. 6. 7–10 n.

35 *No tigress in Armenian dens*: a good example of Ovid's way with
his models. Armenian tigers first figure in Virgil's *Eclogues* (5.
29), but in making them a type of savagery as he does here and
at *Met.* xv. 86 Ovid was thinking of Dido's tirade against
Aeneas as 'suckled by Hyrcanian tigresses' (*Aeneid* iv. 367),
which he later improved in Scylla's outcry against Minos,
whom she accuses of being the offspring of, variously, the
Syrtes, an Armenian tigress, or Charybdis (*Met.* viii. 120–1).
In point of fact tigresses and lionesses may in certain
circumstances kill and eat their cubs; but rhetorical appeals
of this sort are free of the constraints of scientific fact.
Compare Juvenal's excursus on (the absence of) intra-specific
aggression among animals in his denunciation of cannibalism
(15. 159–64).

15

10 *Circe*: i. 8. 5 n. She is called *Aeaea*, as in Homer, after the island
on which she lived (*Odyssey* ix. 31–2, x. 135–6). *Proteus*: a sea-
god who could change his shape at will; hence 'protean'. Ovid
calls him *Carpathius senex* 'the old man of Carpathus', an echo
of the words with which Virgil had introduced him into the

story of Aristaeus in the *Georgics*, where Virgil's phrase *Neptuni . . . uates* 'prophet of Neptune' (iv. 387) in turn refers back to Homer's description of him as 'servant of Poseidon' (*Odyssey* iv. 386). Thus in a single phrase Ovid recalls (for the alert reader) both Proteus' most notable appearances in earlier poetry.

16

1 *I'm at Sulmo*: this elegy is an especially interesting exercise in the recombination of themes from earlier poetry. Its basic motif is central to love-elegy: separation from the beloved (cf. i. 6. 11–12, 13, ii. 2–3, 11, 15, iii. 4, 6, 10). By situating himself in the country and the girl (presumably) in Rome Ovid reverses a scenario exploited by Propertius at i. 11 (Cynthia at Baiae) and ii. 19 (Cynthia in the depths of the countryside). However, the theme of the withdrawal of the lover himself to a remote spot had also been used memorably by Propertius, who had taken it from Callimachus' Acontius (Prop. i. 17, 18). Further, Ovid's idealizing portrayal of his native countryside recalls both Horace's reiterated praise of country life and (more particularly in the elegiac situation) Tibullus' wistful visions of the country as the imagined scene of his happiness with Delia. A traditionally Roman image of rural beauty and virtuous contentment is thus implictly contrasted with the danger and indeed immorality (ii. 11. 1 n.) of travel. On Sulmo see ii. 1. 1 n.; it was one of the three districts into which the Paelignian territory was divided.

13 *between Castor and Pollux*: as a star (cf. ii. 11. 29 n.), like e.g. Ariadne (*Ars* i. 557–8), a traditional divine reward; but with a reference also to the banquets of the gods. Cf. Horace, *Odes* iii. 3. 9–12, where Augustus is pictured as drinking nectar between Pollux and Hercules, all three having earned this privilege by heroic achievement. Ovid's rejection of such preferment verges on imprudence: i. 2. 51 n.

16 *those who scored*: i. 7. 32 n.

23–6 *Scylla . . . Charybdis*: ii. 11. 18 n.

24 *Cape Malea*: the south-east extremity of the Peloponnese, a notorious hazard.

31 *Leander . . . Hero*: Hero was priestess of Aphrodite (Venus) at Sestos, on the other side of the Hellespont from Abydos, the home of her lover Leander. He swam across the straits to her

every night, guided by a lamp on the tower in which she lived, until in a great storm the lamp went out and he drowned. Hero, seeing his body washed up on the rocks under the tower, threw herself down to her death. The story is treated briefly and allusively by Virgil (*Georgics* iii. 258–63), more extensively by Ovid in *Heroides* 18 and 19, by the late Greek poet Musaeus (fifth century AD), and by Christopher Marlowe. In 1982 there was published a fragment of papyrus containing some fifty mutilated verses from what in all probability was the Hellenistic poem in which the story came to the attention of the Augustan poets (*Supplementum Hellenisticum*, ed. Lloyd-Jones and Parsons, 1983, 901A). Byron's well-known comment will bear repetition: 'This morning I *swam* from *Sestos* to *Abydos*. The immediate distance is not above a mile, but the current renders it hazardous;—so much so that I doubt whether Leander's conjugal affection must not have been a little chilled in his passage to Paradise' (letter to Henry Drury, 3 May 1810).

39 *woad-blue*: the Britons' habit of painting themselves with woad had been noted by Caesar (*Bellum Gallicum* v. 14. 3).

40 *the wild rocks*: for stealing fire from Olympus for the benefit of mankind Prometheus was chained to a rock in the Caucasus and tormented by an eagle which came daily to gnaw his liver.

41 *Elms . . . vines*: vines were commonly trained on elms; the poets elevated the association into an image of conjugal devotion.

49 *your trap and lightfoot ponies*: such a turn-out was 'fast' in every sense. Ovid's words (*esseda, manni*) pick up those of similar references by Propertius to Cynthia's comings and goings: ii. 1. 76 (almost immediately following a reference to Prometheus' crag), ii. 32. 5, iv. 8. 15.

17

4 *Paphos and Cythera*: important centres of the cult of Venus; the island of Cythera was her birthplace.

15 *a mortal*: Ulysses (Odysseus); cf. *Ars* ii. 123–42 and n.

17 *Thetis . . . Peleus*: the most celebrated of all such unions, familiar to Roman readers from Catullus' epyllion *Peleus and Thetis* (64).

18 *Egeria with Numa*: Numa Pompilius was the second of the legendary kings of Rome, the nymph Egeria his 'consort and

counsel', *coniunx consiliumque* (Ovid, *Fasti* iii. 276); instructed by her he introduced religious observance and peaceful government to Rome.

19 *Venus . . . Vulcan*: a different sort of inequality and perhaps not the happiest of illustrations (i. 6. 47 n., *Ars* ii. 567–90); it prepares for the metrical conceit that follows.

20 *he limps*: as a result of his fall when Zeus (Jupiter) threw him out of heaven in an Olympian family row (Homer, *Iliad* i. 590–4): 'from Morn / To Noon he fell, from Noon to dewy Eve, / A Summers day; and with the setting Sun / Dropt from the Zenith like a falling Star, / On *Lemnos* th' *Aegean* Ile' (Milton, *P.L.* i. 742–6).

22 *couples . . . perfectly*: the poet is now (at least for the time being) reconciled to the metre, and with it the subject matter, that he had initially rejected: cf. i. 1. 4 n. As in English 'couples', so in Latin *iungitur* 'is joined' is equally appropriate to sexual connection.

29 *There's one I know . . .*: see Introd. p. xvi.

32 *Eurotas*: in Sparta.
   Eridanus: the Po.

18

1 *your poem*: evidently an epic in which the story of the Trojan War was brought down to the point where the *Iliad* takes it up; cf. *Letters from Pontus* ii. 10. 13 'You sing of all that Homer left untreated'.

3 *Macer*: Pompeius Macer, made procurator of Asia by Augustus. He was related to Ovid's wife. See Syme, 73.

4 *the fine themes*: epic of some sort, presumably the Giganto-machia referred to earlier (i. 1. 1, ii. 1. 11–12 nn.); cf. below, 18 n.

13 *the sceptre*: tragedy traditionally dealt with kings and heroes.

18 *Love has triumphed*: in iii. 1 the poet is given leave to postpone or intermit* his tragedy until his elegies are finished, and at iii. 15. 15–20 he duly announces that ·work on it is now to

---

* Nothing in iii. 1 indicates or implies that the poet had actually begun a tragedy. However, whatever the dates of composition of ii. 18 and iii. 1, their placing in the second, definitive edition of the *Amores* entitles the reader to infer that iii. 1 develops ii. 18.

(re)start. If this refers to his lost *Medea*, it implies that it was composed *pari* (or *impari*) *passu* with the *Amores*, but as with the almost certainly non-existent Gigantomachy, it is hazardous to take these references literally. The *Heroides* (below, 21–6 n.) are of course real enough.

19 *the art of loving*: the phrase *artes . . . Amoris* may refer to the *Amores* or the *Ars* or indeed both. If it refers to the *Ars*, then Ovid had produced at least the first two books of that poem by the time this elegy was written. But here too firm inferences as to chronology are hazardous.

21–6 *love-letters*: the *Heroides* or *Epistulae Heroidum* 'Letters of Heroines', appeals of deserted women to husbands or lovers. Those mentioned here are (the numeration is that of modern editions) Penelope to Ulysses (1), Phyllis to Demophoon (2), Oenone to Paris (5), Canace to Macareus (11), Hypsipyle to Jason (6), Ariadne to Theseus (10), Phaedra to Hippolytus (4), Dido to Aeneas (7), and Sappho to Phaon (15; but see below, 26 n.). This leaves six of the extant 'single' letters unmentioned. The easy inference is that those listed here were all that were written when this elegy was composed; but one is not bound to suppose that. Ovid may have selected more or less arbitrarily, including of course all those that had taken Sabinus' fancy.

26 *the loving Lesbian lyrist*: the extant epistle of Sappho to Phaon, placed between those of Hypermestra (14) and Paris (16) by editors since 1629, is transmitted separately from the rest and Ovidian authorship is ruled out by conclusive stylistic arguments. It has evidently supplanted a genuine epistle on the same subject.

27 *from the world's ends*: his replies purport to come from the various recipients, who are scattered all over the Greek world. *Sabinus*: he is mentioned by Ovid at *Letters from Pontus* iv. 16. 13–16 as the author of an epic and a calendar poem. His answers have not survived (those purporting to be by him in old editions are fictitious), but it is tempting to speculate that he gave Ovid the idea for his later series of paired epistles (16–21), Paris answered by Helen, Leander by Hero, Acontius by Cydippe.

37 *guilty*: not just of adultery but of causing the Trojan War.

38 *Laodamia*: wife of Protesilaus (ii. 6. 41 n.); see *Ars* iii. 18 n.

19

9 *Corinna*: see Introd. p. xv f.

25 *fed too richly*: here and at l. 32 (see n.) we may detect an undercurrent of literary allusion, the poet at play with Callimachean poetics. The word used is *pinguis* 'fat': applied in this context to what is repudiated as common and accessible it recalls Apollo's famous admonition to Callimachus in the prologue to the *Aetia* to 'feed the victim as fat as you can, but keep the Muse slender', a conceit taken up by Virgil in the Sixth *Eclogue*, *pastorem*, *Tityre*, *pinguis / pascere oportet oues*, *deductum dicere carmen* (4-5).

27 *Danae*: an oracle had declared that she would bear a son who would kill her father. Acrisius therefore imprisoned her in a brazen tower, but Jupiter made his way to her in the form of a shower of gold, and she became the mother of Perseus; cf. iii. 4. 21-2, iii. 8. 29-34, *Ars* iii. 415-16. The myth was easily interpreted as an image of bribery: see e.g. Horace, *Odes* iii. 16. 1-16.

29 *Io*: i. 3. 21-4, ii. 2. 45 nn.

32 *Drink from a river*: taken in conjunction with l. 25 (see n.) this too recalls Callimachus, specifically his injunctions to shun the great river and seek inspiration from the unfrequented spring. Thus the poem, last in its book but on the face of it purely amatory in content, carries a programmatic implication. The poet-lover, it is hinted, should have no more use for an obvious and easy style of loving than for an obvious and easy style of poetry. Cf. below, 36 n. and see Introd. p. xiv.

36 *What follows me, I flee; what flees, I follow*: a semi-proverbial sentiment; but the wording here renders quite closely the end of a well-known epigram of Callimachus on his preferences in love (*Anth. Pal.* xii. 102=*Epigr.* 31 Pfeiffer).

57 *pimp for husband*: the juxtaposition *lenone marito* imparts a brutal emphasis. Under Augustus' *Lex Iulia de adulteriis* condonation of a wife's adultery by a husband was a criminal offence.

BOOK III

I

1 *There stands an ancient grove . . . .*: a condensed example of the so-called *locus amoenus*, the formal description (*ecphrasis*) of an

idyllically beautiful spot. Cf. ii. 6. 49-50, *Ars* iii. 687-92. Groves were often sacred and apt to be frequented by deities, hence this is an appropriate setting for a theophany.

7 *Elegy . . . 11 Tragedy*: the encounter is modelled on a famous allegorical fantasy by the sophist Prodicus (fifth century BC), the Choice of Heracles (Hercules) between Virtue and Pleasure (Xenophon, *Memorabilia* ii. 1. 21-34). This in its turn looked back to the choice offered to Achilles between death at Troy with eternal fame and a long and obscure life at home (Homer, *Iliad* ix. 410-16). As in i. 1, Ovid gives a new and ingenious turn to the traditional motif of the scene in which Apollo or the Muses give the poet his marching orders.

8 *one foot short*: cf. i. 1. 4 n.

10 *graced . . . by her foot's infirmity*: cf. *Ars* ii. 659-62 and n.

14 *high Lydian buskins*: the thick-soled cothurnus as an item of tragic actors' costume was a late Hellenistic innovation unknown to the great Attic dramatists. Whether it is called Lydian because it was thought to be of Oriental origin or = 'Etruscan' in deference to learned (and unreliable) opinion that drama was introduced into Italy by the Etruscans is uncertain.

33 *smiled slyly*: like Comedy in Reynolds's famous painting of Garrick between Tragedy and Comedy.

34 *a myrtle wand*: i. 1. 29 n.

40 *Your palace . . . my tiny door*: tragedies were commonly set outside a royal palace, whereas much of the action of love-elegy (cf. i. 6) took place outside, or was otherwise concerned with, the doors of private houses.

64 *My narrow throat*: *contracto . . . ore*, a variation on the idea of slenderness as an elegiac (Callimachean) hallmark: see ii. 19. 25 n.

70 *A greater work*: cf. iii. 15. 18 and n.

2

1 *here*: at the Circus. Other poems in the *Amores* are couched as dramatic monologues; this is the liveliest example. The idea is re-exploited more briefly at *Ars* i. 135-62.

3 *to sit beside you*: possible at the Circus; in the theatre the sexes were segregated.

15–16 *Pelops*: Oenomaus, king of Pisa in Elis, offered his daughter
      Hippodamia (cf. i. 4. 8 n.) to whoever could stay ahead of him
      in a chariot race; he had overtaken and speared a round dozen
      suitors before Pelops appeared. Hippodamia was made to ride
      with the challengers to distract them.

18 *through his girl's favour*: she fell in love with Pelops and bribed
   the royal charioteer, Myrtilus, to sabotage the king's chariot,
   with fatal results.

29 *Atalanta*: see *Ars* ii. 185 n. The Latin plays on two senses of
   sustineo, 'hold back' (i.e. detain in the race) and 'hold up' (i.e.
   in bed); cf. *Ars* iii. 775–6.

43 *The great procession*: the *pompa circensis*, in which effigies of the
   gods were carried on wagons from the Capitol and round the
   course.

51 *Phoebe*: Diana.

54 *Pollux . . . Castor*: a variation on a theme recurring in the poets
   from Homer (*Iliad* iii. 237) onwards.

78 *colours*: red, white, blue and green. These teams were the
   subject of intense and sometimes violent partisanship, focused
   especially on the Blues and Greens. Some of the riots of the
   Circus factions in the later Empire throw modern football
   hooliganism into the shade. See A. Cameron, *Circus factions.
   Blues and Greens at Rome and Byzantium* (Oxford, 1976).

3

11–12 *Even the eternal gods . . .*: cf. *Ars* i. 635 n.

17 *Andromeda*: her mother Cassiopeia incurred the jealousy of the
   Nereids by boasting of her beauty. Her offence could only be
   expiated by the sacrifice of Andromeda to a sea-monster. She
   was rescued by Perseus; cf. iii. 6. 13 n., and see *Metamorphoses*
   iv. 614–803.

35 *blasts sacred groves and towers*: that Jupiter's lightning struck
   indiscriminately was noted with sarcastic relish by Lucretius,
   De rerum natura vi. 417–18.

37 *Semele*: she was tricked by Juno into making Jupiter swear to
   come to her in his panoply of thunder and lightning, in which
   she died. See *Metamorphoses* iii. 256–315.

40 *played the mother's part*: he snatched Bacchus from Semele's womb and sewed him into his thigh until it was time for him to be born.

4

19 *Argus*: ii. 2. 45 n.

21 *Danae*: ii. 19, 27 n.

40 *Ilia*: iii. 6. 45–82 n. On the form of the verse see ii. 11. 10 n.

5

This by no means ineffective poem is not by Ovid: see Introd. p. xviii. Inverted commas, like the rest of the modern battery of punctuation marks, were unknown to the Greeks and Romans; an ancient reader had no way of knowing the dramatic situation until reaching line 32, when it is discovered that the dream is being told to a soothsayer. Contrast iii. 2, where the mise-en-scène is immediately apparent.

3–6 *Below a sunny hill . . .*: a classic *locus amoenus* (iii. 1. 1 n.); that it should be the scene of such ill-omened happenings is an Ovidian trait (*Metamorphoses* iii. 407 n.).

30 *In hope some lusher grass to see*: that the grass is always greener on the other side of the fence was already proverbial: *Ars* i. 349.

31 *whoever you may be*: *quicumque es*, a strange thing for the narrator to say; cf. iii. 2. 21, where it is decidedly brusque: 'You on the right there'. This is one of several oddities which tell against the ascription to Ovid.

33 *The interpreter*: the study and interpretation of dreams was taken seriously and professionally. The symbolism of this dream and the soothsayer's interpretation find parallels and analogies in such sources as the *Onirocritica* of Artemidorus (second century AD). For instance, a female animal might stand in a lover's dream for the beloved (Artem. iv *proem.*, p. 240 Pack), and a crow (which was proverbially long-lived) might signify both an old woman (ii. 20, p. 137 P.) and a type of loquacity (iv. 56, p. 280 P.). For a striking analogy with the situation and the dream-symbolism of this poem see also Alciphron (second/third century AD), *Letters of Parasites* iii. 23.

6

5 *Once you were small*: Ovid has ingeniously transposed the theme of the locked-out lover (i. 6) to an open-air setting, with the river as the hard-hearted doorkeeper. The situation is authentic: 'These upper rivers of the hills run high and low according to storms and to the melting of the snows'—readers of *The path to Rome* will be reminded of Hilaire Belloc's adventures in the northern Appennines, including one brush with death—'overwhelmed in the rush of water, it was easy to understand how the Taro could drown men, and why the peasants dreaded these little ribbons of water.' More poetic is Norman Douglas in *Old Calabria*: 'At such moments, these torrents put on new faces. From placid waterways they are transformed into living monsters, Aegirs or dragons, that roll themselves seaward, out of their dark caverns, in tawny coils of destruction.'

13 *the wings of Perseus*: the winged sandals which he wore when he slew the Gorgon Medusa and rescued Andromeda (cf. iii. 3. 17 n.).

15 *the flying chariot*: the car of Ceres (Demeter), drawn by dragons, from which Triptolemus, the mythical inventor (i. 7. 32 n.) of agriculture, scattered the seeds of corn over the earth: see *Metamorphoses* v. 642-61.

25-48 This catalogue of rivers in love is a deliberately bravura display of curious Alexandrian learning; for some of these stories Ovid is our only source. This emphasis on mythological learning and the extended narrative that follows may be a preliminary hint of the forthcoming disengagement from love-elegy: cf. Introd. p. xix.

25 *Inachus*: the river of Argos.

28 *Xanthus*: otherwise Scamander, in the Troad; according to Homer (*Iliad* xx. 74) it was called Xanthus by the gods, Scamander by men. The story is otherwise unknown.

29-30 *Arethusa . . . Alpheus*: fleeing from him she was changed into a spring, flowing under the sea from Arcadia in the Peloponnese to the island of Ortygia near Sicily; he followed and mingled his waters with hers. See *Metamorphoses* v. 572-641.

31 *Peneus*: in Thessaly. The previous engagement is mentioned only here.

33 *Asopus*: in Boeotia. The story is otherwise unknown.

35 *Achelous*: in Aetolia. His fight with Hercules for the hand of Deianira, daughter of Oeneus king of Calydon, was a famous story, told by Ovid at *Metamorphoses* ix. 1–100. River-gods were usually represented with horns.

40 *hides . . . his mighty waters' home*: the source of the Nile remained one of the great geographical riddles of the world until modern times.

41 *Evanthe*: the story is otherwise unknown.

43 *Enipeus*: in Thessaly.

45–82 The culminating place in the catalogue is reserved for an Italian river and a story familiar to every Roman schoolboy, told by Ennius in his *Annales*. Ovid's treatment, needless to say, is anything but solemn. Ilia, or Rhea Silvia, was a Vestal Virgin seduced by Mars. She bore twin sons, Romulus and Remus, whom her uncle Amulius condemned to be set adrift on the Tiber. They were found and reared by a she-wolf and eventually founded Rome. Her attempted suicide appears to be adapted by Ovid from a variant of the legend in which Amulius condemned her to be drowned in the Tiber or the Anio; the common version is that she was married to Anio. See also Ovid, *Fasti* iii. 1–54, ii. 381–422, Livy i. 4.

54 *child of Troy's long ancestry*: Ilion was another name for Troy.

56 *no white band*: she had been stripped of the headbands (*uittae*) worn by priestesses and by Roman women as a symbol of purity; cf. *Ars* i. 31–2 n.

63 *A hundred nymphs or more*: a grand court for this comparatively modest Italian river, challenging the state kept by such as Peneus, of whom Ovid later wrote 'seated here / Within a rock-hewn cavern he dispensed / Justice to all his waters and their nymphs' (*Metamorphoses* i. 575–6). Such scenes look back to the submarine grottoes of Thetis in Homer (*Iliad* xviii. 35–50) and Cyrene in Virgil (*Georgics* iv. 333–44).

7

23–4 *Chlide . . . Libas . . . Pitho*: 'Naughtiness', 'Rivulet', 'Persuasion'. Greek names were de rigueur for girls of the elegiac demi-monde; compare Horace's Pyrrha, Glycera, and co. Pitho was in fact a not uncommon name in real life.

41 *Nestor*: the veteran of the Greek army before Troy, proverbial for long life.

42 *Tithonus*: i. 13. 1 n.

51 *Tantalus*: ii. 2. 44 n.

61 *Phemius*: Odysseus' court bard. This and the following illustration have been lifted from Horace: 'A man with fear or desire has as much pleasure from his house / and possessions as sore eyes from a picture, gouty feet / from muffs, or ears from a lyre when they're aching with a mass of dirt' (*Epistles* i. 2. 51–3 tr. Niall Rudd).

62 *Thamyras*: a bard, blinded for his presumption in challenging the Muses to a singing-match. Cf. *Ars* iii. 399.

69 *Lie down in shame*: compare the witty exploitation of this idea by Robert Graves in his poem 'Down, wanton, down!' (*Collected poems* (1965), p. 101).

8

9 *whose wounds have made his money*: he has made enough by soldiering to buy his way into the order of knighthood, for which the qualification was a substantial personal fortune. Naturally Ovid, a knight of old family (i. 3. 8, iii. 15. 5–6) is resentful of such men. Behind this contemporary figure, however, is discernible a literary stereotype, the mercenary soldier-rival of New Comedy, where he is usually depicted as a braggart. Scorn of the upstart is an even older literary theme: Horace's fourth Epode is a famous example.

15 *his new ring*: the gold ring worn by knights.

23 *the priest of Phoebus and the Muses*: another reference to Horace's famous pronouncement in the character of poet-priest (ii. 1. 3 n.).

28 *Homer*: cf. i. 8. 61.

30 *the girl*: Danae; ii. 19. 27 n.

35 *Saturn*: father of Jupiter; see Ovid's description of the Golden Age at *Met.* i. 89–112.

42 *no surveyor marked a boundary*: i.e. private property was unknown.

43 *No dipping oars . . .*: ii. 11. 1 n.

51-2 *Romulus . . . and Caesar too*: the deification of the first founder of Rome and the father of her second founder is associated with the well-worn theme of impious aspirations (see Horace, *Odes* i. 3. 38 'we seek the sky itself in our folly'). Surely a tactless application? If the couplet is really Ovid's, which some have doubted, he nodded with a vengeance.

61 *strait-laced Sabines*: i. 8. 39 n.

9

This elegy on the death of Tibullus is a serious counterpart to the mock lament for Corinna's parrot (ii. 6); both follow the standard schema of a formal dirge or epicedion. However, it is with i. 8 that the poem is most closely linked. Each stands at the centre of its book (Introd. p. xviii) and begins with a reference to Memnon; in each the central figure is that of the poet-lover, here exalted, there disparaged; in each there is a vision of the elegiac *domina*, there as seen through the cynical eyes of the *lena*, here humorously idealized; each ends with a *uotum*, there a curse, here a blessing. Cf. also Introd. p. xix.

1 *Achilles . . . Memnon*: i. 13. 3-4 n.

4 *Too truly you are named*: referring to the standard etymologies from *eleos* 'pity' or *eu legein* 'praise' sc. the dead. Cf. i. 15. 26 n.

5-6 *Tibullus . . . now . . . is burned*: Tibullus died in 19 BC, but it does not follow that this poem was written then. On its position and role in Book III see Introd. p. xix.

7 *his quiver bears upturned*: reversing arms was and is a military gesture of mourning: cf. Virgil, *Aeneid* xi. 93.

13 *his brother . . . Aeneas*: cf. i. 2. 51 n.

14 *Iulus*: son of Aeneas, also called Ascanius.

16 *slashed Adonis' thigh*: Adonis was a 'dying god' of Eastern origin and a hunter loved by Venus: see *Met.* x. 519-59, 708-39.

21 *Orpheus' great parents*: Apollo and the Muse Calliope.

23 *Ah Linus, Linus*: in the Latin *Linon . . aelinon*, with a reference to the refrain of the ritual laments that were sung for Linus as they were for Adonis. His parentage, like that of Orpheus, was disputed; Ovid probably had in mind the account which made him the son of Apollo and thus Orpheus' brother.

27   *Avernus*: a lake in Campania traditionally identified as one of the entrances to the Underworld.

29   *the toils of Troy*: told in the Iliad.

30   *that slow web*: told in the Odyssey. Penelope's suitors allowed her to defer her decision between them until she had finished weaving a winding-sheet for Odysseus' father Laertes. Each night she undid what she had woven that day.

31   *Nemesis and Delia*: Tibullus' mistresses.

33-4   *What use . . . nights of chastity?*: cf. i. 8. 74 n. The couplet echoes Tibullus' own complaints (Tib. i. 3. 23-6); cf. below, 47-58 n.

45   *Eryx*: a mountain in north-west Sicily with a famous sanctuary of Venus.

47-58   This passage reworks motifs from Tibullus' own poetry, particularly the elegy (i. 3) purporting to have been written by him on a bed of sickness far from home. Whereas he there imagines himself dying with no mother or sister or Delia to comfort him (lines 5-9), here Ovid assembles them all and throws in Nemesis for good measure, with a witty reversal of roles. Tibullus had in another elegy prayed that Delia (the chief inspiration of Book I of his elegies) should hold his hand as he died; Ovid makes Nemesis (the inspiration of Book II) protest that she was *maîtresse en titre* when the time actually came, making her point by quoting Tib. i. 1. 60 back almost verbatim at her rival (58).

62   *Calvus . . . Catullus*: Calvus was best known for his miniature epic *Io*, lost but demonstrably influential on later poets; but he also wrote elegies, and he and Catullus were close friends, frequently mentioned together as here.

64   *Gallus*: cf. i. 15. 9-30 n., Introd. pp. xii, xv. He forfeited Augustus' friendship by his imprudent behaviour, was disgraced, and died by his own hand. This oblique defence of him may not have been wholly politic.

10

2   *lies alone in bed*: such ritual chastity was especially associated with, but not peculiar to, the cult of Isis (i. 8. 74 n.). It is the formal justification for the inclusion in the collection of an elegy whose emphasis is less erotic than aetiological. It points

forward to the wholly aetiological iii. 13; see iii. 13. 1 n., Introd. p. xix.

7 *His corn*: *farra*, 'poetic' plural of *far*, used by ancient writers both of the wild 'emmer' and 'spelt' wheats and also, as at *Ars* i. 758, = 'corn', 'wheat', 'grain' in general. Apart from these two instances and line 40 of this elegy, Ovid only uses the word (but see *Medicamina* 65) in the *Fasti*, where it occurs sixteen times, clearly because of its association (as here) with a primitive stage of culture.

11 *Ceres first taught*: i. 7. 32 n. The allusion to Virgil (*Georgics* i. 147 ff.) calls attention to the originality of Ovid's treatment: see below, 25, 35 nn.

19 *aren't always liars*: a proverbial slander: the author of the Epistle to Titus (1: 12) quotes Epimenides' well-known verse 'The Cretans are always liars, evil beasts, slow bellies'. Cf. *Ars* i. 297-8.

20 *the nurse of Jove*: the infant Zeus (Jupiter) was saved from his father Cronus (Saturn) by being hidden in Crete, where he was suckled by a she-goat (*Fasti* v. 115-28).

25 *She saw Iasius below Mount Ida*: a good example of Ovid's way with his models. The love-story of Ceres (Demeter) and Iasius is treated very briefly by Homer and Hesiod: the initiative seems to have been on the goddess's side—she 'yielded to her inclinations'—but all we are there told of the sequel is that her lover was killed by Zeus for his presumption (Homer, *Odyssey* v. 125-8; cf. Hesiod, *Theogony* 969-74). On to this simple story Ovid grafts motifs borrowed from the more familiar legends of Anchises and Aphrodite (Venus), who fell in love with him when she saw him herding his flocks on the *Trojan* Ida (*Homeric Hymn to Aphrodite* 53-5), and the Rape of Proserpine, in which Ceres went on strike in her grief at the loss of her daughter (*Homeric Hymn to Demeter* 305-33, Ovid, *Met.* v. 474-86; cf. below, 46 n.). See next n.

35 *Deep in the woods*: it was in the glades of the *Trojan* Ida that Venus had dallied with Anchises (Homer, *Iliad* ii. 821). Homer refers to it as a haunt of wild beasts (*Iliad* viii. 47, xiv. 283, xv. 151) and as thickly wooded (xxi. 449, 559, xxiii. 117-22; cf. *Homeric Hymn to Apollo* 34). In transferring the attributes of the Trojan to the Cretan Ida Ovid indicates in the manner of the learned poet that he is well aware that the two were distinct.

36 *Her wreath of grain*: the *spicea corona*, garland of ears of corn, was Ceres' symbol.

40 *spelt*: above, 7 n.

41 *Law-giver Minos*: the legendary wise king of Crete, son of Zeus and Europa. After his death he was made one of the judges of the Underworld.

46 *does she reign*: the story of the Rape of Proserpine (Persephone) by Pluto (Dis), king of Hades, is told by Ovid at *Met.* v. 346–571. The three great empires—heaven, sea, the underworld—were assigned by lot. In the usual evaluation Pluto ranked third, below Neptune (Poseidon), and at *Fasti* iv. 584 Proserpine is said to rank third among the three queens. Here she is second. At *Met.* v. 529 Jupiter's words to Ceres can be read ambiguously: *nec cedit nisi sorte mihi*, 'he yields place to me only because the lots so fell' (Melville) ('only' can refer forward or back, as *nisi* can refer to *sorte* or *mihi*). Such inconsistencies are frequently exploited by the learned poet to demonstrate his mastery of the mythological tradition.

12

15 *Thebes . . . Caesar's exploits*: martial epic themes such as those from which the poet had been deflected in i. 1; cf. Introd. p. xiv.

21–40 A catalogue of generally familiar myths, familiar however only because made so by poets; Ovid affects to take literally a figure common in Latin poetry by which the poet is said to do what he narrates.* The power of poetry to immortalize was a commonplace; cf. e.g. Horace, *Odes* iv. 9. 25 ff., *Amores* i. 3. 21–6, *Ars* iii. 413–16, 535–8, et al. Here the idea is ironically exploited to serve the progressive devaluation of elegiac love and elegiac love-poetry that culminates in the explicit rejection of iii. 15. In the poetry of his exile Ovid was to demonstrate that he seriously believed in it; and there is nothing ironical in the claims of *Amores* iii. 15. 7 ff. The list also serves as a 'trailer' for the *Metamorphoses*, in which several of these stories are treated at length.

21 *Scylla*: she fell in love with Minos when he was besieging Megara, and betrayed the city to him by cutting off and handing over the magic lock of hair on which the power of her

* Cf. Dickens while writing *Barnaby Rudge*: 'I have let all the prisoners out of Newgate, burnt down Lord Mansfield's, and played the very devil' (*Letters* ed. House and Storey, Oxford 1969, ii. 385).

father, king Nisus, depended (*Metamophoses* viii. 6–151). Here she is conflated with another Scylla, the monster who infested the straits of Messina: ii. 11. 18 n., *Metamorphoses* xiii. 900–xiv. 67. Cf. below, 24 n. and *Ars* i. 331.

23–4 *We gave . . . To ride a flying horse*: an allusive reference to the slaying of the Gorgon Medusa by Perseus (iii. 3, 17, iii. 6. 13 nn.). The winged horse Pegasus sprang from the blood that fell from the Gorgon's severed head, but it is not Perseus who is elsewhere recorded as riding him, but Bellerophon. This can hardly be a slip on Ovid's part, for it should be remembered that all these poems had (*a*) probably been read to a select and critical circle before publication, (*b*) certainly been circulated in their individual *libelli* before being collected in this edition. We must rather suspect an allusion to an obscure variant of the story by way of another reminder of his mythological erudition.

25 *Tityos*: he was punished for the attempted rape of Latona (Leto) by having his liver eternally devoured by vultures. He was one of the sights of Hades (*Metamorphoses* iv. 457 ff.).

26 *the hound of Hell*: Cerberus; cf. *Ars* iii. 322.

27 *Enceladus*: a Giant (ii. 1. 12 n.), here given a thousand arms by the poet's license claimed below, lines 41–2.

28 *Lured heroes . . .*: an allusive reference to Ulysses' adventure with the Sirens (*Ars* iii. 313 n., *Remedia* 789).

29 *We bagged . . .*: Aeolus, god of the winds, gave them to Ulysses fastened in a bag except for one favourable breeze; his crew thought there was treasure in the bag and let them out, with catastrophic results (Homer, *Odyssey* x. 1–76, *Metamorphoses* xiv. 223–32).

30 *Tantalus*: ii. 2. 44 n.

31 *Niobe*: she was punished for insulting Latona by the deaths of her children; as she grieved she was turned to stone and her tears became a spring (*Metamorphoses* vi. 146–317).
the girl a bear: Callisto, seduced by Jupiter and turned into a bear by the jealous Juno (*Metamorphoses* ii. 401–535).

32 *Itys*: ii. 6. 7–10 n.

33–4 *Jove self-changed*: i. 10. 7, ii. 19. 27 nn.

35–6 *Proteus*: ii. 15. 10 n.
dragons' teeth: the teeth of the serpent slain by Cadmus which

when sown produced a crop of armed men (*Metamorphoses* iii. 99–130). They also figured, with the fire-breathing bulls, in the ordeals of Jason (vii. 100–42).

37 *Phaethon*: he was killed by Jupiter's thunderbolt when the chariot of the Sun, which he was driving, went out of control and threatened to destroy the world. His sisters, the Heliades, were turned to poplars as they mourned him, and their tears to amber (*Metamorphoses* ii. 340–66).

38 *ships turned to sea-nymphs*: Aeneas' fleet, rescued in this way from the onslaught of Turnus: Virgil, *Aeneid* ix. 77–122, Ovid, *Metamorphoses* xiv. 527–65.

39 *the hellish feast of Atreus*: in revenge for his wife's infidelity he murdered the children of her lover Thyestes, his brother, and served them to him at dinner. In his horror at the sight the Sun turned back in his course. Cf. *Ars* i. 330.

40 *the magic lyre*: of Amphion, whose playing (like that of Orpheus) charmed stones to follow him.

13

1 *The . . . town Camillus took*: in 394 BC. The edifying story of the traitorous schoolmaster of Falerii and his fate at the hands of Camillus is told by Livy (v. 25–6).
    my wife: which of Ovid's wives is meant is less important than the fact of her presence, which signals in one word that this is not a love-elegy. See next n. and Introd. p. xix.

3 *Juno's chaste feast*: Juno was goddess of marriage. Ovid may intend his readers to remember Propertius iv. 7, which begins with what promises to be an aetiological excursus but is then revealed in its true colours by the real reason for Cynthia's visit to Juno's shrine at Lanuvium: 'the pretext was Juno, the real reason was Venus' (16). This elegy is going to be aetiological and nothing but aetiological.

13 *white Falerian heifers*: the breed was famous.

19 *Deep in the woods*: exactly the same words as those used of Ceres' amorous adventure (iii. 10. 35). Whom Juno was escaping is unknown; perhaps Jupiter. Ovid has deliberately chosen an obscure story as his 'trailer' for the full-scale mythological-aetiological *Fasti*.

32 *Halaesus*: Ovid was no doubt aware of such etymological speculations as those of Servius (on Virgil, *Aeneid* vii. 695), by which through the change of H to F the people of Halaesus' foundation were called *Falisci*. Tracing connexions of this kind, real or fanciful, was a favourite antiquarian pursuit. Foundation legends (*ktiseis*) were a staple of Alexandrian historiography and learned poetry.

35 *taught me the ritual / Of Juno*: i.e. he introduced the cult of Argive Hera, who became identified with the indigenous Juno.

15

7 *Catullus . . . Virgil*: in sharp contrast to the extensive list at i. 15. 9–30 (see n.) Ovid here names only two predecessors—Catullus as the first Roman love-poet, Virgil as the supreme Roman poet *tout court*. The latter claim must be taken as carefully weighed: see Ovid's appraisal of himself at *Remedia* 395–6.

9 *who fought with honour*: in the Social War of 91–88 BC.

17 *Horned Bacchus*: i. 3. 11–12 n. Mention of Bacchus implies that elegy, conventionally styled 'light' (*leuis*), cannot claim to be truly inspired. Cupid has been trespassing on the preserves of the proper gods of poetry (i. 1. 15–16); what is now announced—the 'greater field' (*area maior*)—is the real thing.

COSMETICS FOR LADIES

(*Medicamina Faciei Femineae*)

3 *By cultivation*: this is the theme of the first fifty lines, to be redeveloped more briefly at *Ars* iii. 101 ff.

9 *Tyrian purple*: Tyre had a monopoly of the true purple; cf. *Ars* ii. 297–8, iii. 370, *Remedia* 707–8.

11 *In Tatius' time*: *Amores* i. 8. 39 n. For Virgil (*Georgics* ii. 532) and Horace (*Epodes* 2. 41, *Odes* iii. 6. 33–44) the Sabine matron typified the old Italian virtue and frugality. Ovid, as often elsewhere, stands the traditional archetype on its head.

27–8 *Girls dress . . .*: text and sense are uncertain.

30 *Athos*: cf. *Ars* ii. 517n. Ovid was not to foresee that, as the Holy Mountain of Orthodox monasticism, it was to become forbidden territory to women.

35–50 For these sentiments cf. *Ars* ii. 99–120, and for the impermanence of women's beauty iii. 69–76.

38 *of lusting mares*: hippomanes; *Amores* i. 8. 7–8 n.

39 *Marsian incantations*: *Ars* ii. 102 n.

41–2 Interference with the moon's motions was a favourite occupation of witches; Ovid pooh-poohs the popular belief that loud noises, especially that of clashing brass, averted such devilments.

51–100 'It is impossible to conclude an investigation of these recipes without feeling considerable admiration for Ovid's practical knowledge and discrimination' (P. M. Green; see his article '*Ars gratia cultus*: Ovid as beautician', *American Journal of Philology* 100 (1979), 381–92).

58 *make a donkey / Grind it*: humorous exaggeration, as at 72 'slow-turned mills' and 75 'brawny lads'. For these quantities a mortar or a quern would be more practical.

65 *Tuscan seed*: spelt; see *Amores* iii. 10. 7 n.

74 *on Illyrian hills*: Illyrian irises were evidently highly regarded for cosmetic and medicinal purposes (Pliny, *Natural History* xxi. 40).

77 *A sad bird's nest*: Alcyone and her husband Ceyx were changed into halcyons, generally identified as kingfishers (*Metamorphoses* xi. 410 ff.); their plaintive cries were proverbial (Homer, *Iliad* ix. 561–4, Ovid, *Heroides* 18. 81–2). The various theories as to the origin of *alcyoneum* are canvassed by Pliny, *Natural History* xxxii. 86.

94 *salt from Ammon's shrine*: sal ammoniac, so called because found under the sand (*ammos*) of Libya (Pliny, *Natural History* xxxi. 79).

THE ART OF LOVE

(Ars amatoria)

BOOK I

3–8 These images recur throughout the *Ars* and *Remedia*: the progress of the poet, the lover, and the affaire itself is figured in terms of a chariot race or a sea voyage. The chariot metaphor also carries overtones of the car of the Muses or of Fame (cf. e.g. Pindar, *Olympians* 9. 81 etc., Propertius iii. 1. 9–10). Ovid's use of these images is complex: they imply that the poet (as charioteer or helmsman) is very much in control of his enterprise and, being especially affected by didactic poets, they enhance (ironically) the literary pretensions of the poems. Cf. i. 772 n., Introd. p. xxiii.

5 *Automedon*: Achilles' charioteer.

6 *Tiphys*: helmsman of the Argo.

11 *Chiron*: the wise Centaur who educated, among other heroes, Achilles.

28 *on Ascra's mountain side*: Helicon, where Hesiod received from the Muses the symbols of his poetic calling (*Theogony* 23–34). This is another (negative) variation on the conventional epiphany theme: cf. *Amores* i. 1 and Introd. p. xiv.

31–2 *skirt*: the flounce (*instita*) which distinguished the long gown (*stola*) worn by Roman matrons.
snood: the bands (*uittae*) which, in different forms, were worn on the head by all respectable free-born Roman women; cf. *Amores* iii. 6. 56 n., iii. 483. Cf. ii. 600 and the similar warning at *Amores* ii. 1. 3–4. Ovid was to quote lines 31–4 in the elaborate defence of himself and his poetry that he composed in exile (*Tristia* ii. 247–50), substituting however for 'safe intrigues' (*Venerem tutam*) the slightly less compromising 'nothing but what is lawful' (*nil nisi legitimum*).

36 *our new recruit*: *Amores* i. 9. 1 n.

39 *my car*: see above, 3–8 n.

53 *Perseus*: *Amores* ii. 19. 27, iii. 3. 17, iii. 6. 13 nn. Andromeda was in fact Ethiopian, but 'in Latin poetry "Indians" and "Ethiopians" are more or less interchangeable' (Hollis).

54 *the Trojan*: Paris.

57 *Methymna*: on Lesbos.
   Gargara: a mountain in the Troad.

60 *her son*: Aeneas; cf. *Amores* i. 8. 41–2 n.

67 *Pompey's colonnade*: porticoes were an important feature of
   ancient city architecture, public and private, offering protection
   from both sun and rain in season. Pompey built this one as an
   adjunct to his theatre.

70 *Those halls of rich exotic marble*: the portico of Octavia, sister of
   Augustus, and the theatre of her son Marcellus.

72 *the arcade*: built by Augustus and named for his empress. It was
   also an art gallery.

74 *where . . . fierce Danaus waits*: *Amores* ii. 2. 4 n. Augustus is said
   to have boasted that he found Rome brick and left it marble
   (Suetonius, *Augustus* 28. 3), and this temple of Apollo in
   particular was clearly intended as a conspicuous monument of
   his beneficent power (cf. Propertius' description, ii. 31). In
   recommending this and other buildings associated with the
   imperial family as good prospects for pick-ups Ovid may have
   been asking for trouble: cf. *Amores* i. 2. 51, *Ars* i. 81–2, 131 nn.

75–8 Rome was by now a cosmopolitan city, attracting many
   foreigners, especially from the eastern Mediterranean, and
   their cults.

75 *where Venus for Adonis weeps*: *Amores* iii. 9. 16 n. A vivid
   account of the Adonia as it was celebrated in Alexandria is to
   be found in Theocritus' fifteenth Idyll.

76 *his sacred Sabbath*: cf. i. 415–16. The traditional Italian 'week'
   was one of eight days, the interval between one *nundinae*
   (ninth-day market) and the next. The development of the
   modern seven-day week was beginning at about this time and
   was probably assisted by Jewish observance. Jewish settlement
   in Rome had been actively encouraged by Julius Caesar and
   Augustus.

77 *Isis' Memphian shrine*: *Amores* ii. 13. 7–8 n.

78 *what Jove made of her*: Isis was commonly identified with Io; see
   Amores i. 3. 21, ii. 2. 45 nn.

81–2 *the spray / Of Appian waters*: the fountain of the Appiades
   (water nymphs) stood in the Forum Iulium near the temple of
   Venus Genetrix: both were dedicated by Julius Caesar and

completed by Augustus (cf. above, i. 74 n.); cf. iii. 451–2, *Remedia* 660.

101 *With Romulus . . . first*: *Amores* i. 7. 32 n. The Rape of the Sabine Women was a famous episode from the traditional foundation legend of Rome. Ovid's flippant misapplication contrasts sharply with the gravity of Livy (i. 9) and Dionysius of Halicarnassus (*Roman Antiquities* ii. 30). Cf. below, i. 131 n.

102 *wifeless*; Romulus had increased the population of Rome by making it a refuge for displaced persons, most of whom were single men (Livy i. 8).

103–8 *No marble then . . .*: the pastoral simplicity of primitive Rome was a favourite topic of the Augustan poets; cf. iii. 119–20.

104 *saffron*: sprayed on the stage to perfume it.

111 *Tuscan*: a glancing allusion to learned speculation on the origins of drama in Italy; cf. *Amores* iii. 1. 14 n. The Etruscans were credited with a number of important cultural introductions.

126 *lovelier for their very dread*: Ovid all over; cf. e.g. *Amores* i. 7. 13, *Ars* i. 533–4, iii. 153, 429–32.

131 *the prize for soldiers*: *commoda*, 'fringe benefits' over and above basic pay. There had been complaints about these recently: 'Ovid is saying in effect, "If they could offer a pretty girl as a side-attraction nowadays, that would solve the recruiting-problem!"' (Hollis). Another pinprick (i. 74 n.), this one too in connection with Romulus, a figure from the national pantheon (Cicero, *De republica* ii passim, Virgil, *Aeneid* vi. 777–87).

133 *Thus was the fashion started*: the phraseology echoes that of Hellenistic aetiology and elevates Ovid's disrespectful interpretation of the legend to the status of a national institution.

135–62 *Nor miss the ring . . .*: see *Amores* iii. 2 and nn.

171 *mimic warfare*: a re-enactment of the Battle of Salamis on an artificial lake near the Tiber. The occasion was the dedication of the temple of Mars Ultor (the Avenger) in 2 BC.

177 *Lo! Caesar plans . . .*: that Augustus was in fact planning the conquest of Parthia is doubtful. This expedition under the young Gaius Caesar, Augustus' grandson and adopted son, may have been intended primarily to enforce a settlement of the affairs of Parthia and Armenia satisfactory to Rome, and that in fact it seems to have achieved.

179 *Parthia shall pay*: the standards captured by the Parthians when they defeated the Romans at Carrhae had already been restored as a result of diplomatic negotiation in 20 BC.

187, 189 *Hercles . . . Bacchus*: both sons of gods and mortal women, frequently invoked as examples of achievement eventually rewarded by deification, hence prominent in Augustan propaganda. So Anchises compares the future Augustus to both of them (Virgil, *Aeneid* vi. 801-7).

187 *the serpents*: sent to attack him by his jealous stepmother Juno.

190 *his conquering rod*: the thyrsus, a wand wreathed with ivy.

194 *Prince of Youth . . . prince of sires*: Gaius had been dubbed *Princeps Iuuentutis* in 5 BC. The vaguer phrase *princeps senum* may refer to his hoped-for accession to the headship of the Senate or to the Principate itself.

195-8 *Brothers you have . . .*: typical declamatory logic. Phraates V (Phraataces) of Parthia had supplanted his four half-brothers against the wishes of his father Phraates IV. Gaius' devotion to his own father and brothers is supposed to strengthen his resolve to punish the usurper.

197 *Your country's sire*: the title *Pater Patriae* had been officially conferred on Augustus in 2 BC, not long before this was written.

203 *Caesar*: Augustus.

205 *Your triumph*: in the event Gaius died of a wound in AD 4.

209-10 *I'll tell of shafts . . .*: the 'Parthian shot' was a standard Eastern cavalry manoeuvre, pretended retreat converted suddenly into counter-attack. Ovid disparagingly implies that these tactics were treacherous and un-Roman.

220 *towns or hills or streams*: pictures of the conquered territory were carried in the triumphal procession.

225 *the Danaan Crown*: Perses, son of Perseus and Andromeda (i. 53 n.), was the legendary ancestor of the Persian royal house.

231-6 The allegory turns on the personifications of wine and love as gods (metonymy), who wrestle for mastery of the lover's heart. The details are not entirely clear, but the moral seems to be that, though the effects of wine are transitory, the love it inspires may not be.

247 *the three*: Venus, Juno and Minerva; cf. i. 625–6, 683–4, *Remedia* 711–12.

255 *Baiae*: a fashionable resort on the bay of Naples, noted for its hot springs and beaches, and with a raffish reputation.

259 *Dian's sylvan fane*: the famous sanctuary of Diana Nemorensis, Diana of the Wood, at Aricia, whose priest was a runaway slave who had won his office by killing his predecessor. This macabre institution was the starting-point of Frazer's *Golden Bough*: see R. Ackerman, *J. G. Frazer. His life and work* (Cambridge, 1987).

278 *would be reversed*: an ancient and apparently ineradicable male conviction. The examples adduced by Ovid are taken from the extensive literary repertory of stories of unnatural passion.

283 *Byblis*: she loved her brother Caunus (*Metamorphoses* ix. 454–668).

285 *Myrrha*: she bore Adonis (*Amores* iii. 9. 16 n.) to her father Cinyras (*Metamorphoses* x. 298–518).

288 *the perfume*: she was changed into a myrrh-tree.

289 *Ida*: in Crete.

293 *Cnossos . . . Cydon*: Cretan cities.

295 *Pasiphae*: wife of Minos (*Amores* iii. 10. 41 n.).

299 *land of lies*: *Amores* iii. 10. 19 n.

323 *Europa . . . Io*: *Amores* i. 3. 21–4 n.

325 *a wooden cow*: made by Daedalus; cf. ii. 23–4.

326 *the child*: the Minotaur, half man, half bull; cf. ii. 24.

327 *spurned Thyestes' vows*: Aerope, Minos' granddaughter and mother by Atreus of Agamemnon and Menelaus, committed adultery with her brother-in-law Thyestes. See next n.

330 *back to Dawn careered*: *Amores* iii. 12. 39 n.

331 *The child*: the same (clearly deliberate) conflation of the two Scyllas as at *Amores* iii. 12. 21–2 (see n.).

334 *Atreus' son . . . his accursèd wife*: Agamemnon and Clytemnestra; cf. ii. 399–408.

335 *Creusa's love-tale*: she was Jason's second wife, supplanting Medea, who murdered both her and her own children by Jason in revenge.

337 *Phoenix*: falsely accused by his father Amyntor's mistress of seducing her and blinded by his father. Homer's version (*Iliad* ix. 447–95) is somewhat different, but in all these examples of female lust Ovid is drawing on well-known Euripidean tragedies.

338 *Hippolytus*: his stepmother Phaedra, finding his chastity impregnable (*Amores* ii. 4. 32 n.), accused him of raping her. He was killed when his horses were stampeded by a sea-monster invoked by the curses of his father Theseus (*Metamorphoses* xv. 497–529).

339 *Phineus*: he was persuaded by his second wife Idaea to blind his two sons by his first wife Cleopatra. He was later blinded himself. Cf. *Remedia* 355, 454.

364 *The troop-filled horse*: the Wooden Horse; Ovid's readers would be familiar with the story as told by Virgil in the second Book of the Aeneid.

368 *Add oar to sail*: 'with sails and oars' (*uelis remisque*) was a cliché for putting on all possible speed; cf. *Remedia* 531, 790.

376 *The gravest risks*: illustrated by *Amores* ii. 7 and 8. Ovid now affects to consider the matter with didactic gravity.

395–6 *Ne'er on her fellow-criminal . . .*: these lines are not Ovid's.

406 *Venus' month*: the first of April is not mentioned elsewhere as a day for present-giving, but as a festival of Venus it would provide an obvious pretext.

408 *The Circus flaunts the wealth*: apparently a reference to the festival of the Sigillaria in December; the simple clay figurines (*sigilla*) that used to be on sale have been superseded by expensive bijouterie.

413 *that day of woe*: 18 July, when in 390 BC the Romans were defeated by the Gauls at the river Allia in Latium. On such *dies atri* (black days) shops and public offices were closed.

415 *the Syrian Jew*: i. 76 n.

437 *the waxed tablet*: *Amores* i. 11. 14 n.

441 *to restore his child / To Priam*: the ransoming of Hector's body is the subject of the last book (xxiv) of the Iliad.

446 *though a cheat at best*: the rider is pointed; Spes (Hope) was jointly worshipped with Fides (Good Faith) and Fortuna.

457 *Cydippe*: her lover Acontius scratched on an apple (or quince) the words 'I swear by Artemis to marry Acontius' and rolled it in front of her. She picked it up and reading the words aloud, as was usual in antiquity, was bound by her oath, though taken involuntarily. Callimachus included the story in his *Aetia* (fragments 67–75 Pfeiffer), whence Ovid took it to develop it in the *Heroides* (20–1). Cf. *Remedia* 382.

459 *rhetoric*: *bonas artes*, liberal arts. The main end of Roman education was the production of fluent and effective extempore speakers, but authorities such as Cicero and Quintilian insisted that for a real orator a good general education was essential. Here, as elsewhere in the *Ars*, Ovid has quietly subversive fun with conventional values. His advice is indeed in strict accordance with rhetorical doctrine. There was a technical literature on the art of letter-writing, and it was a basic principle of rhetoric that the style of speaking should be appropriate to the matter and the situation.

477 *Penelope*: the archetypal chaste wife; cf. *Amores* i. 8. 47–8 n.

507–8 *Mother Cybele*: the Great Mother, Magna Mater. Her orgiastic cult had reached Italy at the end of the third century BC and her corybantic eunuch priests were a familiar part of the Roman scene: cf. Lucretius, *De rerum natura* ii. 610 ff. and Ovid's elaborate account of her reception at Rome at *Fasti* iv. 181–372.

510 *the Cretan maid*: Ariadne; see i. 527–64 n.

511 *rude Hippolytus*: i. 338 n. In her letter to him the Ovidian Phaedra makes great play with his unkempt masculinity: *Heroides* 4. 69–84.

512 *Adonis*: i. 75 n.

527–64 Ariadne, daughter of Minos king of Crete, helped Theseus to find his way out of the Labyrinth after killing the Minotaur (i. 326, ii. 23–4 nn.) and eloped with him. He abandoned her on the island of Naxos, where she was found and rescued by Bacchus (Dionysus). The lament of the abandoned heroine was a standard poetic theme thoroughly exploited by Ovid in the *Heroides* (*Amores* ii. 18. 21−6 n.) and recurring in the *Metamorphoses*, e.g. Scylla's outburst at viii. 108−42. The story of Ariadne was familiar to Roman readers from Catullus' highly influential treatment in his miniature epic *Peleus and Thetis* (64). The tone of this episode contrasts markedly with the melodramatic style of Ariadne's epistle in the *Heroides* (10); this is high ironic comedy. He was to treat the story again, in more summary fashion, in the *Metamorphoses* (viii. 152−82).

528 *Dia*: another name for Naxos.

533 *Became her*: cf. i. 126 n.

558 *your Cretan Crown*: a constellation between Engonasin (The Kneeler) and Ophiuchus (The Snake-Holder): Aratus, *Phaenomena* 71−3.

566 *at the board*: compare *Amores* i. 4.

567 *the Sire of Feasts*: Bacchus.

582 *your own garland*: *Amores* i. 6. 38 n.

585−8 *It's sure and proved . . . in his pact*: this abrupt access of moral scruple is out of place here; the lines have probably been misplaced. They would follow on quite aptly after line 742 'He trusts your praise and ousts you unaware.'

593 *Eurytion*: a casualty in the brawl between the Lapiths and the Centaurs (*Amores* i. 4. 8 n.)

595 *if you're supple*: *si mollia bracchia*, 'if your arms are pliant'; ancient dancing, like that of India and Indo-China, relied principally on movements of the arms and hands; the Greek word was *cheironomein*, 'gesticulate'. Cf. ii. 305, iii. 349, *Remedia* 334.

610 *give you speech*: a variation on the Elder Cato's advice to 'stick to the matter, and the words will follow', *rem tene uerba sequentur*.

626 *that lost award*: the prize for beauty awarded by Paris to Venus: i. 247 n.

635 *his deadliest vow*: the oath by Styx, held inviolate by the gods. Having forsworn himself to Juno over his affaire with Io, Jupiter decreed that lovers' oaths should be exempt from the penalties for perjury. The idea became, as here, a commonplace. So Shakespeare: 'At lovers' perjuries, / They say, Jove laughs' (*R. & J.* II. i. 92−3). Cf. *Amores* iii. 3. 11−12.

637 *Gods have their uses, let's believe they're there*: expedit esse deos, et, ut expedit, esse putemus. The sentiment was ascribed to the Cynic Diogenes by Tertullian (*Ad nationes* ii. 2), but the idea that it was conducive to political and social stability to observe the forms of public worship is found in Cicero (*De natura deorum* i. 61; see A. S. Pease *ad loc.*) and Epicurus (see next n.) set an example of respect for the traditional gods. Whether or not what is said here represents Ovid's own opinion, it was neither unrepresentative nor particularly startling.

640 *They dwell apart*: the Epicureans held that the gods existed in the spaces between worlds (*metakosmia, intermundia*) and played no part in governing the universe, a doctrine not unnaturally fiercely criticized by other philosophical schools.
God's at hand: numen adest. 'To take [this] as a statement of the poet's own view would be absurd: it is meant to be in inverted commas; this is what we have got to tell people, he is saying' (L. P. Wilkinson, *Ovid recalled* (Cambridge, 1955), p. 191).

647-54 The examples of Busiris and Phalaris are taken from Callimachus' *Aetia*, where they figure together and in the same order (fragments 44-7 Pfeiffer). In Apollodorus' account (ii. 224 in Frazer's edn.) the seer is called Phrasius, with an evident pun on Greek *phrazo*, 'show', 'declare'; other such 'significant' names of prophets are Idmon, 'knowing' (in Apollonius' *Argonautica*) and Polyidus, 'much-witting'. Ovid's words *monstrat . . . piari . . . posse Iouem*, 'showed that Jupiter could be propitiated', indicate that he probably found in Callimachus (the surviving fragments do not include the name), and wrote here, 'Phrasius'.

653 *Phalaris*: unlike the mythical Busiris a historical figure, tyrant of Acragas in Sicily in the early sixth century BC, proverbial for cruelty. The letters ascribed to him date from no earlier than the second century AD; in the 1690s their authenticity was the subject of acrimonious contention between Richard Bentley and the 'wits' of Christ Church. The screams of the victim were supposed to sound like the bellowings of the bronze bull.

673 *it's force that women want*: a defence still sometimes employed in cases of rape and taken seriously by (male) judges.

679 *her sister*: Hilaira; they were abducted by Castor and Pollux.

681 *Though known the tale*: though the story had been handled by Euripides in his *Scyrians*, Ovid's immediate source was a Hellenistic Epithalamium (marriage hymn) of Achilles and

Deidamia of unknown authorship of which 32 verses happen to survive (Hollis *ad loc.* and p. 155). 'Known' is therefore disingenuous, the learned poet's way of drawing attention to his use of an out-of-the-way source.

682 *The Scyrian maid . . . Haemon's thane*: Deidamia, daughter of Lycomedes king of Scyros, and Achilles.

684 *her fatal bribe*: 'fatal' because it precipitated the Trojan war; Venus induced Paris to declare her the winner of the beauty contest (i. 247 n.) by promising him Helen to wife.

687 *the injured husband*: Menelaus, brother of Agamemnon.

689 *a mother's prayer*: his mother, the sea-nymph Thetis, knew that he would be killed if he joined the expedition.

692 *Pallas' other art*: Pallas Athene (Minerva) was goddess of war as well as of the arts.

696 *Pelian*: its distinguishing epithet in Homer; its shaft was of ash from Mt Pelion in Thessaly, Achilles' homeland.

702 *changed the distaff for the sword*: he was tricked into revealing himself by Ulysses: 'Among some girlish gear / I smuggled arms that must excite a man, / And as, in girl's dress still, he held the shield / And spear, I said "My lad, my goddess' son, / Why shrink from overthrowing giant Troy? / Troy, doomed to perish, keeps herself for you!"' (*Metamorphoses* xiii. 165-9 tr. A. D. Melville).

714 *No woman e'er corrupted*: indeed, as the escapades to be narrated in the *Metamorphoses* bear witness, the boot was very much on the other foot.

717 *What's gone . . . reject*: a favourite commonplace which went back to Sappho (R. G. M. Nisbet and Margaret Hubbard, *A commentary on Horace: Odes Book 1* (Oxford, 1970), pp. 368-70.

731 *Side*: Orion's first wife, consigned to Hades by Hera (Juno), jealous of her beauty. The story, like the next one, is obscure and the name has been restored by conjecture. Hunting is a regular occupation for the distraught lover, as in romantic novels of the old school.

732 *Daphnis*: he was the subject of many stories, but who the Naiad referred to may have been is quite uncertain.

743-4 *Patroclus . . . Pirithous*: irony is probably at work here. In the post-Homeric tradition Patroclus and Achilles were lovers (this was the subject of a famous lost play of Aeschylus, *The Myrmidons*); and the love of Pirithous and Theseus, treated allusively by Ovid (Heroides 4. 109–12, *Metamorphoses* viii. 405–6), is made an explicit grievance by Seneca's Phaedra (*Phaedra* 91–8). However, no such implications appear to attach to Pylades and Orestes. The same three pairs are brigaded together by Bion, frag. 12 Gow.

745–6 *Hermione*: wife of Orestes. For the friendship of these two cf. *Remedia* 589.
the Twins: Castor and Pollux.
their sisters: Minerva (Athene) and Helen respectively.

761 *Proteus*: Amores ii. 15. 10 n.

771 *Part . . . part*: *pars* is used in its common sense = 'half'; the couplet has been left unchanged from the first edition of the poem in two books. See ii. 745–6 n.

772 *the barque*: cf. i. 3–8 n. The sailing image is exploited more throughly than that of the chariot; see e.g. ii. 9, Remedia 14, 70 nn.

BOOK II

5 *the Trojan*: Paris.
Amyclae: a town near Sparta, here used for Sparta itself.

9 *our barque*: cf. i. 772 n. The lover himself is now co-navigator; cf. *Remedia* 14.

16 *Love's namesake*: the etymological connection (real or false is immaterial) between Erato and *eros* is as old as Plato (*Phaedrus* 259b). Ovid expects his readers to remember that she is invoked by Apollonius at the beginning of his account of the love of Jason and Medea (*Argonautica* iii. 1). There may also possibly be an arch 'correction' of Virgil, whose commentators, from Servius onwards ('Erato for Calliope or for any Muse') have been hard put to it to explain why he chose to introduce the second, 'Iliadic', half of the Aeneid by invoking Erato (vii. 37). Ovid makes it clear that she has every right to figure in *his* poem and lends it status by the invocation.

23 *pent the monster in*: in the Labyrinth; i. 527–64 n.
fruit of a mother's sin: Pasiphae; see i. 289–328.

24 *Half bull, half man*: Amores ii. 11. 10 n.

27 *a cruel destiny*: he had had to flee Athens after murdering his

nephew Perdix in jealousy of his inventive powers (*Metamorphoses* viii. 235–59).

35 *and ocean*: 'Minos was the first ruler to build a fleet and to take command of the sea' (Thucydides i. 4).

39 *aspire to reach your starred abode*: like the Giants (*Amores* ii. 1. 11–12, 13 nn.). Icarus in his youthful heedlessness does just this and incurs destruction. The story is abruptly introduced, and its moral—the difficulty of Ovid's undertaking (97–8)—seems to be at odds with the confident manifesto that ushered in the poem. In Horace Daedalus figures as a warning of the originally sacrilegious character of seafaring (*Odes* i. 3. 33 ff.; cf. *Amores* ii. 11. 1 n.), and Icarus as a type of the daring that courts destruction (iv. 2. 1–4; cf. ii. 20. 13–16), as he does in Ovid's later comments on his own fate (*Tristia* i. 2. 89–90, iii. 4. 21–4). Rather than taking all this as a serious reflection on 'the limits of *ars*' (Myerowitz) it seems preferable to see it as a mock-solemn warning to the lover to 'follow reason and avoid extremes' (Green). Resort to magic (the next precept) is a case in point: that, like Icarus' attempt to scale the heavens, is impious (*nefas*, 107).

55 *Bootes*: the Wagoner.
   Callisto: the Great Bear; the story of her double metamorphosis is told by Ovid at *Metamorphoses* ii. 401–535.

80 *the isle to Phoebus dear*: Delos, his birthplace. Here and in the later retelling of the story at *Metamorphoses* viii. 220–2 scholars have puzzled over Daedalus' route, which is not altogether easy to square with the geographical facts. Ovid was more concerned with the evocative qualities of the Greek names of these islands than with their precise locations.

96 *the sea his name assumes*: the Icarian Sea, between the Cyclades and south-west Asia Minor.

100 *from brow of foal*: hippomanes; here the reference is to a growth on the forehead of new-born foals, supposed to have magic properties. For its other sense see *Amores* i. 8. 7–8 n.

102 *Marsian enchanter*: the Marsi were a Latin people with a reputation as magicians; cf. *Medicamina* 39.

103 *his Colchian bride*: Medea.

109 *Nireus*: 'the fairest hero of all the Greeks who came to Troy, after Achilles' (Homer, *Iliad* ii. 673–4). He is mentioned nowhere else in the *Iliad*, and no other hero is singled out for

his looks in the Catalogue. In the next verse he is described as a 'weakling', and in the post-Homeric tradition he acquired the reputation of a catamite. In describing him as Homer's 'flame' and in coupling him with Hylas (see next note), as Horace (*Odes* iii. 20. 15) couples him with Ganymede, Ovid is discreetly alluding to this imputation.

110 *Hylas*: the boy-love of Hercules, who took him on the Argonautic expedition; the story of his abduction by water-nymphs is told by Apollonius (*Argonautica* i. 1207–39) and Theocritus (*Idyll* xiii).

122 *both the tongues*: Greek and Latin; cf. Horace's well-known address to Maecenas as 'learned in both tongues' (*docte sermones utriusque linguae*, *Odes* iii. 8. 5)—a reminder of the Greek-oriented character of Roman culture and of its exclusiveness. In exile Ovid was to discover that there were languages other than Greek or Latin and even to write poetry in one of them (*Epistulae ex Ponto* iv. 13. 19 ff.).

124 *Ocean's nymphs*: Circe and Calypso; cf. *Remedia* 263–88 and n. This episode is an Ovidian embroidery on the passage in the Odyssey in which Odysseus takes his departure from Calypso (v. 202 ff.); see ii. 131 n.

130 *Rhesus*: king of Thrace, a Trojan ally. Odysseus and Diomedes killed him and many of his followers and carried off his famous white horses in a night surprise. Cf. *Metamorphoses* xiii. 239–52 and ii. 135 n.

131 *a cane perchance he bore*: *uirga*, one of the withies used to construct the bulwarks of his raft (*Odyssey* v. 256); 'perchance' (*forte*) is wittily disingenuous (Sharrock, *Mnemosyne* 40 (1987), 406–12).

135 *Dolon*: a Trojan spy captured by Odysseus and Diomedes and killed after betraying to them the location of Rhesus' camp. *Iliad* x, in which the episode is narrated, was traditionally called the Doloneia.

155 *strife's the marriage dower*: an evergreen view of marriage bequeathed (so far as the literary tradition is concerned) to the elegists by Greek New Comedy and its Roman derivatives.

166 *Fine words I gave*: in Latin *uerba dare*='deceive'.

185 *Atalanta*: a fiercely chaste huntress. Ovid has borrowed the idea of Milanion as a paragon of devotion from Propertius (i. 1. 9 ff.); the better-known variant of the story is that in which

he won her hand by beating her in a race with the trick of the three golden apples (*Metamorphoses* x. 560–707; the hero is there called Hippomenes). Ovid appears in the *Metamorphoses* to distinguish between this Atalanta and the one who took part in the Calydonian hunt (viii. 317 ff.), in so far as he does not overtly identify them and their stories are widely separated in the poem; but he must have been well aware of the differences among the literary authorities, and in not explicitly naming her on her first appearance (viii. 317 *Tegeaea* 'the Arcadian girl') he was probably hinting at his awareness by declining to make a positive identification. (For a convenient summary of the myth and its variants see J. G. Frazer's edition of Apollodorus, ii. 398 n. 2.) Cf. *Amores* iii. 2. 29–30, *Ars* iii. 775 for his scabrous gloss on the relationship.

191 *Hylaeus*: a Centaur, his rival.

192 *Another*: Cupid.

203 *the numbered ivories*: dice of the modern kind, with faces numbered one to six.

205 *knucklebones*: these had only four numbered faces, 1, 3, 4, and 6. Cf. iii. 353–6.

207 *chessmen*: 'Bandits', *lusus latrunculorum*, a boardgame analogous to chess; see the fuller reference at iii. 357–60.

216 *In freeborn hands*: this, and the preceding services (including the hand-warming?), were usually performed by slaves.

217 *his step-dame*: Juno, at whose orders Eurystheus imposed on Hercules his Twelve Labours.

218 *that he'd . . . sustained*: on the quest for the Golden Apples of the Hesperides, which Atlas fetched while Hercules held up the sky in his stead.

219 *'Mid Lydian maids*: in expiation of a murder committed in a fit of madness Hercules was sentenced to serve Queen Omphale of Lydia for three years. In the *Heroides* Ovid places in the mouth of his wife Deianira a catalogue of the indignities that he submitted to (9. 53–118).

221 *Tirynthian*: Eurystheus (ii. 217 n.) was king of Tiryns in Argos.

233 *Love is a warfare*: the theme of *Amores* i. 9, of which there are several echoes in these lines.

239 *the lord of Pherae*: Admetus, king of Pherae in Thessaly. That Apollo was in love with Admetus must be inferred here from the context, but the story was familiar: Callimachus, *Hymn to Apollo* 49, Tibullus ii. 3. 11 ff., Ovid, *Metamorphoses* ii. 683. See also iii. 19 n.

249 *Hero . . . Leander*: *Amores* ii. 16. 31 n. This embellishment is of course purely Ovidian.

256 *St Fortune's day*: 24 June. As Ovid explains elsewhere (*Fasti* vi. 781–4), the cult of Fortuna was supposed to have been established by King Servius Tullius, who (as his name indicates) was born of a slave mother, and it was therefore popular with slaves and humble folk generally.

257–8 *the day the Gaul / . . . was cozened to his fall*: 7 July. After the withdrawal of the Gauls in 390 BC, Rome was attacked by her neighbours, who demanded the surrender of all the freeborn women and girls. The maidservants of Rome, dressed in their mistresses' clothes, went instead. In the night they signalled to the Romans, who surprised and routed the enemy as they lay asleep—the maids having seen to this. This version (in Plutarch and Macrobius) is intrinsically more probable than Ovid's ascription of the defeat to the Gauls themselves; but he may possibly, as elsewhere, be following an otherwise unattested alternative version.

266 *a West-End street*: the Via Sacra; *Amores* i. 8. 100 n.

267 *Amaryllis*: Virgil's shepherd Corydon, courting the disdainful Alexis, promises to send him chestnuts 'which my Amaryllis used to like' (*mea quas Amaryllis amabat*). The allusion ironically underlines Ovid's message, that town-girls nowadays expect something more lavish than such old-fashioned rustic offerings.

271 *on childless dotards trade*: legacy-hunting, if the satirists may be believed, was a national industry. According to Petronius, at Croton the whole population was divided into the hunters and the hunted: 'aut captantur aut captant' (*Satyricon* 116. 6–7). Cf. below, ii. 332 'Thus many into wills have found their way.'

277–8 *This truly is the Golden Age . . .*: the poet-lover's recurrent complaint of the venality of women is broadened into a declamatory commonplace which in fact represents a considerable body of serious historical theorizing on the connection between luxury, greed, and civil war.

298 *silks*: *Coa*, semi-transparent stuffs produced on the island of Cos.

309 *Medusa*: the Gorgon killed by Perseus.

330 *egg*: the superstitious wife in Juvenal purifies herself with a hundred eggs to avert disaster (*Satires* 6. 517–21).

353 *Phyllis . . . Demophoon*: she was daughter of Sithon of Thrace, he the son of Theseus; on his way home from Troy he engaged himself to marry her, but never returned to fulfil his engagement. In desperation she hanged herself. Her letter to Demophoon is *Heroides* 2. Cf. iii. 37–8 n., 459–60, *Remedia* 591–606.

355 *his lady*: Penelope, the writer of *Heroides* 1.

356 *her absent chief*: Protesilaus; *Amores* ii. 18. 38 n. Laodamia is the writer of *Heroides* 13. See iii. 18 n.

361 *forth to wend*: to Crete; see *Remedia* 773–4. The imagined correspondence of Paris and Helen while he was Menelaus' guest at Sparta is one of the liveliest products of Ovid's imagination (*Heroides* 16–17).

381 *Colchian spouse*: Medea; cf. i. 335 n.

383 *That swallow*: Procne; see *Amores* ii. 6. 7–10 n.

384 *blood-marks*: chestnut-brown in fact. The conceit seems not to antedate Virgil (*Georgics* iv. 15).

396 *more is read*: because the previous writing on the wax has not been completely erased; cf. *Amores* i. 11. 14 n.

399 *Atreus' son*: Agamemnon.
    She: Clytemnestra.

401–4 *She'd heard . . .*: forced to restore the captured Chryseis to her father Chryses, priest of Apollo, when the god sent plague on the Greeks, Agamemnon compensated himself by taking Briseis from Achilles. This precipitated Achilles' withdrawal from the war and so prolonged it. Cf. *Remedia* 467–84, 777–84.

405 *Cassandra*: cf. *Amores* i. 9. 37 n. The confrontation had been memorably represented in Aeschylus' *Agamemnon*.

407 *Aegisthus*: son of Thyestes by an incestuous union with his own daughter. He had murdered Atreus in revenge for his treatment of his father; cf. i. 327, 330 nn., *Remedia* 161–8.

410 *deny the whole affair*: as brilliantly demonstrated at *Amores* ii. 7.

420 *Eryx*: *Amores* iii. 9. 45 n.

421 *Alcathous*: son of Pelops and builder of the walls of Megara.

422 *The plant of love*: *eruca sativa*, rocket. Most reputed aphrodisiacs are of doubtful efficacy, but this one is vouched for by Norman Douglas: *Venus in the kitchen or Love's cookery book* (1952), p. 151 'Salad rocket is certainly a stimulant.'

426 *On the inside*: i.e. I must not digress; for the image cf. i. 3–8, 39 nn.

467–80 *At first the world . . .*: a brilliant condensation of Lucretius' account of the creation of the world and the life of primitive man: see *De rerum natura* v. 432–508, 925–72, 1011–27.

491 *Machaon*: he and his brother Podalirius, sons of Asclepius, were doctors to the Greek army before Troy (Homer, *Iliad* ii. 731–2); cf. ii. 735.

500 *to know yourself*: a reference to the famous maxim *gnothi seauton*, inscribed on Apollo's temple at Delphi.

501 *wisely . . .* 511 *in prudent wise*: *sapienter*, i.e. philosophically, a contradiction in terms if love is viewed as a kind of insanity. The pomposity reinforces the didactic pose.

517 *Athos*: Mt Athos, at the south end of the easternmost promontory of Chalcidice, now the Holy Mountain and the foremost centre of monasticism in Greece. It is mentioned in the *Medicamina* (30) as the back of beyond; its richness in hares is otherwise unattested.
Hybla: in Sicily; cf. iii. 150.

528 *hang . . . roses*: cf. *Amores* i. 6. 68 n.

540 *on Jove's own hill*: i.e. you will triumph; the triumphal procession ended at the temple of Capitoline Jupiter.

541 *Sacred Oaks*: the oracle of Zeus (Jupiter) at Dodona in Epirus. The claim to speak with oracular authority is Lucretian: *De rerum natura* i. 734–41, v. 110–13.

546 *kindly slumber*: feigned by the complaisant husband; cf. *Amores* ii. 19. 57 n.

561–92 *a far-famed tale*: briefly and brilliantly retold from Homer, *Odyssey* viii. 266–369; cf. *Amores* i. 6. 47 n. Ovid retold it again at *Metamorphoses* iv. 169–89.

563 *Our Sire*: Mars, the father of Romulus and hence of the Roman people.

567 *her husband's legs*: *Amores* ii. 17. 20 n.

573 *who can e'er escape the Sun?*: a frequent conceit from Homer onwards.

585 *one who laughed*: in Homer it is Hermes, who remarks to Apollo 'I'd be bound in three times as many chains with all Olympus looking on, if I could sleep with golden Aphrodite' (*Odyssey* viii. 339–42). Possibly Ovid refrains from naming the speaker because in one version of Venus' genealogy she was Hermes' (Mercury's) sister? Cf. *Amores* i. 6. 47.

600 *skirt*: i. 31–2 n.

601 *Ceres' rites*: the Eleusinian Mysteries.

602 *Samothrace*: the island was an important centre of the cult of the Cabiri, ancient non-Greek gods known to the Greeks as the 'Great Gods' (Megaloi Theoi). Their mysteries were commonly associated, as here, with those of Demeter (Ceres).

606 *Tantalus*: *Amores* ii. 2. 44 n.

609 *coffered sacraments*: cult-objects kept in caskets and forbidden to the sight of the uninitiated.

610 *clashing cymbals*: associated with orgiastic cults such as those of Cybele and Bacchus; cf. i. 537–8.

614 *curtaining the view*: a favourite pose for statues of Venus, of which Praxiteles' Cnidian Aphrodite was the prototype. In the original it was with the right hand that the 'view' was 'curtained'; the left rested on the urn which formed part of the composition. In the later adaptations the pose was reversed, with the left hand doing the curtaining and the right shielding the breasts. It is this later, more obviously erotic, model that Ovid has in mind here. See Robertson, op. cit. (*Amores* i. 14. 34 n.), i. 391–4 and Plate 127.

643 *Andromeda's complexion*: i. 53 n.

645 *too tall*: the heroines of old were proverbially fine figures of women (cf. *Amores* ii. 4. 33–4); that Andromache was above the average in this respect seems to be an Ovidian fantasy, lubriciously exploited at iii. 777–8.

659–62 *Be Tow-heads . . . the nearest good retreat*: the lover's euphemism has a long literary history, starting with Plato

(*Republic* 474d, there in connection with boys), and continuing through Lucretius (*De rerum natura* iv. 1160–70, mordantly satirical) and Horace (*Satires* i. 3. 38–53, urbanely humorous). Cf. the neat reversal at *Remedia* 325–30. This is a special application of the rhetorical ploy in which the speaker assumes 'for the purpose of praise or blame, that qualities which closely resemble the real qualities are identical with them, for instance, that the cautious man is cold and designing, the simpleton good-natured', etc. (Aristotle, *Rhetoric* i. 9. 28–9; cf. Quintilian, *Institutio oratoria* ii. 12. 4).

Tow-heads . . . Minervas: this renders *flaua* 'fair', but that is not a disparaging epithet. Ovid actually wrote *raua* 'tawny-eyed', i.e. with a forbidding stare; the word is used by Horace of wolves (*Odes* iii. 27. 3) and lions (*Epodes* 16.33). The traditional epithet of Minerva (Athene) was 'grey-eyed'.

Cross-eyes . . . Venuses: *straba*, 'squinting'; the cast in her eye, with goodwill, becomes a languishing sidelong glance, an ogle. Cf. Petronius, *Satyricon* 68. 8 (Habinnas on a favourite slave) 'I don't mind his squint; that's how Venus looks.' The word used there, *paeta*, is a milder equivalent of *straba*. Cf. Horace, *Satires* i. 3. 44–5 *strabonem / appellat paetum pater*.

664 *the censor*: the duties of the Censor, formerly one of the most important magistrates of the Republic, had been taken over by the Princeps. They included maintaining a register of citizens, but it did not in fact include women and children.

669–74 *Work hard . . . this is manhood's test*: these lines are of doubtful relevance here and may have been displaced from somewhere else in the poem; possibly they originally followed line 702 '. . . if he will but wait'.

680 *ne'er did artist limn*: images of copulation abounded in ancient art, as emerges from more than one recent coffee-table book. Propertius, wearing for the moment his moralist's hat, execrates the inventor of the genre (ii. 6. 27–8).

684 *makes me loth*: *Amores* i. 1. 20 n.

700 *her mother*: Althaea; but it is not clear why Ovid singles her out for special mention in this connection.

734 *myrtle*: *Amores* i. 1. 29 n.

735–8 *Podalirius*: 491 n. *Nestor*: *Amores* iii. 7. 41 n. *Automedon*: i. 5 n. *Calchas*: he plays a prominent role in the quarrel of Agamemnon and Achilles in *Iliad* i, but thereafter does not reappear, except when Poseidon impersonates him (xiii. 43 ff.).

743 *an Amazon*: the image is taken up at iii. 1-2 (see n.), *Remedia* 676.

745-6 *Lo! Now the fair ones . . .*: Syme takes the words of iii. 811 'As once [*quondam*] your brothers . . .' to indicate a fairly long interval between Books I-II and III, supporting his hypothesis that the original edition of I-II appearerd as early as *c.*7 BC, i. 171-228 (see nn.) having been added later (Syme, 13-19). However, the sense of *quondam* cannot be pressed to this extent: cf. Virgil, *Aeneid* xi. 74, where it refers to an interval of months rather than years.

BOOK III

1-2 *Greeks . . . Penthesilea's band*: the Amazons came to the aid of the Trojans; their queen Penthesilea was killed by Achilles. Battles between Amazons and Greeks were a favourite theme in art: Robertson (op. cit. *Amores* i. 14. 34 n.), Index I s.v. 'Amazonomachy'.

10 *each woman's case*: Ovid, trained in the schools to argue any case *in utramque partem*, is just as ready with his Legend of Good Women as he was with the villainesses of i. 283-342.

11-12 *Atreus' second son*: Menelaus.
Her sister . . . the first: Clytemnestra and Agamemnon.

13 *Oecles' son*: Amphiaraus. His wife Eriphyle was bribed by Polynices to induce him to take part in the expedition of the Seven against Thebes, in which he was (as he, being a seer, knew) fated to perish. He was precipitated alive into Hades through a chasm which Zeus opened up on the battlefield. See *Metamorphoses* ix. 406 ff. Cf. *Amores* i. 10. 52 n.

17 *Phylacides*: Protesilaus. See next n.

18 *Followed*: ironical. Homer mentions the wife he left behind him (*Iliad* ii. 700), a detail recorded in the Catalogue of no other hero. The gods, pitying Laodamia's grief, allowed Protesilaus to return from the dead for a short while; when his time was up she killed herself.

19-20 *For Pheres' son . . . the wife*: her sacrifice of herself to save Admetus' life and her rescue by Heracles is the subject of Euripides' *Alcestis*.

21-2 *'Oh take me . . . upon the fire*: Capaneus was one of the Seven against Thebes, which he boasted he would take and burn whether the gods liked it or not (Aeschylus, *Septem* 423-34).

For his blasphemy Zeus struck him down as he scaled the city wall.

33 *False Jason*: Amores ii. 14. 29 n.

35 *his spouse*: Ariadne; see i. 527–64 n.

37 *'Nineways'*: because she went down to the sea to look for Demophoon nine times (*Remedia* 601) before killing herself; cf. ii. 353 n. The place was identified with the site of Amphipolis in Thrace.

39 *Dido's guest*: Aeneas; cf. *Remedia* 57–8.

40 *Both sword and motive*: this is Ovid's epigrammatic improvement on Virgil's poignant 'a gift not meant to be so used' (*non hos quaesitum munus in usus*, *Aeneid* iv. 647). The conceit is repeated here from *Heroides* 4. 195–6 and was to be used again at *Fasti* iii. 549–50.

50 *in a happier key*: the Greek poet Stesichorus was said to have been struck blind by the deified Helen for a poem in which she was blamed for the Trojan war. He recovered his sight when he wrote a recantation, his Palinode, in which not Helen herself but a wraith of her was said to have gone to Troy. It began 'The story is not true: you did not embark in the well-benched ships nor come to the citadel of Troy' (Plato, *Phaedrus* 243a). Therapnae near Sparta was her home.

53 *myrtle*: Amores i. 1. 29 n. Having at the beginning of Book I disclaimed divine inspiration, Ovid now conforms with convention in receiving these symbolic gifts—but just as Cupid had stood in for Apollo or the Muses in the *Amores*, so Venus does here. Cf. i. 28 n.

69 *The time will come . . .*: a standard threat of the rejected lover; cf. Horace's Ode to Lydia (i. 25) and Propertius' bitter dismissal of Cynthia (iii. 25).

78 *The roebuck's youth survives*: stags were popularly supposed to live nine times as long as men.

83 *him of Latmos*: Endymion; Amores i. 13. 43 n.

86 *Aeneas*: her son by Anchises.
Harmonia: her daughter by Mars.

93 *lighting flare from flare*: an ethical commonplace. 'A man who shows another the way when he has lost it, is in the same position as if he had given him a light: his own light burns no

less brightly for having kindled the other's' (Ennius, quoted by Cicero, *De officiis* i. 51).

96 *water*: cf. *Amores* iii. 7. 83-4.

98 *costs you nought*: except possibly an unwanted pregnancy; see *Amores* ii. 13. 2 n.

101 *care: cultus*; with the following lines compare *Medicamina* 1-50.

112 *seven ox-hides*: his famous shield of seven layers.

118 *Tatius: Amores* i. 8. 39 n.

119 *grazed on Palatine*: i. 103-8 n.

126 *upon the ocean's blue*: wealthy Romans liked to build out into and over the water; the virtual tidelessness of the Mediterranean no doubt favoured the habit. As another example of the violation of natural boundaries (*Amores* ii. 11. 1 n.) this was a common target for moralists and satirists before and after Ovid.

127 *refinement: cultus* again (iii. 101 n.); the repetition rounds off the excursus, the device known as 'ring-composition'.

138 *Laodamia*: iii. 18 n. This is an Ovidian invention; the point presumably is that 'a simple parting' suits her character as an exemplary wife.

150 *Hybla*: ii. 517 n.

151 *than I can count the fashions*: this is borne out by the wealth of hair-styles represented in surviving Roman portrait busts.

153 *tangles can be charming*: i. 126 n. The 'spent the night under a hedge' look is not a twentieth-century innovation.

156 *Iole*: when her father Eurytus, king of Oechalia, refused Heracles' offer of marriage to her, he sacked the city and carried her off.

158 *the Cretan waif*: Ariadne; see i. 527-64 n.

163 *Dutch shampoo: Germanis herbis* 'German herbs'; on the predilection for blonde hair cf. *Amores* i. 14. 45, 49 nn.

168 *Hercles' and the Muses'*: their temple, with its portico, stood near the portico of Octavia (i. 70 n.). They are supposed to be shocked by the spectacle of wigs openly on sale.

176 *from fierce Ino fled*: they were the children of Athamas by his first wife Nephele ('Cloud'), who rescued them from death at

the hands of their stepmother Ino. In their flight on the back of the golden-fleeced ram Helle fell into the sea named after her, the Hellespont, and was drowned.

183 *Amaryllis*: ii. 268 n.

189 *Briseis . . .* 191 *Andromeda*: Ovidian fantasy and love of piquant antithesis is well exemplified here. Andromeda, being Ethiopian, was nothing if not a 'brunette' and naturally should wear white to set off her complexion. Briseis, called 'fair-cheeked' by Homer, is made a blonde (Ovid's word is *niuea* 'snow-white') and dressed in black for contrast. Their situations both resemble and contrast with each other: both were carried off, Briseis as a slave, Andromeda into freedom. The whole forms a neat and balanced diptych.

192 *Seriphos*: in art she is usually shown just after being released from her rock (so also in Propertius, i. 3. 3−4); for the sake of the parallel with Briseis, Ovid sets her in Seriphos, the island ruled by Polydectes, which Perseus revisited after rescuing her to punish the king for his treachery (*Metamorphoses* v. 242−9).

196 *Mysian dwellers*: representative provincials, living in north-west Asia Minor. Caicus, however, was a river of some stature, one of those noted by Aristaeus in Cyrene's grotto (Virgil, *Georgics* iv. 370) and included in Ovid's great catalogue of rivers (*Metamorphoses* ii. 243; cf. xv. 278).

204 *Cydnus*: in Cilicia. Saffron seems odd for eye-liner.

205 *A little guide*: the *Medicamina*.

209 *But let no lover find . . .*: contrast *Remedia* 351−6.

213 *the grease*: lanoline, but clearly a far cry from the modern refined product.

215 *deer's marrow*: a standard ingredient in cosmetics and ointments; cf. Pliny, *Natural History* xxviii. 185, recommending a preparation of veal suet, deer's marrow, and whitethorn leaves for facial blemishes.

219 *Myron*: a sculptor famous for the realism of his work; his chef d'œuvre, a statue of a cow, is the subject of a series of thirty-one epigrams in the Greek Anthology (ix. 713−42).

224 *a Venus nude*: *Amores* i. 14. 34 n. and below, lines 401−2.

239 *bullying the maid*: cf. *Amores* i. 14. 16. Such behaviour was memorably satirized by Juvenal in his great diatribe on women, *Satires* 6. 490 ff.

244 *Bona Dea*: the 'Good Goddess', a personification of fertility; men were strictly exluded from her rites.

250 *a head sans hair*: cf. 1 Cor. 11: 15 'But if a woman have long hair, it is a glory to her'; Ovid's is a rather more moderate panegyric than the almost hysterical adulation of hair by Lucius in Apuleius' *Metamorphoses* (ii. 8–9).

251–2 *No Semele nor Leda . . .*: i.e. the sort of girl that might take Jupiter's fancy needs no instruction from me. *her*: Europa.

270 *Egypt's fabric*: linen.

272 *cross-bands*: periscelides, ornamental bindings.

281 *even laughing*: the Homeric epithet for Aphrodite (Venus) is 'laughter-loving'. With Ovid's examples compare Nabokov's 'a dazzling flow of unsuspected lovely laughter transfiguring Josephine, who was not pretty, while Eileen, who was, dissolved in a jelly of unbecoming giggles' (*Pnin*).

295 *It's winsome*: 'At first he thought her lisp was affected, and that she ought to be whipped, but he soon got used to it, and then thought it rather pretty indeed' (Surtees, *Mr Facey Romford's Hounds*).

313 *Ulysses*: following the advice of Circe, he had himself tied to the mast to listen to their song, while the crew, their ears stopped with wax, rowed on (Homer, *Odyssey* xii. 36–54, 153–200).

316 *a better procuress*: 'Her voice was ever soft, / Gentle and low, an excellent thing in women' (Shakespeare, *King Lear* V. iii. 273–4).

318 *light Egyptian beat*: Egyptian music and dancing were accounted particularly sensuous; Propertius had an Egyptian *auletes* for his ill-starred orgy (iv. 8. 39).

320 *quill*: the plectrum with which the strings were plucked.

322 *hound with triple head*: Cerberus; Orpheus charmed his way past him to win his wife Eurydice back from Hades.

324 *who justly venged*: Amphion; cf. *Amores* iii. 12. 40 n. He avenged the sufferings of his mother Antiope at the hands of her wicked aunt Dirce by tying Dirce to the horns of a wild bull (Propertius iii. 15. 11 ff.). This gruesome punishment was the subject of a group of statuary which was to be seen in Rome in Ovid's day (Pliny, *Natural History* xxxvi. 34).

326 *Arion*: he was saved from drowning by a dolphin that he had charmed by his playing; Ovid introduces his retelling of this famous story with the question 'What sea, what land, does not know Arion?' (*Fasti* ii. 83). The dolphin was rewarded by being turned into a constellation (ibid. 117–18).

329–48 *Next you must con . . .*: the list invites comparison with that at *Amores* i. 15. 9–30 (see n.); though it is included for a different reason, there is, not surprisingly, a considerable overlap. At *Remedia* 759–66 most of the same names are placed on the Index Librorum Prohibitorum.

329 *The bard of Cos*: Philetas (or Philitas), fl. *c.*280 BC, 'the coryphaeus, as it were, of the Alexandrian school of poetry' (W. V. Clausen). Quintilian ranked him as an elegist second only to Callimachus (*Institutio oratoria* x. 1. 58), and Propertius names them together as his chief models and sources of inspiration (ii. 34. 31–2, iii. 1. 1–2).

330 *Teos' vinous sage*: Anacreon, fl. *c.*530 BC, the poet par excellence of wine and love.

331 *Sappho*: fl. *c.*570 BC. This characterization ('whom all wantonness inspires' = *quid enim lasciuius illa?*), evident in the pseudo-Ovidian epistle of Sappho to Phaon (*Heroides* 15; see *Amores* iii. 18. 26 n.), represents a debased, tribadic, view of her art. She deserves to head any list of love-poets for her description of Eros as 'bittersweet' (*glykypikros*), the simple but profound paradox to which all writing about love ultimately returns.

332 *him*: Menander; cf. *Tristia* ii. 369 'Every one of Menander's plays has a love-interest.'

333 *Propertius*: presumably alive when *Amores* i. 15 was written (ibid. 9–30 n.), he had died about 16 BC.

335 *Varro's tale*: this would seem to show that Varro's treatment followed that of Apollonius in giving prominence to the love of Jason and Medea.

337 *the noblest lay*: no doubt Ovid had in mind principally the love of Dido and Aeneas, heavily indebted in Virgil's treatment to Apollonius. Cf. *Tristia* ii. 533–6 '. . . the poet . . . brought his armed hero to the bed of the Tyrian queen, and no part of his whole work is more read than that which tells of love united by unlawful compact' (tr. S. G. Owen).

339 *And with those names shall mine perchance be classed*: 'I remember once being with Goldsmith in Westminster-abbey. While we

surveyed the Poets' Corner, I said to him, "*Forsitan et nostrum nomen miscebitur istis.*"

When we got to Temple-bar he stopped me, pointed to the heads upon it, and slily whispered me, "*Forsitan et nostrum nomen miscebitur* ISTIS." '

(Boswell, *Life of Johnson*, ed. Birkbeck Hill (Oxford, 1887) ii. 238).

345 *an Epistle tunefully recite*: literally 'sing with well-schooled voice'. The *Heroides* would have been particularly suitable for delivery as monodies.

346 *A novel form*: Ovid's inspiration for the *Heroides* was Propertius' elegy (iv. 3) in the form of a letter from 'Arethusa' to her soldier-husband 'Lycotas'. His claim to originality is ambiguously worded (*nouauit* = both 'invented' and 'gave a new lease of life to'); but it is improbable that the heroic epistle would have had such a long and flourishing life in post-classical times as a literary form if Ovid had not (in his usual manner) exploited Propertius' idea so thoroughly and masterfully. See, for a comprehensive history of the genre, H. Dörrie, *Der heroische Brief* (Berlin, 1968). Cf. *Amores* ii. 18. 21-6 n.

348 *the Nine*: the Muses.

355 *three*: dice were thrown in threes, knucklebones in fours; cf. ii. 203-6.

356 *challenge . . . reinforce*: presumably a reference to betting on the game, but the precise sense is unclear.

357 *chessmen*: ii. 207 n.

361 *disturbing none beside*: this sounds something like spillikins, but it is not easy to envisage how such a game might be played with balls.

363 *A game*: the 'twelve-line game', *ludus duodecim scriptorum*, an ancestor of backgammon. See R. C. Bell, 'Board and tile games', *Encyclopaedia Britannica* 15th edn., *Macropaedia* ii. 1150.

365 *A smaller board*: a 'position' game, something like Nine Men's Morris; see Bell (previous n.) 1152-3.

375 *the air resounds with cries*: *resonat clamoribus aether*, an epicizing tag adapted from Virgil (*Aeneid* iv. 668, v. 228). The effect was not lost on Pope: (Belinda takes a trick at ombre) 'The Nymph exulting fills with Shouts the Sky, / The Walls, the

Woods, and long Canals reply' (*The Rape of the Lock* iii. 99–100). Cf. E. F. Benson's expert observation of the card-table: 'All semblance of manners was invariably thrown to the winds by the ladies of Tilling when once bridge began; primeval hatred took their place' (*Miss Mapp*).

385 *Maiden's icy flow*: the Aqua Virgo, an aqueduct famous for its cool water.

387 *Pompey's Porch*: i. 67 n.

389 *Phoebus' palace-shrine*: i. 74 n.

390 *sank the barques of Egypt*: Apollo had a famous shrine on the promontory overlooking the scene of the battle, and it was part of Augustan mythology that the victory of Actium in 31 BC was won under his auspices (cf. Virgil, *Aeneid* viii. 704 ff., Propertius iv. 6).

391 *the arcades*: of Livia and Octavia (i. 67, 72 nn.) and of Agrippa.

392 *his laurelled sailor son*: actually son-in-law through his marriage to Julia, decorated for his naval victory over Sextus Pompey in 36 BC.

394 *the three theatres*: of Pompey (i. 67 n.), Marcellus (i. 70 n.) and Balbus.

395 *the Ring*: the arena; i. 163–4.

399 *Thamyras*: a mythical singer from Thrace, deprived of his powers of song by the Muses when he challenged them (Homer, *Iliad* ii. 594–600).
Amoebeus: a famous Athenian musician of uncertain date.

410 *next great Scipio*: P. Cornelius Scipio Africanus Major (236–183 BC), the conqueror of Hannibal, had a statue of Ennius placed on his tomb. On Ennius see *Amores* i. 15. 9–30 n.

413 *who'd know Homer's name*: the poet shares the immortality which he has power to confer on his subjects; cf. *Amores* i. 3. 21–6, iii. 12. 21–40 nn.

429 *Andromeda*: cf. *Metamorphoses* iv. 672 ff. 'When Perseus saw her, had a wafting breeze / Not stirred her hair, her eyes not overflowed / With trembling tears, he had imagined her / A marble statue. Love, before he knew, / Kindled; he gazed entranced; and overcome / By loveliness so exquisite, so rare, / Almost forgot to hover in the air' (tr. A. D. Melville)

431 *at funerals*: this is how one young lover in comedy, Antipho in Terence's *Phormio*, first sees and falls in love with the girl he marries (95–111).

440 *Cassandra*: priestess of Athena (*Amores* i. 7. 18 n.) and prophetess; her prophecies were invariably correct, since her powers were conferred by Apollo, but when she rejected his advances he decreed that she should never be believed. Cf. iii. 789 n.

452 *Her nymphs around her*: the Appiades; i. 81–2 n.

463 *the sleepless Vestal fires*: Vesta (Hestia) was the goddess of the hearth; the undying flame in her temple symbolized the life of Rome herself, so that to extinguish it would have been high treason.

479 *cultured but colloquial way*: cf. i. 459 n. Cicero (*Brutus* 211, *De oratore* iii. 45) and Pliny (*Letters* i. 16. 6) both noted the purity of the Latin spoken by ladies of good family. See the letter of Cornelia to Gaius Gracchus (quoted and translated by A. S. Gratwick, *The Cambridge History of Classical Literature*. ii *Latin Literature* (Cambridge 1982) 146–7 = *The early Republic* (1983) 146–7).

483 *wedlock's honoured ties*: *uittae*; cf. i. 31–2 n. A witty paradox: the ladies of the demi-monde have just as much right to deceive their lovers (the point is assisted by the ambiguity of *uir*) as married women their lawful husbands. This is in keeping with traditional literary stereotypes of marriage (ii. 155, 546 nn., iii. 613–4), but rather detracts from such disclaimers as that at i. 31–4.

492 *'gainst the armed to arm*: the Twelve Tables laid down that a burglar might be lawfully killed by night (xii. 12) and that a thief who defended himself with a weapon might be lawfully killed by day (xii. 13). In this more generalized form the principle cannot be traced further back in the legal sources than the second century AD (*Digest* 43. 16. 1. 27); but Cicero's appeal to the authority of the Twelve Tables at *Pro Milone* 9 and the casual nature of Ovid's reference suggests that it was a commonplace of the courts. Few have taken the principle to greater lengths than the septuagenarian Mr Purcell of Co. Cork, who in 1811 was knighted for killing four burglars with a carving knife (Kenny, *Outlines of criminal law*, 18th edn J. W. C. Turner (1962), p. 137 n. 4).

496 *two messages*: ii. 396 n.

506 *Pallas*: Athene (Minerva) invented the pipe (the *aulos* or *tibia* was not a flute but something more like an oboe) but threw it away on seeing her face reflected while playing it; see Ovid, *Fasti* vi. 649–710.

519 *Tecmessa . . . Andromache*: having previously pilloried them as dowdy soldiers' wives (iii. 109–12), Ovid now compounds his denigration by characterizing them as what Uncle Pentstemon called 'grizzlers': 'The wust sort's the grizzler . . . If ever I'd 'ad a grizzler, I'd up and 'it 'er on the 'ead with sumpthin' pretty quick' (H. G. Wells, *The Story of Mr Polly*). Tecmessa and Andromache are associated in literature with the tragic deaths of their husbands, and in Homer's famous depiction of the parting of Andromache and Hector (*Iliad* vi. 390–502) she is despondent and tearful; but the libel on her here is of a piece with the fantasy of iii. 777–8. This is the poet's license (*Amores* iii. 12. 43–4) seen in all its vigour.

536–7 *Nemesis . . . Cynthia . . . Lycoris*: the names under which Tibullus, Propertius and Gallus respectively wrote of their mistresses; cf. *Amores* i. 15. 9–30 n., Introd. p. xv.

538 *Corinna*: see Introd. p. xvi.

547–50 *Be kind . . . has its source*: the sentiment is conventional (e.g. Plato, *Phaedrus* 245a, Cicero, *Pro Archia* 18, al.) and the application flippant; but Ovid's consciousness of his vocation was serious and deeply felt. Cf. *Remedia* 389–96 n., Introd. pp. xv, xix–xx.

604 *Thais*: a famous Athenian courtesan, mistress of Alexander the Great and subsequently of Ptolemy I Soter of Egypt; Menander entitled one of his plays *Thais*. Cf. *Remedia* 385–6.

608 *the trembling gallant's clapped*: a stock situation from mime, referred to by Horace (*Satires* ii. 7. 59), Propertius (ii. 23. 10) and Juvenal (*Satires* vi. 44), and subsequently exploited by Apuleius (*Metamorphoses* ix. 5. 4, 23. 2) and Boccaccio (*Decameron* v. 10, vii. 2, viii. 8).

615 *an ex-housemaid*: literally 'just redeemed by the rod', i.e. manumitted from slavery. On the social status of the elegiac mistress see Introd. p. xxii.

620 *in your bath*: literally 'when you are given time to wash'; the expression *aquam sumere* is used by Ovid and others specifically of washing after intercourse (*Amores* iii. 7. 83, *Ars* iii. 96). The

ironical implication is that the intervals of dalliance with one lover should be used for correspondence with another.

627 *new milk*: the sap of a plant such as *tithymallus* (a kind of spurge); 'It is said, that if letters are traced on the body with its milk and then allowed to dry, on being sprinked with ash the letters become visible. And it is by this means, rather than by a letter, that some lovers have preferred to address unfaithful wives' (Pliny, *Natural History* xxvi. 62 tr. W. H. S. Jones).

631 *his daughter*: Danae.

635 *your rattle*: the sistrum; *Amores* ii. 13. 11 n.

637 *Bona Dea*: iii. 244 n.

639 *guards your clothes*: bathers both in Greece and Rome had to be perpetually on guard against this hazard. The irony is that the guard is set over precisely what the girl who is out to misconduct herself can best dispense with. Mixed bathing was not considered respectable, and from time to time Emperors forbade it, but it persisted.

643 *picklocks*: *adultera clauis*, piquantly exploiting the double sense of *adulter*, 'adulterous' and 'counterfeit'.

646 *on Spanish hills*: the Romans generally classed Spanish wine as plonk.

653-4 *Both gods and men . . . yield to pelf*: an almost verbatim quotation from Euripides' *Medea*: 'They say that gifts persuade even the gods, and gold has more power over mortals than many thousands of words' (964-5). The sentiment became proverbial.

659 *I once complained*: at i. 739-54.

672 *the Lemnian crew*: an unflattering comparison. The women of Lemnos were afflicted by Aphrodite with an evil smell for failing to honour her. When their husbands imported girls from Thrace to console themselves, the women killed all the men on the island.

686 *Procris*: this episode is only part of the legend; Ovid retells it in a much more elaborate version at *Metamorphoses* vii. 665-865. There we learn that the death of Procris was Aurora's revenge on Cephalus for rejecting her love (*Amores* i. 13. 39 n.) and that the spear that killed her was a magic weapon that could not miss. It is striking that the last of the narrative illustrations in the poem is in tragic vein. Cf. *Remedia* 453 n.

687–94 *Hard by Hymettus . . .*: a classic example of the *locus amoenus* (*Amores* iii. 1. 1 n.). As often in the *Metamorphoses* it forms a background to violence.

698 *wanton air*: *mobilis aura*, which could be heard as 'supple Aura', a plausible girl's name (and a shortened version of Aurora). In the *Metamorphoses* his address to the breeze is a good deal longer and richer in the sort of double meanings in which Ovid took pleasure.

710 *Mad as a thyrsus-stricken Maenad*: cf. i. 312 (Pasiphae) 'like a hag-ridden bacchanal.'

725 *Hermes' offspring*: by Herse; but he had an alternative parentage, of which Ovid's identification implicitly indicates awareness.

755 *eat with finger-tips*: knives and forks being centuries in the future. It would be interesting to have more information on the etiquette of eating with the fingers; that society paid close attention to such things is shown by the acid remarks of Lucian in his satire on the treatment of Greek clients by Roman patrons (*De mercede conductis* 15).

777 *Hector's bride*: Andromache.

786 *Like the swift Parthian*: i. 209–10 n.

789 *horned Ammon*: an Egyptian god, identified with Zeus (Jupiter). His oracle at the oasis of Siwa in Libya came to rank with those at Delphi and Dodona.
Phoebus' tripods: at Delphi. In making this claim Ovid was echoing Lucretius: *De rerum natura* i. 736–9, v. 110–12. Cf. iii. 440 n.

809 *You swans*: the poet's chariot (i. 3–8 n.) is now revealed as drawn, like that of Venus (cf e.g. Horace, *Odes* iii. 28. 13, iv. 1. 10), by swans, which were also sacred to Apollo and credited by the poetic tradition, in defiance of ornithological fact, with the power of sweet song. This error has been canonized in English by such soubriquets as the Swan of Avon (Shakespeare) and the Swan of Lichfield (Anna Seward).

THE CURES FOR LOVE

(*Remedia Amoris*)

4 *your standard bore*: *Amores* i. 9. 1 n.

5 *hurt your mother*: Amores i. 7. 31 n.

12 *unweaves work done before*: like Penelope; Amores iii. 9. 30 n.

14 *sail before the wind*: Ars i. 772, Remedia 70 nn.

17, 19 *a noose . . . a sword-blade*: Ovid for once allows his readers to remember examples for themselves. If a modern instance be wanted, the newspapers of 9 July 1988 carried the story of the suicide by hanging of two rejected lovers of the same woman.

27 *Your stepfather*: Mars; Amores i. 2. 24 n.

34 *husband*: uiro; for the ambiguity cf. Amores i. 4. 1 n.

40 *'Complete', he said, 'the work your heart desires'*: et mihi 'propositum perfice' dixit 'opus'. The line echoes and varies Cupid's parting words in their earlier encounter: 'quod'que 'canas, uates, accipe' dixit 'opus' (Amores i. 1. 24). There the poet was (ostensibly) conscripted protesting into the service of Love, now it is Love who defers to the experienced instructor and past master of his subject—and master of Love himself; cf. Ars i. 7-8, Introd. p. xix f.

48 *cured his woes*: Amores ii. 9. 7 n.

55-68 Another catalogue, this time of women who came to grief because they knew no better; instruction in time would have saved them. This ironical deflation of some of the world's great legends of love and jealousy is pointed by the reference in line 54 to 'A heart to its infirmities enslaved'; the phrase *seruum uitii* is both a pun on *seruitium*, the 'state of emotional bondage' (Henderson) professed by the elegiac lover, and also a glance at the philosophical commonplace that men are the slaves of their baser passions; 73 n.

55 *Phyllis*: see 591-608.

57 *Dido*: cf. Ars iii. 337. There would have been an agreeable and undemanding relationship, enjoyed without commitment and terminated without acrimony—and what would have become of the *Aeneid*?

59 *a mother's vengeance*: Medea; Amores ii. 14. 29 n.

70 *let ship and crew progress*: cf. 14 n. The image is now enlarged to include the poet's readers, with a suggestion of himself as Ulysses that becomes more explicit later on (699, 737-40, 789 nn.).

73 *the Emancipator*: *publicus assertor*; specifically legal terminology adds a contemporary twist to the traditional images of enslavement (55–68 n.). The *assertor libertatis* 'was he who, in a trial about the status of an alleged slave, asserted and defended his liberty', which he did by touching him with a rod (*uindicta*). The same form was observed, by agreement, in the ceremony of manumission. See A. Berger, *Encyclopedic dictionary of Roman law* (Philadelphia, 1953), s. vv. *Adsertio*, *Manumissio vindicta*. Ovid has a predilection for legal language and metaphor: *Amores* i. 4. 40 n.

78 *they both belong*: a neat application of the god's traditional attributes.

111 *Philoctetes*: a famous archer, who inherited the bow and arrows of Hercules. On the way to Troy he was bitten by a snake and marooned on the island of Lemnos on the advice of Ulysses because of the smell of his festering wound. He was brought to Troy when Calchas revealed that the city could not be taken without him, and cured by Machaon (*Ars* ii. 491 n.). Cf. 699 n.

131 *largely one of timing*: cf. *Ars* i. 357 'She'll tell the times with true physician's art'; a medical commonplace as old as Hippocrates, which passed into something like a proverb.

137 *Leisure breeds love*: another ancient commonplace, to which in what follows Ovid imparts a characteristically Roman colour. Cf. Catullus' ironical exploitation of the idea at the end of *c.* 51.

141 *As planes love wine*: that it was thought beneficial to plane-trees to pour wine on their roots is attested by Pliny (*Natural History* xii. 8) and others; there may also be an allusion to the role of the plane, the shade-tree par excellence of the Mediterranean region, as the natural gathering-place for drinkers. Cf. Virgil, *Georgics* iv. 146 'planes already / Providing welcome shade for drinking-parties' (tr. L. P. Wilkinson).

151–210 This catalogue of occupations comprises most of the *negotia* and *officia* recognised as useful and fulfilling by conventional Roman opinion—those of 'the law, the legion, and the land' (Henderson). The lawcourts were no longer, as in Cicero's day, a political arena, but they remained central to Roman public life, as is shown, a couple of generations later, by Quintilian's treatise on the education of orators and the career of the Younger Pliny. Farming had been canonized— whatever dark undertones modern analysis may detect in

Virgil's celebration of Italian agriculture—by the *Georgics*; to live on and take a personal interest in the improvement of one's estates was looked on at least by the traditionally-minded, as Pliny's Letters show, as morally estimable. Military service also retained its traditional image, and indeed Augustus laid down a period with the colours as a *sine qua non* for a senatorial career. Hunting—'the image of war with only five-and-twenty per cent of the danger'—was naturally considered a toughening pursuit for manly young men. With grave irony Ovid systematically exalts the very values which as elegiac lover-poet he had no less systematically sabotaged; cf. *Amores* i. 15. 3–8 n.

156 *sees Caesar's soldiery*: *Ars* i. 177 n.

160 *her lover*: Mars.

161 *Aegisthus*: Ovid makes free with the traditional motivation of the story, in which Aegisthus' enmity to Agamemnon was at least as powerful as his love of Clytemnestra; cf. *Ars* ii. 407 n.

169–96 *There's pleasure too . . .*: this highly idealized picture of country life would have been recognized by Ovid's readers as a pretty pastiche of themes from earlier poetry, especially the *Georgics*.

200 *Phoebus' sister*: Diana (Artemis), goddess of the chase.

203 *strings of feathers*: to frighten the game into the nets.

214 *There's travel too*: though young men of good family, as Ovid himself had done, frequently finished off their education with a sort of Grand Tour in Greece and Asia Minor, travel was not an occupation, a *negotium*. Philosophical opinion, summed up in Horace's famous verse *caelum non animum mutant qui trans mare currunt*, 'emigrants only change their scenery, not their outlook' (*Epistles* i. 11. 27, tr. N. Rudd), held that change of scene solved nothing—a maxim equally applied by the poets to love. Here Ovid takes up an independent position.

219 *a foreign Sabbath*: *Ars* i. 76 n.

220 *Allia's catastrophe*: *Ars* i. 413 n.

224 *the Parthians fly*: *Ars* i. 209–10 n.

249 *herbs of Thessaly*: traditionally the home of witchcraft; cf. Apuleius' satirical description of Lucius' absurd fantasies, wondering 'whether the stones I kicked against were really,

perhaps, petrified men, and whether the birds I heard singing were people in feathered disguise—like Procne, Tereus and Philomela in the myth' (*Metamorphoses* ii. 1. 4, tr. R. Graves).

263–88 This episode with Circe is a product of Ovid's lively imagination; in Homer she tells him by no means to stay longer if he does not wish to (*Odyssey* x. 489). The imagined scene on the seashore is a doublet of that with Calypso in the *Ars* (ii. 124 n.), and Circe's resignation of her hopes of marriage and her plea for delay are indebted to Virgil's and Ovid's Dido (*Aeneid* iv. 431–6, *Heroides* 7. 167–80).

279 *you've cause to fear them*: because of his shipwreck at the hands of Poseidon (Neptune).

291 *The world's great mistress*: *domina . . . in Vrbe*, with a play on the two senses of the word.

306 *a salesman*: then, as now, the travelling salesman was stereotyped as a philanderer: Horace, *Epodes* 17. 20, *Odes* iii. 6. 29 ff.

310 *Just suffer—you'll be fluent*: cf. *Ars* i. 610 n.

323 *neighbour to the good*: *Ars* ii. 659–62 n.

334 *move her arms*: *Ars* i. 595 n.

354 *Greases*: *Ars* iii. 213 n.

355 *Phineus*: cf. *Ars* i. 339 n. He was tormented by the Harpies, monstrous birds with women's faces, who befouled his food, leaving a horrible stench behind them. Ovid's readers would remember Virgil's vivid description (*Aeneid* iii. 210 ff.).

366 *Zoilus*: a rhetorician of the fourth century BC known as Homeromastix 'Scourge of Homer'.

367 *the poet*: Virgil. One Carvilius Pictor had attacked the *Aeneid* in a book called, no doubt with Zoilus in mind, *Aeneidomastix*, and others made collections of alleged faults and plagiarisms. See the survey in the edition of Virgil's works by J. Conington and H. Nettleship, vol. i (5th edn. rev. F. Haverfield, 1898), pp. xxix ff.

369 *strikes at the peaks*: proverbial from Herodotus onwards: (Artabanos to Xerxes) 'You see how it is the lofty that god blasts' (vii. 10e).

375 *its buskins*: *Amores* iii. 1. 14 n.

378 *swift-footed*: the pure iambic trimeter associated particularly
with Archilochus (first half of the seventh century BC).
with last foot lame: the 'limping' iambus (scazon, choliambus),
in which the last foot was a spondee, associated particularly
with and invented by Hipponax (fl. *c.*540 BC).

387 *If my Muse matches* . . .: Ovid's defence of the Ars is grounded
on a technical point of literary propriety: if the verse medium
and the style fit the subject-matter, there is no breach of
literary decorum and criticism has not a leg to stand on. This
defence rests on tacit acceptance of the premiss, explicitly
argued in Ovid's apologia, that his poetry and his life were
two distinct things: 'My life is virtuous, though my Muse is
free' (*Tristia* ii. 354, tr. S. G. Owen). This was a classic
position, also taken by Catullus (16. 5-6) and later—surprisingly
and amusingly—by the Younger Pliny (*Letters* iv. 14. 4, v. 3.
2); see Owen's n. on *Tristia* loc. cit.

395-6 *Now Elegy owes me* . . .: a bold claim, but one fully justified
by Ovid's subsequent career. His preaching is orthodox:
'judge matter by the metre' (372), i.e. respect the traditional
genres invented by the Greeks, with the material and
treatment proper to each. His practice was less inhibited: he
enormously extended the scope of elegy, and might indeed in
the event have claimed to excel Virgil as a poetic empire-
builder, for the Eclogues, Georgics and Aeneid all belonged in
genres for which the hexameter was the accepted medium.
That cannot be said of the subject-matter of the *Ars* and
Remedia; and the *Heroides* and the poems of exile each represent
in different ways radically new departures in elegy. Even the
Fasti and the *Ibis*, though formally indebted to Callimachus,
are original in scale and scope.

398 *on your proper circuit*: Ars i. 3-8 n. The poet's 'panting steeds'
seem somehow to have strayed off the race-course and on to
the lower slopes of Parnassus (393-4). He now humorously
recalls them, and himself, to order.

402 *have first go*: Ovid deliberately uses a crude word, *inire* 'enter'.

411 *wide open*: we have come a long way since the first romantic
encounter with Corinna, *Amores* i. 5. 3-8.

450 *the heights above*: the Capitol, i.e. he has triumphed; cf. *Ars* ii.
540 n.

453 *Procris*: *Ars* iii. 686 n. A casual allusion to a variant of the story in which she was Minos' lover.

456 *Callirhoe*: a passing allusion to a complicated story; see *Metamorphoses* ix. 414 ff. for part of it.

457 *Oenone*: a nymph of Ida, abandoned by Paris for Helen; she is the writer of *Heroides* 5.

459 *Procne*: *Amores* ii. 6. 7–10 n.

461 *instances that tire me?*: by cutting short the list the poet draws attention to himself. After the previous catalogues (*Ars* i. 283 ff., iii. 11 ff., *Remedia* 55 ff.) his mastery of the mythological material can now be taken for granted.

476 *save one syllable*: *Bris*eis for *Chrys*eis. An unlikely point for a Homeric hero to take!

482 *Thersites*: a subtle touch, Ovid crediting Homer's hero with his own knowledge of Homer's text. This episode is loosely based on the quarrel between Agamemnon and Achilles in the first Book of the Iliad; Thersites, 'the ugliest man who came to Troy' (*Iliad* ii. 16; contrast Nireus, *Ars* ii. 109 n.), makes his first and only appearance in Book ii, where he abuses Agamemnon and is beaten for his insolence by Odysseus (212 ff.).

487 *my textbook*: the *Ars Amatoria*.

531 *sail before it*: *Ars* i. 368 n.

550 *in Venus' name:* it was dedicated to her as Venus Erycina, Venus of Eryx (*Amores* iii. 9. 45 n.). Lethean Love, *Lethaeus Amor*, is however a creature of Ovid's fantasy. His epiphany is introduced to counterbalance that of Apollo at *Ars* ii. 493 ff.

552 *in cold water*: from Lethe, the Underworld river of forgetfulness. This is a striking paradox; normally water had no power over the fire of Cupid's torches (*Amores* iii. 6. 25–6, 41–2; Apuleius, *Metamorphoses* iv. 33. 2, v. 25. 2).

556 *And not a dream*: *somnus*—or possibly Somnus, the god of sleep, who brings oblivion from care. Ovid may, as suggested by Henderson, be exploiting the ambiguity in the interests of his fantasy. Cupid and Sleep (represented as a winged youth; cf. Statius' famous invocation, *Silvae* v. 4) share certain attributes—'boyish vision' (575 *puerilis imago*) suits either— and the god's words do not positively identify the speaker.

573   *Your brothers*: according to Homer, Priam had fifty sons, nearly all killed at Troy (*Iliad* xxiv. 493 ff.).

577   *Our ship's lost Palinurus*: a fresh turn to the pervasive nautical metaphor, but the point is not clear. Palinurus was Aeneas' pilot, drugged and pushed overboard by Sleep (*Aeneid* v. 835–61). The episode is one of the most enigmatic in Virgil's poem, and Ovid's allusion to it, apparently *identifying* Cupid/Somnus with Palinurus, is hardly less puzzling. Suggestive ambiguity or carelessness? Many readers have felt that as the end of the *Remedia* comes in sight Ovid's treatment becomes increasingly more perfunctory.

593   *Biennial*: in several places in the Greek world the birth of Dionysus (Bacchus) was celebrated every other year; why is unclear.

615   *themselves are wounded*: pseudo-science apparently stemming from Epicurean theory; Lucretius, *De rerum natura* vi. 779–80 'and there are many things not to be touched or looked at'.

625   *a fire*: with a play on the metaphorical sense of fire = love; cf. 649.

667   *the double tablets*: holding the legal formula of *uadimonium*, the security to be given for a defendant's appearance.

680   *loose*: the mark of the dandy. At *Ars* ii. 433 ff. women had been warned against professed fops.

699   *like Ulysses*: when he tricked Philoctetes out of his weapons on his mission to bring him to Troy (111 n.).

704   *come, healing*: he was the god of medicine as well as of poetry and prophecy.

705   *lyre sounding, quiver rattling*: a double allusion, to Callimachus— 'Apollo joins the dance; I hear his lyre' (Frag. 227. 1 Pfeiffer)— and (ominously ?) Homer, who describes Apollo coming to punish the Greeks for Agamemnon's refusal to give up Chryseis, daughter of his priest (*Ars* ii. 401–4 n.), with the words 'His arrows rang on his shoulders as he moved on in his wrath' (*Iliad* i. 46–7).

707   *the vats of Sparta*: actually on Cythera. The industry there had been established by the Phoenicians, but the true purple was a Tyrian monopoly; cf. *Ars* ii. 297–8, *Medicamina* 9.

712   *them*: Juno and Minerva.

721 *Althaea . . . Meleager*: her son Meleager killed her two brothers in a quarrel over the disposal of the trophies of the Calydonian boar-hunt. In revenge she threw on the fire the half-burned log on which his life depended. The story is told at length by Ovid, *Metamorphoses* viii. 260–546. The comparison is highly rhetorical and not really very apt—another sign of haste?

724 *Laodamia*: *Ars* iii. 18n. That she fed her love by gazing on Protesilaus' picture is an effective stroke of Ovid's imagination, repeated from *Heroides* 13. 152.

735 *Caphereus*: a cape at the south-east tip of Euboea. Palamedes had exposed Ulysses when he feigned madness to avoid joining the Trojan expedition, for which Ulysses later contrived his execution on a false charge (*Metamorphoses* xiii. 55–60, 308–12). In revenge Palamedes' father Nauplius lit a signal fire on the headland which lured many of the Greek fleet to destruction. In this and the two following couplets the recurrent navigational metaphor is elaborated.

737–40 *Scylla . . . Syrtes . . . Thunder Mountains . . . Charydis*: a recycling of *Amores* ii. 11. 17–20 (see nn.).

743–6 Another unexpected twist is given to now familiar examples: if Phaedra (*Ars* i. 338n.) and Pasiphae (*Ars* i. 289–326) had been poor, discretion would have been forced upon them. Unexpected also is the company in which these regal heroines find themselves (next n.).

747–8 *Hecale*: the poor old woman who put Theseus up for the night on his way to encounter the Bull of Marathon; she gave her name to Callimachus' influential miniature epic (fragg. 230–376 Pfeiffer).
Irus: the loud-mouthed beggar who provoked and was thrashed by the disguised Odysseus (Homer, *Odyssey* xviii. 1–116). The thought that Hecale, who had known better days (fragg. 254–5), had missed her chance through poverty, is apt; Irus serves as a largely formal complement to her.

755 *The dancers there*: the reference is to pantomime, in which stories from myth were enacted in dumb-show by a dancer while the text was sung to a musical accompaniment by a chorus (see *Oxford Classical Dictionary* s.v. Pantomimus). Ovid's own poems were performed in this way (*Tristia* ii. 519–20).

759–66 *Avoid Callimachus . . .*: a reversal of the advice given at *Ars* iii. 329–48 (see n.).

764 *whose theme was Cynthia alone*: Propertius.

772 *another*: Neoptolemus; her letter to Orestes is *Heroides* 8.

773–6 *Why, Menelaus, moan? . . .?* cf. *Ars* ii. 361 n.

777 *What riled Achilles*: *Ars* ii. 401–4 n.

783–4 *He swore upon his sceptre*: the oath is from *Iliad* xix. 258 ff.,
the sceptre from Achilles' oath of revenge on Agamemnon at i.
233 ff. The conflation is more likely than not to be deliberate;
Ovid takes comparable liberties with the Homeric narrative in
the debate over the arms of Achilles at *Metamorphoses* xiii. 1–
398.

789 *Lotus-eaters*: 'Whoever ate the sweet fruit of the lotus had no
wish to report back or return but desired only to stay with the
Lotus-eaters feeding on the lotus and forgetting return'
(Homer, *Odyssey* ix. 94–7).
Sirens: *Ars* iii. 313 n.

790 *row . . . and set full sail*: *Ars* i. 368 n.

794 *kiss him*: a normal greeting between men.

799 *rocket*: *Ars*. ii. 422 n.

811 *garland the weary vessel*: more apt perhaps than Ovid intended?
the image itself seems by now somewhat 'tired'.

GLOSSARY AND INDEX OF NAMES

This list includes all names of any importance. The references are to the pages on which they occur. As a guide to pronunciation, the stress is indicated by an accent; and in some cases syllables are divided by a hyphen or the number of syllables is specified. Many names end in 'eus'; unless otherwise shown, this is one long syllable which rhymes with 'deuce', e.g. Perseus. A final vowel, unless otherwise marked, is to be pronounced as a separate syllable, whether it follows another vowel or a consonant, e.g. Pasiphae and Penelope.

258   GLOSSARY AND INDEX OF NAMES

264   GLOSSARY AND INDEX OF NAMES

PROTESILÁ-US, the first Greek killed at Troy, 36
PRÓTEUS, a sea-god, 48, 79, 107
PÝLADES, friend of Orestes, 36, 107, 167

RÉMUS, brother of Romulus, 62
RHÉSUS, prince of Thrace, 18, 111
ROME, 13, 27, 33, 40, 45, 62, 82, 88, 91, 99, 137, 157, 159, 161
RÓMULUS, son of Mars, the founder of Rome, 62, 71, 89, 90

SÁBINES, a powerful people of central Italy, 15, 20, 32, 71, 83, 89
SABÍNUS, a contemporary poet, a friend of Ovid, 52
SACRED WAY, a fashionable shopping street in Rome, 17
SÁMOS, an Aegean island, 110
SÁMOTHRACE, an Aegean island (three syllables), 124 [cf. PALATINE]
SÁPPHO, poetess, 53, 136, 171
SÁTURN, father of Jove, 71
SÁTYRS, 101, 132
SCÍPIO, Roman general, 138
SCÝLLA, (1) opposite Charybdis, 43, 49; (2) daughter of Nisus, 78, 152
SCÝROS, an Aegean island, 105
SCÝTHIA, a country in the north beyond the Black Sea, 50, 67
SÉMELE, mother of Bacchus, loved by Jove, 60, 134
SEMÍRAMIS, queen of Babylon, 9
SERÍPHOS, an Aegean island, 133
SÍDE, bride of Orion, 106
SÍDON, a city in Phoenicia, 134
SILÉNUS, a satyr, guardian of Bacchus, 101
SÍMOIS, river of Troy, 27, 111
SÍRENS, sea-nymphs whose singing lured sailors to destruction, 78, 136, 172
SÓPHOCLES, poet, 27
SPÁRTA, a city in the southern Peloponnese, 163, 170
STYX, a river in the Underworld, 109
SÚLMO, birthplace of Ovid, 28, 49, 50, 82
SUN, 123, 158
SYGÁMBRIANS, a German tribe, 26
SÝRTES, gulfs with notorious quicksands off the coast of Africa, 43, 49, 171

TÁGUS, Spanish river, 27
TÁNTALUS, father of Niobe, famous for his punishment, 30, 79, 124
TARPEÍA, Roman traitress, 20
TÁTIUS, king of the Sabines, 15, 83, 131
TECMÉSSA, loved by Ajax, 141

THE WORLD'S CLASSICS

A Select List

JANE AUSTEN: Emma
Edited by James Kinsley and David Lodge

J. M. BARRIE: Peter Pan in Kensington Gardens & Peter and Wendy
Edited by Peter Hollindale

WILLIAM BECKFORD: Vathek
Edited by Roger Lonsdale

JOHN BUNYAN: The Pilgrim's Progress
Edited by N. H. Keeble

THOMAS CARLYLE: The French Revolution
Edited by K. J. Fielding and David Sorensen

GEOFFREY CHAUCER: The Canterbury Tales
Translated by David Wright

CHARLES DICKENS: Christmas Books
Edited by Ruth Glancy

MARIA EDGEWORTH: Castle Rackrent
Edited by George Watson

ELIZABETH GASKELL: Cousin Phillis and Other Tales
Edited by Angus Easson

THOMAS HARDY: A Pair of Blue Eyes
Edited by Alan Manford

HOMER: The Iliad
Translated by Robert Fitzgerald
Introduction by G. S. Kirk

HENRIK IBSEN: An Enemy of the People, The Wild Duck,
Rosmersholm
Edited and Translated by James McFarlane

HENRY JAMES: The Ambassadors
Edited by Christopher Butler

JOCELIN OF BRAKELOND:
Chronicle of the Abbey of Bury St. Edmunds
Translated by Diana Greenway and Jane Sayers

WITHDRAWN

A complete list of Oxford Paperbacks, including The World's Classics, OPUS, Past Masters, Oxford Authors, Oxford Shakespeare, and Oxford Paperback Reference, is available in the UK from the Arts and Reference Publicity Department (BH), Oxford University Press, Walton Street, Oxford OX2 6DP.

In the USA, complete lists are available from the Paperbacks Marketing Manager, Oxford University Press, 200 Madison Avenue, New York, NY 10016.

Oxford Paperbacks are available from all good bookshops. In case of difficulty, customers in the UK can order direct from Oxford University Press Bookshop, Freepost, 116 High Street, Oxford, OX1 4BR, enclosing full payment. Please add 10 per cent of published price for postage and packing.